J&K

INVISIBLE FAULTLINES

J&K
INVISIBLE FAULTLINES

Edited by
Sandhya Jain

PENTAGON PRESS

J&K invisible Faultlines
Editor: Sandhya Jain

ISBN 978-93-86618-85-6

First Published in 2019

Published by
PENTAGON PRESS
206, Peacock Lane, Shahpur Jat,
New Delhi-110049
Phones: 011-64706243, 26491568
Telefax: 011-26490600
email: rajan@pentagonpress.in
website: www.pentagonpress.in

Printed at Aegean Offset Printers, Greater Noida, U.P.

Contents

Editor's Preface

This book attempts to acquaint the general reader with hitherto suppressed facts regarding some historically mistreated personalities and neglected regions and groups of Jammu and Kashmir (J&K) State. Foremost amongst these is the last ruler of the state, Maharaja Hari Singh, about whom the British Resident said, "In the recent past it has happened for the first time that the State of Jammu and Kashmir is seen as a well-organised State, and the ruler who is ruling the State has got all the power.... The Administration of the State is in much better condition than that of many other princely states. There is no doubt about the fact that Maharaja is intelligent and he has got ability to do work. He is influential amongst the people and he has got the ability to determine the course of this important border State". History, however, has been unkind to Hari Singh and readers are invited to draw their own conclusions.

In 1947, the provinces of Jammu and Ladakh sought unity with the Indian motherland at par with British India and the other Princely States that acceded to India The saga of their neglect at the hands of valley-centric regimes forms the template of this book. The authors offer cogent narratives on the lingering problems of these regions, from the discrimination suffered by citizens on account of Article 370 and Article 35-A; the sufferings of the Pakistan-occupied regions of J&K over which India has legal title; the harassment of Hari Singh over the accession and perversion of the document by Louis Mountbatten; the strategic importance of Jammu and Ladakh regions for the security of India; the unequal delimitation of constituencies; the suppression of the Praja Parishad movement; the forced exodus of the Kashmiri Pandits, and the demographic threat posed by the illegal immigration of Rohingyas.

An immediate trigger was the murder of a child in Rassana village, Kathua district, Jammu, and its projection on the national and international plane as a cold-blooded, premeditated, and communal crime. Indeed, communal passions were fuelled with high decibel and one-sided debates in the print and electronic media, often devoid of fact and reason. Social activists who visited the village found a different reality, with sharp discrepancies in the versions of the State Police and hyperactive activists who were feeding the media frenzy, including in the international media. That contrived narrative is now falling apart. What emerges is the outline of a sinister plot to change the region's demography to help Pakistan encroach on Indian territory via this remote border village; Kathua is a border district that was attacked during the Indo-Pakistan war of 1947-48.

This volume is a humble attempt by the authors to present facts suppressed in the officially sanctioned narrative and fill some of the gaps in public knowledge. I would be failing in my duty if I did not acknowledge the generous help extended at various times by friends who include, in no particular order, P.P. Wangchuk, Sonam Wangchuk Shakspo, Claude Arpi, Prof. Hari Om, Ashutosh Bhatnagar, Capt. Alok Bansal, B.S. Slathia, R.K. Raizada, Ajatshatru Singh, A.K. Sawhney, Aseem Sawhney, Senge Sering, Kulbhushan Mohtra, Ankur Sharma, Pankaj Jamtani, and above all, Ranjan Chauhan, who painstakingly read the manuscript multiple times and gave valuable suggestions. Any errors or shortcomings are mine alone.

New Delhi
February 2019

Sandhya Jain

List of Contributors

Colonel (Retd.) Jaibans Singh, an analyst of Indian defence and security affairs, has an abiding interest in national security, internal security, geopolitical developments and defence strategy. His specialty lies in the region of Jammu and Kashmir and as a corollary, Pakistan and China. He is the Editor-in-Chief of the popular defence portal, www.defenceinfo.com, and writes for a number of newspapers and magazines and often comments on defence matters on various television channels.

Sandhya Jain is Senior Fellow, Nehru Memorial Museum and Library, New Delhi. An author, she writes a fortnightly column for *The Pioneer*, New Delhi, on political and contemporary affairs.

Sarjana Sharma is an award-winning journalist with vast experience in print and electronic media, in leading Indian (Zee) as well as international (BBC, USIS) media houses. She was key person in producing a 45-minute TV women's magazine ASMITA (1995), and produced, directed and scripted an internationally famed program, Manthan, on Indian heritage and culture for Zee News. Her blog, *Rasbatiyan* (http://rasbatiya.blogspot.in/) is widely read.

Nidhi Bahuguna is a social media activist, blogger, and freelancer who writes on current affairs, Jammu and Kashmir, and geopolitics.

Abha Khanna is a senior journalist and Media Director, Jammu Kashmir Study Centre, Delhi.

Pankaj Gupta is a Ph.D. scholar at the Department of Social Work, University of Delhi, Delhi, and a social activist.

Yashraj Singh Bundela practises law in the Supreme Court of India.

Shakti Munshi is a Kashmiri Pandit, entrepreneur, independent director on the Board of the Dedicated Freight Corridor Corporation of India Ltd., environmental activist ("Save Powai Lake"), and social activist working in the field of children's education. She is a Life Member of Ladies' Wing, Indian Merchants' Chamber, Mumbai.

Divya Roy is an advocate practicing in the Supreme Court of India.

Kuldip Chand Agnihotri is Vice Chancellor, Central University of Himachal Pradesh. He is an author and contributes columns to many regional and national newspapers.

CHAPTER ONE

The Geo-strategic Significance of Jammu and Ladakh

Jaibans Singh

The overwhelming preoccupation with Kashmir, both at the national and international levels, has given short shrift to the Jammu and Ladakh regions of the state. The hype created over Kashmir is the result of a carefully calibrated, foreign-driven psychological campaign dependent predominantly on the media. It is definitely not the result of any deep study of the actual significance of the region. It has refused to factor the more populous, larger and strategically important regions of the state that have been reduced to the status of poor country cousins. It is imperative to correct the one-sided narrative and the implications of a failure to do so. This chapter attempts an overview of the Jammu and the Ladakh regions, their history of violence contested with grit and determination, their implicit loyalty to the Indian Union and the manner in which they can positively impact the fortunes of the Indian nation.

JAMMU REGION

Jammu region enjoys a central strategic importance in the state of Jammu and Kashmir as well as in the nation. Its importance flows from its location and its abundant natural resources. It is because of its strategic importance that it remained the seat of power of the erstwhile Princely State of Jammu and Kashmir and compelled the British to maintain good relations with the Maharaja. Post-independence, its strategic importance for India increased on account of the sensitive national and international situation. It is the best communication route to Kashmir Valley and Ladakh, and provides essential sustenance to these areas; it has a vibrant agricultural economy while also being the hub of trade activity for the entire state. Post-partition, Pakistan correctly gauged the strategic significance of Gilgit-Baltistan and, due to the ineptness of our leaders at that time, managed to secure and retain control over the area after the 1947-48 war, thus fulfilling its strategic objectives.

Contrary to the popular perception, the next in importance for Pakistan is not Kashmir, but Jammu region. It is here in Jammu that the River Chenab flows, whose waters are a lifeline for Pakistan, far more than the Jhelum or the Indus. This, too, is little known. And it is through Jammu that Pakistan can reach out to Punjab on one side and Kashmir/Ladakh on the other. The natural resources and deep forests add to the economic value of the area.

The greatest fear that impels the Pakistan army into a perpetual conflict with India is the country's lack of strategic depth due to its geographic location. In this regard, Pakistan is most vulnerable from the Jammu region. The important city of Sialkot is within walking distance from Jammu and its control opens the way to Pakistan's Punjab. It is no wonder, then, that the second campaigning season of the Indo-Pakistan War of 1947-48 witnessed the most ferocious battles being fought in Jhanger, Nowshera and the famous Haji Pir Pass that connects Uri and Poonch to other parts of the Jammu region.

The first set of heroes in the military folklore of independent India fought in battles for the Jammu region during the Indo-Pakistan War of 1947-48. Prominent among them are Brigadier Mohammad Usman, MVC (posthumous), also called the "Lion of Nowshera," and Naik Jadunath Singh, PVC (posthumous), the hero of the Battle of Jhanger. Pakistan had every intention of extending its domination beyond Mirpur and its surrounding areas that now form Pakistan-Occupied Jammu and Kashmir (POJK). It was these brave hearts and many like them who fought under very difficult conditions and defeated Pakistan's concerted attempt to fructify its evil designs in the Jammu region.

In the war of 1965, even though Operation Gibraltar (that involved sending mercenaries into Jammu and Kashmir) was initiated from the Kashmir Valley, the most strategic battles of Chamb and Haji Pir were fought in the Jammu region. The return of the Haji Pir Pass to Pakistan by Prime Minister Lal Bahadur Shastri is looked upon as his gravest mistake in the Tashkent negotiations. In the Indo-Pakistan War of 1971, when the western front opened up, Pakistan chose to attack Akhnoor first. The fact that Pakistan has not given up on its strategic intent to wrest the Jammu region from India can be gauged from the fact that it continues to call the international border (IB) a "working boundary" and is consistently building military pressure all along the same.

Jammu: Oasis of Peace and Tranquility

After the war of 1947-48, as the early partition era began to stabilise, Jammu region emerged as an oasis of peace, tranquility and communal harmony. It was, in fact, a city and a region where nothing exciting ever happened. To quote one instance, the visit of Prime Minister Indira Gandhi led to super-excitement in Jammu for weeks on end; she travelled along the main road in an open vehicle with people throwing flowers and garlands towards her and she extended her hand to touch those standing on the roadside. Compare this with the kind of security any visiting dignitary, let alone the prime minister of the country, is provided with nowadays in Jammu and Kashmir.

There was almost zero crime in Jammu. Everybody seemed to know everybody else, so nothing was hidden. The city was compact since population was sparse; there were no high-rise residences since land was freely available. Winters used to witness more activity since many from Kashmir used to come down to Jammu, the winter capital, and the secretariat area would become vibrant. The poorer section of Kashmiri Muslims used to come down and look for jobs; they were simple hardy people called "*Hathos*" (hands, or handymen) who would be employed for wood cutting. They also worked as coolies in the bus stand and for load carrying in the *mandis* (trading areas). Schools were a mix of Dogras, Kashmiri Pundits and Kashmiri Muslims, Gujjars, Sikhs and some Christians. Student life was peaceful, and children of senior government officials studied for six months in Jammu and six months in Kashmir.

Jammu witnessed its first major upheaval in the late 1980s and early 1990 when the Kashmiri Pundit population suddenly descended on the region. As a result, there was a spate of admissions in all schools. The Pundits were very intelligent students who gave the easy-going Jammu kids a run for their money in studies. The city started extending its boundaries at a very fast pace and quickly went many kilometers beyond its original limit. News of rising violence in Kashmir coupled with the chanting of anti-India slogans had begun to trickle in from Kashmir. Since there was no television or visuals, nobody took it seriously for a long time. The seriousness of the situation hit the people only in the late 1980's and early 1990's when the army was deployed along the border in Jammu as part of Operation Rakshak.

Pakistan-sponsored Terrorism

Terrorism in Kashmir captured the attention of the nation as well as the international community. The atrocities committed by the terrorists, the courageous efforts of the people and the security forces to challenge this menace, the aspiration of the people to follow democratic norms, all this and much more has been scrupulously chronicled and commented upon all through the period of turmoil. What is not very well-known is that the Jammu region was central to Zia-ul-Haq's policy of "a thousand cuts." It is for this reason that this area emerged as a prime target for the infiltration of Pakistani terrorists.

The Jammu region south of the Pir Panjal, which also suffered similar atrocity, pain, deprivation and loss at the hands of terrorists and whose people put up an equally brave fight, has not received the attention it deserves. There is very little awareness about the plight of these people who also suffered due to terrorism, even less about the fight that they have so courageously put up, in concert with the Army and with great loss of their lives and property. It is notable that areas of the Line of Control (LoC) that fall south of the Pir Panjal, and especially the area around Krishna Ghati, were very active infiltration routes for Pakistani terrorists. The higher reaches of the Pir Panjal range that are covered with thick forests and inhabitable terrain became safe havens for terrorists who remained hidden there and crossed over to the Kashmir Valley from there. The situation remained volatile for more than a decade until the Indian army totally eradicated terrorism from the area in the early years of this millennium.

Even today, the general impression is that terrorism was confined to the Kashmir Valley and that the Jammu region was safe. There is also a misplaced belief that due to this problem, only Kashmiri Pandits were forced to abandon their homes and hearth. A few specific incidents can bring out the helplessness faced by the locals of the Jammu region at the hands of the terrorists. In one ghastly incident on July 29, 2005, terrorists massacred five men of a minority community, including two brothers, near Kandi in the Rajouri district. The obvious reason was to orchestrate an exodus of the minority community from the region.

The massacre of innocent Hindus at Kulhand in early May 2006 was also aimed at engineering an exodus of the minority community. Kulhand is about

15 km from Doda. It had and continues to have a predominantly Hindu population. The specifically targetted area of Pauchra had and continues to have a mixed population of Hindus and Muslims who lived in separate clusters, whereas the second village, Tawa, is totally Hindu. The villages had poor communications and were totally dependent on foot tracks with no telephones, etc. The people were and continue to be very poor, with indifferent education and dependence on agriculture. The village had no previous history of terrorist violence. However, the terrorists came dressed as security personnel and herded the unsuspecting members of the Hindu community into one room where they opened indiscriminate fire, killing 22 innocent persons in one go.

There are a number of instances that go to prove the manner in which the insatiable thirst for blood propelled the terrorists towards the most ghastly crimes without discrimination between the minority and the majority community. Rubina Kooser, a Muslim resident of village Ludkoti, Rajouri, was abducted from her home by eight terrorists on November 21, 2005, forced to marry one of them, raped repeatedly and beaten brutally for one month, till she managed to escape from the clutches of her tormentors. On July 26, 2006, terrorists entered the house of Wali Mohammad at village Sajon in Doda, and slit the throat of his daughter, Zubadia, in a cowshed. It seems likely that she had resisted their carnal advances and they ended her life in a fit of rage.

The aforementioned incidents have been narrated from amongst innumerable others with the specific purpose of giving an insight into the magnitude of the sufferings of the people of the Jammu region, due to terrorism. Though picked at random, they serve to establish the grip of terrorism during the period when it was at its peak. It also proves that terrorists have targetted people regardless of their caste and religion and that their reign of terror enveloped the entire area from Poonch to Doda and beyond, on the southern slopes of the Pir Panjal.

Even as the terrorist leadership has maintained stony silence on these terrible atrocities, the reasons are not difficult to fathom. While the minority community was targeted with the objective of triggering a mass exodus and as part of the agenda of ethnic cleansing, the majority community was targeted for assisting in the security of the minority community, for being informers of the security services, and for having opted for recruitment in the Army.

During the course of this long and debilitating battle, many families of the region were totally wiped out, many lost their earning members, others witnessed their property being pillaged and destroyed and a whole lot were forced to migrate from their homes and hearth. Migrants from Poonch, Doda, Rajouri and Udhampur continue to live under very difficult conditions in refugee camps. Miscreants have reportedly encroached upon and taken possession of the lands and property of the people who had to flee from these areas.

Challenges along the IB

The International Border (IB) in the Jammu sector is about 198 km long. The Border Security Force (BSF) is manning the border with about nine units. In pursuance of its policy of constantly keeping the Jammu region under pressure, Pakistan has never accepted the IB. Despite having agreed to the terminology during the Shimla agreement of 1972, Pakistan calls it a "Working Boundary". This provides it with the justification to keep the area "heated up" and leads to consistent and intense ceasefire violations as also attempts towards infiltration, smuggling and such activities. Pakistan also targets the border villages to create an adverse political situation in India and add to its vulnerability by keeping communal fires alive.

Before the 1980s, the IB did not have fencing; it was marked by pillars. Deployed on the border was the BSF on the Indian side and Rangers on the Pakistani side. The threat then was more of animals crossing over, and smuggling. On either side of the border in both India and Pakistan, there is an area about five kilometers in breadth (more in some places) which, in military language, is called the forward zone. Behind the forward zone, both countries have built fixed defenses called the Ditch-cum-Bandh (DCB). The DCB comprises a moat in front with bunkers behind, quite akin to the fortifications of ancient forts. The entire IB segment in the Jammu region has a DCB, which extends through Punjab to part of Rajasthan as well.

When Operation Rakshak was invoked, the BSF continued to be on the IB while the army was told to man the DCB. This indicates that even in those days, there was a perceived threat of infiltration and other misadventures by Pakistan. Exchange of fire became routine from 1996 onwards. The ceasefire came into existence from 2003 and lasted, by and large, till 2014 even though intense violations occurred sporadically. In July 2014, heavy firing was initiated from the Pakistan side to which BSF has been retaliating effectively.

The exchange of fire adversely affects and interferes with the routine life of the population that has long been settled in the area. While the Pakistani side is underdeveloped and almost barren, the Indian side has fertile, irrigated agricultural land right up to what has now become the border. Pakistan has cleverly allotted land along the border to its ex-servicemen who are trained to protect themselves against Indian shelling and remain in constant touch with the Rangers. On the Indian side, the inhabitants are civilians with families, including women and small children, who are most adversely affected by the shelling. This adds a very critical dimension to the security of the region. There are many instances when the people, due to heavy shelling, have had to vacate their houses and take refuge in ad hoc refugee camps, leading to immense suffering, damage to property and huge economic loss.

The BSF carries out routine border domination operations during the day and the night, which includes patrols and ambushes. Pakistan objects to any kind of defence works and interdicts all such attempts with heavy fire. The Pakistan Rangers are equipped with sophisticated surveillance devices that assist it in keeping the border under constant watch. The BSF is also fully equipped, but our vulnerability is that we have to maintain a proactive and consistent border management posture to thwart infiltration bids, which necessitates domination of every inch of the IB. Pakistan, however, has no threat of infiltration from India; it therefore goes for deployment in depth rather than in a linear fashion. The situation makes the job of the BSF much more difficult and dangerous than that of the Rangers.

The restive population creates political pressure on the state government and also on the Centre. Many political parties have had to face the flak. The Bharatiya Janata Party–led National Democratic Alliance (NDA) government announced construction of bunkers for civilians and use of bulletproof vehicles for evacuation during shelling. The construction of bunkers comes with its own set of problems, land acquisition being foremost. The local residents are not ready to part with their fertile land, especially when the bunker would put the surrounding area also at risk. Secondly, no civilian construction agency is likely to come forward to take up the contract due to fear of enemy shelling on the construction site. It remains to be seen as to how much this would help.

Challenge to Social Cohesion

The magnificent Pir Panjal Range lies south of the Himalayas and extends from POJK through the State of Jammu and Kashmir to Himachal Pradesh. The northern slopes of this breathtaking mountain fall into the exquisite

Kashmir Valley. The southern slopes fall into the Jammu region where the beautiful peaks and valleys are the abode of communities like the Gujjar/ Bakarwals, the Pathowari-speaking Muslims, Hindu Dogras and Sikhs, who have coexisted peacefully from times immemorial. Major townships on the peripheries of the mountain range include Poonch, Rajouri along the LoC and extending eastwards to Reasi, Doda, Kishtwar, Bhaderwah etc.

Pakistan's main problem is that the Jammu region boasts of a nationalist population. The country's notorious spy agency, the Inter-Services Intelligence (ISI), does not have in this area as many paid stooges to do its dirty work of engineering dissension as it has in Kashmir. This inability has, by no means, reduced the ambition of bringing about a communal divide in the region, especially at this stage as terrorism has not produced the desired results. The area south of the Pir Panjal has been stable security-wise for about a decade now. However, the complacency that has crept into the administration due to the relatively peaceful conditions can be ominous. It would be foolhardy to lower the guard so long as terrorism is alive in the state as it is just across the Pir Panjal mountain range. If terrorists can cross over the range to go to the Kashmir Valley, they can carry out a reverse movement also. Further, Pakistan has by no means renounced its intention to wrest the Jammu region from India or at least keep it in a destabilised condition. The huge spread of the area, the difficult forested terrain in the mountainous region and its slopes, the diverse population, the lack of communication and infrastructure, poverty and lack of access of the government are factors that the ISI intends to leverage in fructifying its intentions.

The settlement of the Rohingya Muslims from Myanmar against all legal tenets of the state, which is protected from outside migration by Article 370, has added another dimension to the problem. There is a feeling that this entire exercise has been carried out at the behest of the ISI. There are regular instances of a communal situation erupting in many areas. Intelligence inputs point towards the existence of terrorist sleeper cells in areas of Doda and onwards towards Kishtwar. If such is the situation in areas deep in the hinterland, one really cannot feel safe about the frontier areas of Poonch and Rajouri. The Kathua incident and its mismanagement by the government is an instance that can be played up by enemies of the nation to great advantage. That it has been engineered by the enemies themselves is not beyond the realm of possibility.

The army has been successful in containing the influx of foreign terrorists, but the communal fissures within can turn the region into a veritable tinderbox in favour of the Pakistani terror-mongers. The situation essentially has a law-and-order dimension and would logically come under the ambit of management by the local police force. The question that arises here is whether the Police force can meet the challenge or not. While one does not have any doubt about the capability of the Police Force, its capacity is quite worrisome. It does not seem as if the Police have adequate manpower (boots on ground) or technological wherewithal to offset the lack of manpower. There is also an urgent need to enhance the training levels in order to create the necessary expertise required to deal with the situation. As things stand, the *thanas* (police stations) are themselves vulnerable, being without proper fortification or even fencing; how can they be expected to deal with adverse conditions? There is local pressure and political pressure to contend with, which adds to the problem and as a corollary to the vulnerability of the force.

Way Ahead

The need of the hour is to meet the multiple challenges posed by foreign powers to engineer dissension and divisiveness in the Jammu region. This would entail a concerted effort by the government, while keeping the people at the centre of gravity. While the threat of infiltration is being met with quite effectively by the Indian Army, the internal fissures would need to be identified and addressed in the political and social domain. Development is one important factor but not central to the problems of the region. It is for this reason that a holistic approach is very necessary.

The key to the problem lies in maintaining the age-old integration between the people and to thwart all attempts to disrupt the same. More interaction and ensuring a level playing field in work and opportunities for all three regions, namely Jammu, Kashmir and Ladakh, should be the first step taken by the government in this direction. There is need for better cohesion and coordination between the police, the administration, and the other security forces. The standard operating procedures need to be re-tuned to be responsive and not reactive, since reaction may amount to a case of "too little too late". Lack of manpower needs to be offset by the introduction of technology. There has to be flexibility to change deployment patterns and concentrate on a point of decision rapidly, for which multi-tasking would be an imperative tool of training. Most important is the aspect of morale and instilling in every policeman the concept of authority and responsibility.

Border management needs to be given immediate and urgent attention; upgrades in technology and building of fortifications, despite the challenges involved, are absolutely imperative. The local population needs to be educated on the long-term benefits that would accrue from such an initiative. They would be able to avoid constant relocation and also suffer fewer casualties.

The central government needs to escalate the means and methods to exert more international pressure on Pakistan to force the latter to adopt a more civilised posture towards the border state of Jammu and Kashmir. The international community needs to be made aware of the larger areas of the state beyond Kashmir that is being affected by border shelling, terrorism, and psychological operations to engineer dissension and divisiveness. It needs to be emphasised that the humanitarian crisis that the world is facing due to Pakistani intransigence has a larger connotation than the stories that keep flowing out of Kashmir alone. When the dam bursts in the Jammu region, the flood will be impossible to control.

The aforementioned are only some aspects that need to be taken into consideration in building up the law-and-order structure to address the challenges of an exacerbating communal divide, followed by dissension and divisiveness with a foreign-sponsored signature in the Jammu region. There are other aspects of socio-political responsibility that also need to be looked into. Only a concerted effort will be successful in meeting the critical challenge looming in the region.

The people of Jammu region are intrinsically peace loving and habitually secular. They love the togetherness that has developed between communities from times immemorial, which is why repeated attempts to tear the communal fabric in the region have failed to produce results. The repeated failure has not led to any lack of motivation in the enemy and attempts continue unabated. In fact, the intensity has increased substantially over the years and new methods are being devised to achieve the desired results. Jammu cannot remain unaffected by these machinations. At times, the situation has veered to a crisis point but has fortunately not exploded, once again due to the resilience of the people. An ostrich-like approach and procrastination by the government in dealing with the sensitive and volatile situation would be very dangerous; the challenges being thrown by a very determined enemy need to be identified and credible action needs to be taken to eradicate them by their very roots.

LADAKH REGION

The politics of a democracy is normally people-centric. It is the population that defines the political interest in a particular region. It is here that Ladakh, with its huge landmass and scant population, becomes an enigma, a region that has huge geo-strategic importance for India, but tends to be ignored in view of its insignificance in the politics of the ballot.

Ladakh forms what is mostly referred to, with utmost pride, the crown of India. As the northern frontier of the country, it constitutes the largest division of the state of Jammu and Kashmir with an area of 49,146 km^2. Jammu region is a little over half of this landmass and the Kashmir Valley is one-third. Bordered by the Karakoram chain of mountains in the north and the Himalayas in the south, Ladakh constitutes two districts of the state of Jammu and Kashmir: Leh and Kargil. Integral to India is also the region of Gilgit-Baltistan that forms part of Greater Ladakh and is under Pakistani occupation; this region has a land mass of 72,971 km^2. Apart from this, 37,555 km^2 of the area in Aksai Chin is under Chinese occupation. The population of this huge landmass is a mere 300,000 in view of the extreme cold conditions prevalent there. It is predominantly Buddhist with a sizeable segment of Shia Muslims in the Kargil region.

Strategic history of Ladakh

Historically, Ladakh comprises Leh, Kargil, Gilgit, Hunza and Skardu and was a part of the greater Central Asia since ancient times. The great empires in Russia, China, Tibet and India are known to have fought to gain and retain domination of the strategic region. When viewed in the modern context, one can trace realisation of the importance of Ladakh to the Sikh Empire of Maharaja Ranjit Singh, who called upon his Dogra vassals of Jammu to keep the region in the control of his Empire, despite the logistical difficulty in doing so. The strategic importance was not lost to Gulab Singh, the Dogra Prince who purchased the state of Kashmir from the British after their annexation of Punjab. He cleverly included the territories of Ladakh in the deal and then proceeded to annex it in totality. It was while doing so that Zorawar Singh, a mighty general of Gulab Singh, carved a unique place in military history for himself by his various forays in Ladakh and Tibet where he also met his end, but not before establishing Dogra supremacy over the region.

It did not take the British long to understand the blunder that they had committed in giving away Ladakh to the Dogras. As Russian power increased, giving way to the diplomatic situation known as the Great Game in Central Asia, the British got wary of the dangers posed to the northwestern borders of the empire and prevailed upon the Dogra dynasty to allow establishment of an Agency in Gilgit and a Commission at Leh. It was in this situation that the post-Independence Indo-Pakistan War (1947-48) was fought. The government of the day failed to push the gains accrued by the great victory of the Indian forces in the war, to take control of the entire state of Jammu and Kashmir. As a result, the Gilgit-Baltistan region of Ladakh and some other parts of the state remained under occupation of Pakistan and are today known as Pakistan-Occupied Jammu and Kashmir. This single act of strategic negligence caused the biggest geo-strategic set back to nascent India whose tremors are being felt till date.

China annexed Xinjiang and Tibet and constructed a road called Highway 219 through Aksai Chin to connect the two areas. Post-independence, a proposal by Chinese premier Zhou En-lai to settle the border issue between the two countries by recognising Indian control over Arunachal Pradesh in return of Aksai Chin remaining under Chinese control was rejected by Prime Minister Jawahar Lal Nehru. Escalating tensions led to the brief and bloody Indo-China War of 1962 in which the Indian defeat is well recorded. The Aksai Chin area continues to remain under Chinese occupation as border talks over the years remain inconclusive. Chinese make periodic thrusts into the territory under Indian control that are managed diplomatically by being termed as differing "perceptions" of the Line of Actual Control (LAC).

In the modern context, Ladakh, though disintegrated due to the machinations of Pakistan and China, has significant geo-strategic importance because of its huge land mass and location. Great world powers like USA, China, Iran, Turkey, Russia, Pakistan and India have great interest in the Central Asian Republics (CAR) and wish to expand their trade signature in the region. The world is in the throes of what can be termed as the new Great Game, which is larger in both form and context than the previous one. Ladakh has boundaries touching China in the North, Tajikistan and Afghanistan in the west and Pakistan in the South. It, as such, has the potential of being a hub and the bridge between Central Asia, South Asia, China and the Middle East. It is from here that the mineral wealth of countries like Uzbekistan, Turkmenistan and Kazakhstan can flow into India and onwards to the rest of the world. It can also become a hub for gas pipelines to China and Central Asia.

Siachen Saga

In April 1984, the gallant soldiers of the Indian Army, by establishing their writ over the Siachen Glacier, accomplished a feat of valour that has few parallels in the annals of military history. Colonel Narendra Kumar, a reputed mountaineer and Commandant of the Indian Army's High Altitude Warfare School (HAWS), in 1977, came across a map in the possession of a German that showed a dotted line joining NJ 9842 to the Karakoram Pass, thus depicting that the India–Pakistan boundary line ended at NJ 9842. With great energy, he launched a couple of expeditions from 1977 onwards and unearthed the Pakistani plan to control the unmarked territory. Pakistan had already taken the first few steps by opening the area to mountaineering expeditions by civilians and was inching towards gaining military control.

Under these circumstances, Operation Meghdoot was launched on April 13, 1984, to establish control over Indian territories in the icy heights of the Siachen Glacier. The plan was based on maps, photographs and videos provided by Colonel Kumar. In an unimaginable feat of grit and bravery, the Indian Army gained control over the dominating heights on the main passes of the Saltoro Ridge, Sia La and Bilafond La, in a short period of time. Pakistan denounced the Indian action as a violation of the Shimla agreement that barred the use of force to bring about a change in the line of control.

Three years later, Pakistan tried to gain a dominant position by forcibly occupying a height that it called the Quaid Post. The Quaid Post was regained by a five-member team of 8 Jammu and Kashmir Light Infantry led by Naib Subedar Bana Singh. This almost superhuman effort came after the unit had suffered initial setbacks and even lost an officer, Second Lieutenant Rajiv Pande. It is now a part of military folklore. The post was renamed Bana Post.

Pakistan, being in a position of disadvantage, consistently makes calls for demilitarisation of Siachen. There have been instances where the Indian political leadership has exhibited signs of vacillation. On June 12, 2005, while on a visit to the glacier, then Indian Prime Minister Dr. Manmohan Singh openly expressed a desire to see the demilitarisation process through. "Now the time has come that we make efforts that this battlefield is converted into a peace mountain," he said. The Indian Army, however, has remained steadfast in its insistence that demilitarisation, if considered, will be done only after authentication on a map of the Actual Ground Position Line (AGPL) along which troops are presently deployed.

Pakistan is insisting on a withdrawal to the positions held in 1984, which is clearly not acceptable to India because such an act would validate occupation of the Saltoro range by the Indian forces as a violation of the Shimla agreement. Having achieved the first step, Pakistan will declare the region as disputed territory. After this, a jihadi intrusion to fructify expansionist designs is definitely not beyond the realms of possibility, regardless of the assurances given. Control over the area would constitute a major strategic achievement for Pakistan as it would breathe down the Indian Army's positions in Ladakh while denying India the capability to monitor the sensitive Pakistan-China axis.

Avalanche or no avalanche, hollowness or no hollowness, diplomacy or no diplomacy, Pakistan will always look upon Indian presence on the Saltoro Ridge as a forcible occupation. No agreement will be strong enough to deter Pakistan from attempting, at some point in time, to restore the status quo ante. Pakistan is not averse to building international pressure against India on the subject, especially by firing from the shoulders of the United States or by involving China as a partner in the dispute. It is, presently, actively pursuing both options, though Washington is no longer so amenable to its desires.

Indian expenditure and effort to regain the Saltoro Ridge, if demilitarised, would escalate in algebraic progression. This will happen in terms of building a new line of defence further down that will require more infrastructure and troops involving prohibitive expenditure. As and when the conflict escalates, the money saved over the years will go down the gutter in nanoseconds. A much larger number of soldiers will be called upon to sacrifice their lives than the few who are becoming unfortunate victims of the weather presently. More dangerous is the fact that this may well trigger a scary sub-continental conflict. The matter has taken an even more critical turn for India with Pakistan having illegally ceded to China the Indian territory of Shaksgam Valley, which is under its forcible occupation since Independence. As a result, China is in a position to bridge the Aksai Chin–Gilgit-Baltistan gap and dominate the Karakoram Pass. India cannot allow such a strategic misadventure to take place. Thus, holding the Siachen Glacier becomes even more important. The NDA government, fortunately, is not taken in by Pakistan's duplicity and there has been no talk of withdrawal from Siachen since it came to power in 2014.

Kargil War

On May 3, 1999, two shepherds reported to the army an unusual movement of people with a soldierly bearing in the Batalik Sector. Further investigations exposed blatant intrusions amounting to a full-fledged breach of the Line of Control (LoC) by Pakistani forces in the trans-Himalayan sector. A war, not of its choosing, was once again thrust upon India. The war that lasted for almost three months was a battle of epic proportions fought at extreme high altitude. It culminated with Pakistan lamely announcing withdrawal of its battered Northern Light Infantry (NLI) formations when there was very little left to withdraw. July 26, 1999, was a fateful day when the Indian Army put paid to the audacious misadventure by Pakistan. The war witnessed fighting in heights up to 18,000 feet with extremely low temperatures. The Indian soldier fought with traditional bravery, fortitude and sense of duty, without complaint under almost impossible conditions. Victory was achieved with the sacrifice of 537 brave sons of India; no less than 86 gallantry awards were won during the course of the war.

It would be appropriate here to revisit the treachery, duplicity and deceit that went into the planning and execution of the war by Pakistan. Even as India was being feted with an olive branch with the promise of a negotiated peace, Pakistani troops were already on their way to stealthily occupy Indian territories. Pakistan went into the war with a fair realisation of the risks and gamble involved. An eminent Pakistani writer, Altaf Gauhar, has suggested that contingency planning for the Kargil conflict was formulated way back in 1987. The plan, however, was set aside as militarily untenable and irrational as also internationally indefensible.

Why then did Pakistan decide to take this gamble after 12 long years? The reason was the then Chief of the Pakistan Army, General Pervez Musharraf. He had been part of the initial planning and had all through considered the plan to be operationally tenable. The Pakistan Army, under the leadership of General Musharraf, factored in a normal winter, a weak and vacillating Indian reaction, a strong element of surprise, and most likely a strong international intervention for fear of a possible nuclear escalation—all tenuous probabilities not based on rational military analysis. Having decided on the operation, Islamabad sent in troops of the NLI, which comprises exclusively of troops from Gilgit-Baltistan and Pakistan-Occupied Kashmir. Being from a backward and underdeveloped area, their education levels are low. They are hardy, innocent and well-disciplined troops who exude a great sense of loyalty.

However, they are looked down upon by their Punjabi counterparts and are given the status of low-grade soldiers. The Pakistani military hierarchy decided to sacrifice them at the altar of its grand ambitions, as cannon fodder.

A captured diary of a captain serving with one of the NLI units tells a chilling story. He was in the vanguard of the operation launched in February when winter was at its peak. Only trained mountaineers, specially clothed, equipped and rationed could have risked a passage in the treacherous terrain. The Captain's untrained and ill-equipped column lost 11 men in the approach march itself. The remainder suffered terrible physical torture. The terrain was so inhospitable that the intruders would not have been able to survive without comprehensive and sustained re-supply operations. Those who reached their objective found themselves without support and assistance. These poor soldiers were unaware that right from the word go, the operation was undertaken with woefully inadequate planning for logistic support, a situation considered suicidal in military terms.

The Indian response was swift, courageous and spirited. The tactical advantage of the enemy sitting on high ground did not deter the resolve of the Indian soldiers to throw him out of Indian soil. No sooner was the battle joined, the intruders realised the harsh reality of the treachery of their own leaders. The result for this hapless body of troops was ignominious death under conditions of great deprivation and humiliation. Even after denigrating their loyal troops in such a dastardly manner, Pakistan declined to receive the bodies of its regular soldiers from the Indian side. Islamabad took 11 years to acknowledge that it lost soldiers in the conflict. In November 2010, it listed on its official website the names of 453 soldiers and officers as killed in the operation. The actual figure, according to informed sources, was well over 2000. The then Prime Minister, Nawaz Sharif, publicly acknowledged complete lack of information about the operation; Benazir Bhutto openly condemned the same.

Strategic Policy for Ladakh

The Ladakhi people are proud Indians with no sympathy or feeling for Pakistan. They have proved their nationalism in all hard times. The Ladakh Scouts, which form part of the Indian Army as its youngest regiment, comprises exclusively of Ladakhi troops who are responsible for the defense of the region and are doing a magnificent job. In view of the distinguished performance of the regiment, it was honoured with the Presidents Colours in August 2017, by President Ram Nath Kovind at the Regimental Centre in Leh.

The strategic policy for any region needs to be based as much on the aspirations of the people as on national imperatives. The people of Ladakh, who are basically peace loving, do not wish to see their land as a place for confrontation of big powers; they want it to be a trade hub so that the Central Asian region can benefit along with them. With a sizeable military presence in the region, India can work towards fulfilling this aspiration by reaching out to the many players in the field, including China. New Delhi and Beijing must move beyond the current diplomatic détente and boost regional trade with the Central Asian region, especially in the energy segment. India can successfully blunt the value of the China Pakistan Economic Corridor (CPEC) with an alternative corridor from an Indian sea port to China through Ladakh. Most of the road infrastructure is already in place on both sides; a little adjustment will make it operational. India needs to move fast in this direction in view of the Chinese forays into Gilgit-Baltistan in the name of CPEC.

Ladakh gives New Delhi the leverage to blunt the Kashmir call for *Azadi* (freedom). Ladakh is the keystone of regional stability and the kernel of India's strategic outreach, as has been often suggested by Phunchok Stobdan, a Ladakh resident and strategic expert. India must also carefully calibrate Ladakh's historical linkage with Gilgit-Baltistan. Over the years, successive Indian governments have made the mistake of ignoring Ladakh. Its strategic value must be leveraged and its seamless integration with the Indian Union assured so as to alleviate the sense of isolation experienced by the people.

*

CHAPTER TWO

Rohingya Shadow over Jammu

Sandhya Jain

Ethnic cleansing in Myanmar

Nine months after the current Rohingya crisis seized global eyeballs, following a self-invited calamity in which Rohingya militants made a coordinated pre-dawn attack on 30 Myanmar police posts and an Army base and unleashed unprovoked brutalities upon their mild-mannered Hindu and other non-Muslim neighbours in the western state of Rakhine (Arakan), Amnesty International admitted that the Rohingyas were guilty of massacring men, women and children across villages near the Bangladesh border. The Rohingya have a pre-colonial history of conflict with the dominant Buddhist community there. But the attacks on the tiny non-Muslim villages bear eerie similarities with the anti-British agitation in Kerala's Malabar region in 1921, when the Mappilas (Moplahs) turned on their Hindu neighbours for reasons that defy understanding to this day. India, which hosts at least 40,000 illegal Rohingyas (over 7,000 in the Jammu province alone; unofficial figures are higher) and another unwanted 20 million illegal migrants from Bangladesh, is concerned over the security implications of this uncontrolled ingress.

In its report,[1] released on May 22, 2018, Amnesty International admitted what the Myanmar government stated in September 2017 that a militant organisation, the Arakan Rohingya Salvation Army (ARSA), now designated as a "terrorist" organisation by Myanmar, slaughtered dozens of Hindus even as it fought with the Army. Amnesty International's report is based on interviews with several Hindus, including survivors, who witnessed the killings, and other evidence, such as photographs of mass graves. The ARSA has admitted targetting Myanmar security personnel but denied the killing of non-Muslim civilians. The Myanmar government did not allow human rights activists to visit the conflict zone, but David Mathieson, a Yangon-based security analyst who had access to Amnesty's report said, "What Amnesty have clearly shown is the group was involved in evident atrocities against Hindu civilians in the early stages of the area clearance operation". Hence, ARSA "should be properly investigated for all the many abuses it has been accused of, in the same way the Myanmar security forces and auxiliaries should be properly investigated and brought to account".

The ARSA attacks of August 25, 2017, were carefully planned and began within hours of the release of the final report of the Advisory Commission on Rakhine State, led by former UN Secretary-General Kofi Annan. The Commission, appointed by the Myanmar Government in 2016 to suggest ways for peace and development in the backward Rakhine State after a bout of violence, suggested that the government revisit the 1982 Citizenship Law and alleviate the region's poverty, and urged "all communities to move beyond entrenched historical narratives". Instead, ARSA launched its premeditated attacks; the army response has been seen by the UN and much of the Western world as "ethnic cleansing", which triggered an exodus of Rohingyas to Bangladesh (estimated at around 7 lakh). However, within this armed conflict between ARSA and the Army, the former mobilised Rohingya villagers to terrorise their Hindu and other non-Muslim neighbours and ethnically cleanse a host of villages.

ARSA, previously Harakah al-Yaqin or Harakatul Yakeen (faith movement), sprang to fame in October 2016 after it attacked border police posts in the northern Rakhine State, which resulted in a fierce military response "amounting to crimes against humanity", according to Amnesty International.[2] ARSA was set up in 2012 after violence between the Buddhist and Muslim communities in Rakhine State; it has hundreds of trained fighters with access to small firearms and home-made explosives. In the August 25, 2017 attack, it mobilised several thousand villagers armed with bladed weapons or sticks. Amnesty International documented many of the human rights abuses by ARSA, including unlawful killings and abductions of unarmed Hindus in the northern Rakhine State. Amnesty also, in April 2018, visited Sittwe, the capital of Rakhine State, and met with survivors from the Hindu, ethnic Rakhine, Khami, Mro, and Thet communities; many faced threats and intimidation from the militant group. Reports of ARSA-related killings of suspected government informers in the refugee camps in Bangladesh further petrified them.

Collating reports of the massacres, Amnesty International stated that on August 25, 2017, ARSA attacked the Hindu community in village Ah Nauk Kha Maung Seik in the Kha Maung Seik village tract in northern Maungdaw Township, at around 8 am. This was just a few hours after the assault on the border police posts and army base camp. Some attackers were dressed in black and the rest in ordinary clothing. They rounded up all 69 Hindu men, women, and children then present in the village, executed the majority within the next few hours, and abducted the rest. The same day, the Hindu community of village Ye Bauk Kyar nearby (46 men, women, and children) disappeared without a trace. Their relatives and other Hindus in the northern Rakhine State suspect that they have been murdered by the same gang.

Kha Maung Seik had a mixed population of Hindu, Rohingya, and ethnic Rakhine villagers. Bina Bala, 22, one of eight women abducted and taken to Bangladesh by ARSA members, told Amnesty, "They came to our house. Some were wearing black and others were wearing normal clothes. ... I recognized them [from the village]". They confiscated the family's mobile phones; all Hindu villagers were gathered in the courtyard. "[The men] held knives and long iron rods. They tied our hands behind our backs and blindfolded us. I asked what they were doing. One of them replied, 'You and [ethnic] Rakhine (Buddhists) are the same, you have a different religion, you can't live here'. He spoke the [Rohingya] dialect. They asked what belongings we had, then they beat us. Eventually I gave them my gold and money". Rika Dhar, 24, said, "We didn't have a chance to run. Muslim people took our gold .... I was blindfolded, and they tied my hands behind my back". She said some of the attackers were members of the Rohingya community living in the Kha Maung Seik village tract.

After binding, robbing, and blindfolding the Hindu villagers, the ARSA militants marched them to a creek area on the outskirts of the village; burned their ID cards; divided the men, women and children and brought the women into the forest. Thereafter, they executed 53 of the hostages, including 20 men, 10 women, and 23 children, 14 of whom were under the age of 8 years. Only 16 persons – eight women and eight of their children – were spared on the condition that the women agreed to "convert" to Islam and then marry people selected by ARSA fighters. All eight women corroborated the accounts of the slaughter.

The survivors were held inside a house for two nights and then forced to go with their captors to the Kutuparlaung refugee camp in Bangladesh. Five of the women said they fled on a day when helicopters were seen flying over the village. San Nyunt, Village Administrator of Min Kha Maung village, agreed that helicopters were seen in the area, evidence that the Myanmar Army had no control of the area at the time of the massacre. This is pertinent because on arrival in Bangladesh on August 28, the eight Hindu women were forced to lie on video and allege that the massacre had been carried out by ethnic Rakhine villagers (i.e., Buddhists). Bina Bala said, "[One of the kidnappers] told us that if anyone asks we should say that the Rakhine and the military attacked us ... or you will be killed". When the video surfaced on Facebook, Hindus in the northern Rakhine State alerted friends in Bangladesh who found the survivors and moved them to a camp reserved for Hindu refugees, where they were protected by Bangladeshi security forces. In early October 2017, all sixteen survivors were repatriated to Myanmar with help from the Bangladesh and Myanmar authorities.

Meanwhile, in Myanmar, members of the Hindu community in the northern Rakhine State and members of the Myanmar security forces went to the site of the massacre on September 23 and unearthed four mass graves with the remains of 45 people. On September 27, the authorities briefly permitted local and international journalists to visit the mass graves. Amnesty International assessed that all 45 bodies belonged to persons from Ah Nauk Kha Maung Seik or persons visiting the village at the time of the attack. The bodies of the other eight persons killed were not found; the villagers from Ye Bauk Kyar are still missing.

Despite ARSA's denials of any hand in the killings in its Twitter account, Amnesty International said that careful scrutiny of evidence gathered in Bangladesh and Rakhine State showed that ARSA fighters were responsible for the massacre, especially as the survivors identified specific individual perpetrators. Amnesty International was able to confirm that one of these was a Rohingya from the Kha Maung Seik village tract. Hindus in Sittwe told Amnesty International, "I never imagined this could happen, we had a good relationship [with the Rohingya]. Why did they attack us?" Shawlyee Shawltee from Kha Maung Seik was emphatic that she did not want to return to her village, "I lost everything, my house, all our property. My husband is suffering [psychologically] after all his family members died".

On account of their tense relationship with the Myanmar State (as we shall see), Rohingyas do not have citizenship or the right to buy and legally own property. Yet their Hindu neighbours, on the basis of personal and business relations, helped them to get property deeds surreptitiously. But after the wanton, premeditated executions, the minuscule minorities displaced inside Rakhine, mostly in Sittwe, told Amnesty International that they could never again contemplate living beside Rohingya neighbours.

There were other attacks. On August 26, 2017, ARSA fighters shot six Hindus (two women, a man, and three children) and injured another Hindu woman on the outskirts of Maungdaw town, near Myo Thu Gyi village. The victims were members of an extended family of twelve who had fled from the U Daung village tract in Maungdaw after being threatened by ARSA. Tirana Hassan, Crisis Response Director at Amnesty International, acknowledged,

> Our latest investigation on the ground sheds much-needed light on the largely under-reported human rights abuses by ARSA during northern Rakhine State's unspeakably dark recent history. It's hard to ignore the sheer brutality of ARSA's actions, which have left an indelible impression on the survivors we've spoken to. Accountability for these atrocities is every bit as crucial as it is for the crimes against humanity carried out by Myanmar's security forces in northern Rakhine State.[3]

The plight of Hindus in Myanmar was, however, ignored for many months. Israel Resource News Agency correspondent Rachel Avraham lambasted the international community for not treating all Myanmar refugees equally. A woman, who fled on foot to Bangladesh despite being seven months pregnant, said, "They dug three holes. One to dump the bodies of women, one to dump the bodies of children and a third one for the men they kill. All of the holes are overflowing. That is where I last saw my husband's body".[4] Avraham said Rohingya militants have ties with Islamist groups like the Islamic State, al-Qaida, Lashkar-e-Taiba (LeT) and Pakistan's Inter-Services Intelligence (ISI).

The Indian Home Ministry has uncovered links of Rohingyas with jihadi groups and the ISI of Pakistan. Many believe that the Rohingyas' illegal entry into India was organised by a group backed by the ISI, with the objective of spreading fundamentalism in areas where they settled and launching pan-Islamisation of the region, which involves creating religious and political strife to force Hindu exodus and alter regional demography. Rohingyas are reported to be affiliated to the Bangladesh Islami Chhatrashibir (ICS), which has links with the Bangladesh Jamaat-e-Islami, which is linked to acts of violence in Bangladesh. In September 2017, Zakir Musa, commander of Al-Qaida affiliate, Ansar Ghazwat-ul-Hind, released a 10-minute audio message on YouTube channel Ansar Ghazwa, warning India against deporting Rohingyas from Jammu; he made unsavoury references to Prime Minister Narendra Modi.

Lt. Gen. Prakash Katoch believes that the discovery of the mass graves of Hindus massacred in Rakhine State "may not be all".[5] The rugged terrain of the Chittagong Hill Tracts is famous for terrorist sanctuaries and has often been used by ISI and Al-Qaida instructors. The former joint director of the Intelligence Bureau, M.K. Dhar, in his book, *Open Secrets – India's Intelligence Unveiled*, mentioned that in 1992-1993, the "SIMI had already started deputing 'volunteers' to Pakistan for training along with the mujahideen, Taliban, and Al-Qaeda cadres. They established firm linkages with Islamic Chhatra Shibir, Al-Qaida–affiliated Harkat-ul-Jihad al-Islami (HuJI), Al-Badr, Al-Jihad and other organisations in Bangladesh and were trained in facilities located inside Bangladesh and under the very noses of the DGFI and BDR".[6] During the Bangladesh Nationalist Party rule, four large anti-India terrorist training camps were run in the neighbouring country.

India and the Rohingyas

The International Crisis Group (ICG) has pointed out that the entire Rohingya Movement is controlled by around twenty wealthy Rohingya businessmen settled in Mecca, Saudi Arabia. The ARSA first emerged in October 2016 when it attacked three Myanmarese police outposts in the Maungdaw and Rathedaung townships, killing nine police officers. Their leader, Ataullah Abu Ammar Jununi, is a Pakistani national who has received billions of dollars from Saudi Arabia. He defended the assault in a video, stating, "For over 75 years there have been various crimes and atrocities committed against the Rohingya ... that's why we carried out the October 9, 2016 attack – to send a message that if the violence is not stopped, we have the right to defend ourselves".[7] Ataullah was born in Karachi, but the family settled in Saudi Arabia. He returned after the conflicts of 2012, with huge sums of money, but had a bad experience with the Afghan and Pakistani Taliban and Kashmiri separatist groups like LeT, and thought poorly of Rohingya groups such as the Rohingya Solidarity Organisation (RSO) whom he met in Karachi. Analysts feel his vanity and recklessness has "provoked the worst crisis for the population probably in its history".

Diaspora Rohingyas living in Dubai and Pakistan persuaded the Jamaat-ud-Dawa (JuD) to take up the cause of their co-religionists in the sub-continent. Indian intelligence officers observed that Firdous Sheikh, Dubai-based president of the Rohingya Federation of Arakan, visited Pakistan in November 2017 and attended some functions in Pakistan-occupied Kashmir and Islamabad, in support of Rohingyas.[8] He met Naveed Qamar, JuD "amir", and Noor Hussain, Pak-based leader of RSO and president, Burmese Muslim Welfare Organisation. Naveed Qamar revealed that JuD charity Falah-e-Insaaniyat Foundation (FIF) was operating in Teknaf, Bangladesh and Indonesia. However, none of the Islamic nations that are aiding and abetting the jihadi attacks in Rakhine state are willing to give refuge to any of the Rohingyas who now need succour.

India's Rohingya crisis is almost certainly part of the global jihad mission of Pakistan's ISI-LeT and Al-Qaeda. This is why LeT cadres have been busy along the Bangladesh-Myanmar border. They would like to derail Sheikh Hasina Wajed because of her zero tolerance policy towards terrorist organisations in her country. In 2013, Dhaka had alerted New Delhi that LeT was behind Rohingya violence in Myanmar. LeT's Abdul Kareem Tunda admitted travelling from Pakistan to Bangladesh to recruit Rohingyas for jihad. Pakistani terrorist Hafiz Saeed and his organisation, JuD, listed as a terrorist outfit by the United Nations and the United States, has been collecting funds in the name of the Rohingyas, thus lending credence to fears that Rohingyas were being pushed into Jammu province by militant groups as part of a mission to convert the State into an Islamic province. Spokesperson Abdul Rahman said the JuD and its charity arm, FIF, was conducting a charity drive for Rohingyas in "every district of Pakistan".[9] It was also helping Rohingyas in other countries. "Our brothers have reached Indonesia and we have constructed temporary wood and fibre houses for them, arranged for their monthly groceries and set up a bread plant for them", besides running kitchens to feed 63,000 Rohingyas in refugee camps along River Naf that separates Bangladesh and eastern Myanmar. Bangladeshi journalists denied this claim and insisted that all eight feeding centers in the area were run by the Bangladesh government and military.

However, Musadik Malik, a spokesman for the Pakistan government, admitted that the Ministry of Interior was aware of the fund collection and had instructed police to take action against anyone collecting money in the name of these organisations. Islamabad, he said, had closed down 66 accounts operated by JuD and "cancelled licenses of weapons of anyone associated with JuD and taken over their headquarters in Muridke, Punjab". The truth, however, is that Hafiz Saeed continues to operate with impunity inside Pakistan and even launched a political party, the Milli Muslim League, some of whose members contested the 2018 national elections in Pakistan under the banner of a little known registered party. In Lahore, the Milli Muslim League held a rally in April 2018, where it announced that it was sending its cadre to Myanmar to "help" the Rohingyas.[10] Indian intelligence agencies viewed this as a move to arm the Rohingyas; they have evidence of links between Rohingyas and LeT (mother organisation of JuD) and similar groups in Pakistan. Intelligence reports suggested that Jaish-e-Mohammed leader Masood Azhar was also recruiting Rohingyas.

Zabiullah alias Hamza, a LeT terrorist arrested in Kupwara (J&K) in March 2018, told the National Investigation Agency (NIA) that Hafiz Saeed and Zakir-ur-Rehman Lakhvi, accused in the Mumbai 2008 terror attacks, were recruiting youth under the aegis of JuD for war against India: "JuD leaders openly invite boys from 15-20 age group of Pakistan to join 'jihad' [who] are willing to sacrifice themselves. They write down their names, address and phone numbers". The recruits are given two-year training at seven places, including Mudrike and Muzaffarabad.[11] The training comprised a seven-tier hierarchy headed by Hafiz Saeed (Amir Sahab, Amir-e-Masgar), with instructors (*masool*) or recruiters at zonal, district, tehsil, town and sector levels. The recruits were handpicked from madrassas by the town *masool* and taken to the training centre at Muridke. Zabiullah alias Hamza was sent by his father, a town *masool* in Multan. In each training place, army and ISI personnel helped, and at the last stage, Lakhvi and Saeed would arrive to motivate the recruits against.

The critical question is who helped nearly 40,000 Rohingyas to safely cover a distance of over 2,500 km from Rakhine province in Myanmar and settle down unmolested across India (officially 7,096 in Jammu), and why? Rohingya infiltration began over a decade ago, much before the alleged "ethnic cleansing" by the Myanmar Army. Rohingya settlements are known to exist in Jammu (J&K), Hyderabad (Telangana), Mewat (Haryana), western Uttar Pradesh, Okhla (Delhi) and Jaipur (Rajasthan). Intelligence agencies believe that many Rohingya Muslims have moved towards Kerala, Tamil Nadu, Karnataka and even the strategic Andaman & Nicobar Islands. Clearly there is a subversive agenda behind this meticulous movement.

Intelligence sources state that there is a well-oiled and organised network of "handlers" based in Myanmar, Bangladesh and India's West Bengal behind this influx. The infiltrators were able to get Aadhaar cards, ration cards and voter cards. There is a danger that they will be used by Pakistan-based terror groups to carry out strikes in India. It may be recalled that in October 2015, one of two foreign militants killed in an encounter with security agencies in Tral town of south Kashmir was identified as Chota Burmi (Abdul Rehman-al-Arkani).[12] The same year, Hafiz Saeed reportedly met with Maulana Abdul Quddus, a Rohingya who went to Pakistan and set up the Harkat-ul-Jihad-al-Islami Arakan to liberate the Muslim-dominated Rakhine. Both Lashkar and Jaish are luring Rohingyas to work for them; both have trained recruiter teams and have sent emergency supplies to Rohingyas in Bangladesh via NGOs, including FIF (of Lashkar). Radicalisation is taking place in Bangladesh camps.

Jammu-based advocate Hunar Gupta, who filed a petition in the Jammu and Kashmir High Court for deportation of the Rohingyas, observed that many of them had managed to get small patches of land in their name – something impossible under Article 370 of the Constitution. This clearly suggests collusion by the authorities. In previous years, the Rohingyas were quite frank and would admit that they were brought by middlemen who told them that they would be much safer in Jammu rather than any other part of India. Strategic expert Brahma Chellaney said Rohingyas have a long history of jihadism and have ties with Islamic State (ISIS), Al-Qaeda, and other terrorist organisations. They are funded by militant-linked organisations in Saudi Arabia and Pakistan; in fact, the ARSA is led by a Saudi-based committee of Rohingya émigrés.[13] These links compelled the Government of India to declare Rohingyas a serious security threat, a perception shared by Bangladesh.

Colonial legacy

Chellaney pointed out that the Rohingya problem was a legacy of British colonialism. More than a century ago, the British transported people from then East Bengal to work on rubber and tea plantations in Burma, then administered as an Indian province till 1937. In 1947, Rohingyas tried to drive the Buddhists out of the Muslim-dominated Mayu peninsula in northern Rakhine, so that it could secede and be annexed by East Pakistan (now Bangladesh). When they failed, they took up arms and declared jihad, attacked government troops and seized territory in northern Rakhine to set up a state within a state. Soon after Myanmar became independent in 1948, it declared martial law in Rakhine region, but could regain territorial control only in the early 1950s. Rohingya Islamic militancy has since continued intermittently. Chellaney feels Myanmar will have to create an inclusive national identity to break the cycle of ethnic tensions that are driving Rohingyas toward jihadism. Currently, Myanmar officially recognises 135 ethnic groups, but not the Rohingya, who were stripped of citizenship in 1982 due to growing concerns over illegal immigration from Bangladesh. During the military genocide that led to Bangladesh's independence in 1971, thousands of Rohingyas fled to Pakistan. Chellaney states that even as the international community pressurises State Councillor Aung San Suu Kyi to take measures to protect the Rohingyas, the latter's long history of Islamist extremism will also have to be resolved.

The roots of the current ethno-religious conflict can be traced back to World War II. The Japanese military seized the Arakan in 1942; later, when the British launched a counter-offensive, the local Buddhists supported the Japanese while the Rohingyas sided with the British. Hence, the Raj recruited Rohingyas into its guerrilla force (the "V" Force) to ambush and kill Japanese troops. When Britain retrieved control of Arakan in 1945, they rewarded Rohingyas by appointing them to the main posts in the local government. This tempted the Rohingya militants to settle old scores with the Buddhists and in July 1946, they formed the North Arakan Muslim League to seek secession of the Muslim-dominated northern Arakan from Myanmar.[14] In the run-up to the partition of India in 1947, the Rohingyas tried to expel the Buddhists from northern Arakan in an attempt join East Pakistan. Jinnah, however, shunned their requests to join the new Islamic nation as he did not want to alienate Britain. Thereafter, the Rohingya established the Jamaat-e-Islami to agitate for a separate Islamic nation in North Arakan. Supported by East Pakistan–based radical outfits, they attacked the local Buddhists who retaliated to ensure that the nation's geography was not altered or compromised. It was only when their separatist movement failed that Rohingyas sought Burmese citizenship. But after the 1962 coup, they were declared a non-national race and denied citizenship, a position reiterated in the Citizenship Act of 1982.

Myanmar's Buddhist Bamar majority feels threatened by the faster reproduction, migration and over-population of Muslims. The Rohingya are seen as Bengalis settled by the British, who do not speak Burmese. Gautam Mukhopadhyaya, former Indian envoy to Myanmar, points out that "Rohaing" (hence 'Rohingya') is a Bengali dialect spoken on both sides of the Naf river and up to Mayu river in Rakhine. Currently, Myanmar recognises 135 national "races" (but not Rohingya). The Citizenship Act of 1982 puts all "settlers", including people of Indian origin (mostly poor Tamils and Bengalis), at a disadvantage for having originated outside Myanmar.[15] The Hindus of Indian origin, according to Mukhopadhyaya, improved their status by identifying with the Buddhist majority and accepting the protection of the Buddhist Sangha, though their integration into the mainstream is still far from complete. The Myanmar–International Kofi Annan Commission has mooted a revision of the 1982 Citizenship Law.

Danger to India

The Border Security Force (BSF) caught 87 Rohingyas along the Indo-Bangla border between January and October 2017 and sent 76 of them back to Bangladesh. The Director General of the BSF, K.K. Sharma, said the Force has intensified operations against this illegal movement into India as their links with terror organisations cannot be ruled out.[16] The BSF has revealed that "agents allure Rohingyas with good job opportunities in India and motivate that they will work with their own Muslim community in some of the states such as Jammu and Kashmir, Tamil Nadu and West Bengal". Rohingyas go to Jammu – but never to the Muslim-majority Kashmir valley – as some Rohingyas have already been staying there for some years. There is an economic consideration in the form of job opportunities and better pay. This tempts them to send out invites to other relatives to come and settle in the province.

It is significant that, in November 2017, in view of the growing animosity towards the Rohingyas in Jammu, some officers from the United Nations High Commission for Refugees (UNHCR) approached Rohingya refugees in Jammu with an offer: "You may face problems or dangers in Jammu, move out if you want, we will fund you".[17] They suggested that the Rohingyas move to Delhi, Hyderabad, or Mewat, and that the UNHCR would assist in the travel expenses, help to build a shack in the new place, and provide rations for one month. However, the offer was politely refused, "We are used to Jammu, we know everyone over here, why would we leave?"

This is not surprising, given the manner in which successive State Governments have gone out of the way to ensure that the Rohingyas are accommodated in every respect. In May 2017, Vikram Randhawa, member, Legislative Council, lambasted the previous National Conference government for forcing the administration of Government Middle School, Kiryani Talab, Narwal Bala, to admit the children of illegal Bangladeshi and Rohingya immigrants.[18] During a surprise visit to the school, Randhawa was astonished to note that 80 percent of the 200-odd students in the school were from illegal immigrant families. He observed that there was clearly a greater conspiracy to settle aliens in Jammu.

It is now widely recognised that a well-oiled machinery in Kolkata and Guwahati facilitates Rohingya infiltration from Bangladesh and Myanmar. The arrangements include transit accommodation and providing the illegal aliens with fake Indian identity cards and other documents, and linkages to local Muslim organisations.[19] West Bengal shares 1,900 km of the 4,000-km India–Bangladesh border, with two important entry points for Rohingyas and a flourishing trade in infiltration. According to intelligence sources, on settling down in India, Rohingyas become active in Tablighi activities through local mosques. This was noticed in Jammu, Hyderabad and Chennai. Wherever they settle in substantial numbers, they trigger Hindu migration, as already reported from some villages of Jammu. Funds for their stay are arranged through the *hundi/hawala* route by local outfits such as Jamaat Ahle Haider, Yateem Trust and Kashmiri Welfare Trust. Police suspect terrorist outfits may also be funding the Rohingyas as raids in Jammu's Channi Himmat area yielded Rs 30 lakh in cash from some families illegally settled in Narwal, near the Sunjwan military camp that was attacked on February 10, 2018.[20] The residents said that Rohingyas in Kiryani Talab also had huge sums of money. A television channel, Zee News, reported that several Rohingya crossed the India–Bangladesh border into India at a rate of Rs 25,000 per person, with cattle smugglers doubling up as agents in Malda district of West Bengal.[21]

In September 2017, at a seminar organised by the National Human Rights Commission (NHRC), Union Home Minister Rajnath Singh clarified that Rohingyas are not refugees, but illegal immigrants: "The Rohingyas are not refugees. They have not come here after following proper procedures. No Rohingya has applied for asylum. They are illegal immigrants". He insisted that India was within its rights to deport Rohingyas as it was not a signatory to the UN Refugees Convention 1951 and its 1967 protocol. Strangely, the NHRC issued notice to the Centre over plans to deport Rohingyas from various parts of India. Undeterred, in October 2017, Rajnath Singh directed the government of Jammu and Kashmir to collect all personal details of Rohingyas/foreigners living in the state illegally, in a prescribed form. Emphasising its seriousness on the issue, the Union Home Ministry reminded the state government on June 4, 2018, that it is yet to receive the personal data forms of each illegal migrant,[22] but the coalition government fell on June 19 when the Bharatiya Janata Party withdrew support.

In December 2017, while on a visit to West Bengal, Rajnath Singh directed the five eastern states bordering Bangladesh to ensure that Rohingyas and other illegal immigrants did not slip through the porous border. Speaking to the media at the state secretariat, Singh said, "West Bengal chief minister has assured me of all necessary cooperation on making land available both for setting up new border outposts (BOPs) as well as for raising barbed fence at the unfenced borders. I have requested the representatives of all the five states having borders with Bangladesh to take personal interest to expedite land acquisition in the interest of national security". So far, only 3,006 km of the 4,096-km Indo–Bangladesh border has been fenced with barbed wire, roads, floodlights, and so on. Parts of the border will be protected by radar, day-night cameras and sensors.

India has refused to succumb to international pressure to ignore its own security concerns regarding illegal immigrants, but needs the cooperation of both Bangladesh and Myanmar in order to control insurgency in the North-East. Both Bangladesh and Myanmar are part of the Bay of Bengal Initiative for Multi-Sectoral Technical and Economic Cooperation (BIMSTEC) and an intrinsic part of Prime Minister Narendra Modi's Act East policy. India abstained from voting on a Dhaka-backed UN resolution condemning human rights violations in Myanmar, especially against Rohingya Muslims; but the motion was passed as 33 countries voted in favour. As part of its endeavours to develop infrastructure and promote trade and economic development in the region, India is building the Kaladan Corridor linking its North-East across Rakhine State with the Bay of Bengal, through the deep-water Sittwe port it has constructed in Myanmar. India has committed to help develop Rakhine province, which could assuage Rohingya grievances. The area is witnessing considerable economic investment with Beijing building a huge energy/transportation corridor from Yunnan to Kyaukpyu port in Rakhine State.

Supreme Court

Rohingyas started entering India illegally over a decade ago. They came in small groups and quietly spread out in different parts of the country. At some stage, those "managing" their ingress began to push them towards Jammu province. Intelligence agencies have observed that this infiltration is being organised by foreign-funded agencies and is supported within by certain political forces, with the result that Rohingyas have received Aadhaar cards, ration cards, voter identity cards, and even got their children admitted to government schools in Jammu province at the cost of the local population. The local people view the rising numbers of Rohingyas and Bangladeshis as a concerted design to alter the demography of the province and create communal disharmony in a strategic border state. Grievances are aggravated by the fact that around 2 lakh Hindu refugees to the State – legitimate citizens of undivided India who were forced out of the new nation of West Pakistan in 1947 and after – languish from neglect and discrimination by successive Governments of Jammu and Kashmir.

In September 2017, the Government of India announced its decision to expel the 40,000-odd Rohingyas (official figure) who have entered India illegally over the past few years and have penetrated far deeper into the country than warranted by recent troubles in the Rakhine province of Myanmar. Surprisingly, the NHRC opposed the Government's decision to deport the illegal infiltrators. The serial bomb blasts in Bodh Gaya, Bihar, in 2013 were the handiwork of extremists from the banned Students Islamic Movement of India (SIMI) who wanted to take revenge against a Buddhist sacred site for the recurrent conflicts between Rohingya Muslims and Buddhists in Myanmar. On June 1, 2018, five convicted persons were sentenced to life imprisonment.

Nonetheless, oblivious to the danger to national security posed by the intruders, some activists approached the Supreme Court of India to challenge the Centre's decision to expel the Rohingyas. However, the Government of India insisted that this decision lay in the domain of the Executive; affected State Governments have been asked to prepare modalities for deportation. On December 5, 2017, the Supreme Court (bench comprising Chief Justice Dipak Misra and Justices A.M. Khanwilkar and D.Y. Chandrachud) admitted a plea by two Rohingya illegal immigrants, Mohammad Salimullah and Mohammad Shaqir, opposing the Centre's decision to deport over 40,000 migrants.[23] The Supreme Court, on October 13, 2017, observed that there was a need to balance national interest and human rights as the issue involved national security, economic interests and humanity. It suggested that the migrants should not be deported, but Additional Solicitor General Tushar Mehta urged that this should not be written in the order as it could have international ramifications. Others who have approached the apex court on this issue include K.N. Govindacharya of Rashtriya Swabhiman Andolan; Democratic Youth Federation of India, youth wing of the CPI(M); West Bengal Commission for Protection of Child Rights and BJP member Ashwini Kumar Upadhyay.

North-eastern States

India's north-eastern states that are in close proximity to Bangladesh, and hence easy to access by determined Rohingyas and their settlement managers, are also in danger of an influx. Aware of the danger, Union Home Minister Rajnath Singh met with the Chief Ministers of five north-eastern states, namely, West Bengal, Assam, Tripura, Meghalaya and Mizoram, in December 2017 to enhance the border protection grid to check illegal infiltration. India's 4,096-km border with Bangladesh includes West Bengal (2,217 km), Assam (262 km), Meghalaya (443 km), Tripura (856 km) and Mizoram (180 km). Besides the India–Bangladesh border, infiltration also takes place through the India–Myanmar border. Much of the apprehension is due to a decade-old free movement regime between India and Myanmar that permits ethnic communities living on either side of the border to travel 16 km across the boundary without a visa.[24] There are 150 formal and informal border crossings; Rohingyas, including militants, could slip in through these passages.

In November 2017, Mizoram Home Minister R Lalzirliana said that nearly 400 Rohingyas had entered the state's Lawngtlai district from Arakan, Myanmar.[25] They included three Arakan Army militants who were injured in fighting with the Myanmar Army. When hostilities began in August 2017, around 200 Christians crossed the border for safety. In Tripura, Railway police caught six minor Rohingya Muslims, three boys and three girls, from the Dharmanagar railway station in North Tripura district.[26] They entered India through Sonamura border in Sepahijala district and reached Dharmanagar by bus, from where they intended to go to Hyderabad.

In April 2018, Gorkha Janmukti Morcha leader Bimal Gurung issued a statement alleging that Rohingyas were being settled in West Bengal's Darjeeling and Kalimpong districts as part of a conspiracy to alter the demography for "vote bank politics" and marginalise the native Gorkha, Adivasi, Rajbongshi and Indian Bengali communities.[27] Gurung urged Prime Minister Narendra Modi and Home Minister Rajnath Singh to scuttle these "sinister designs", especially in view of the strategic location of Darjeeling, Terai and Dooars that share international boundaries with Bhutan, Nepal, Bangladesh and Tibet. The demand was supported by S.S. Ahluwalia, Union Minister of State for drinking water and sanitation and also the BJP MP from Darjeeling, who stated in a letter to the Prime Minister that more than 320 families have been settled in places such as Deolo, Lava forest, Melli and Rangpo.[28] The claims were strenuously denied by Binoy Tamang, chairman of the board of administrators, Gorkhaland Territorial Administration, which is backed by the Trinamool Congress government.

What is undeniable is that eight Rohingya families comprising 29 adults and 11 children have been settled in a new colony in Kulari village under the Baruipur police station area in South 24-Parganas.[29] Local police say the new group has refugee cards from the UNHCR. Their overt supporters include the Desh Bachao Samajik Committee headed by a local paint supplier, Hussain Gaji, who said, "There are 16 rooms and eight Rohingya families. My organisation constructed the colony on 15 cottahs of land which belong to me. All of this has been built with donations from individuals and various organisations in West Bengal. More such colonies are being set up. At present, there are around 4,000 Rohingya in Bengal and many others, who do not have any documents, are in jail". The Rohingyas, who refused to show their "refugee cards" to the media, expressed gratitude for receiving jobs with welfare organisations. Momena, who came to Kulari via Bangladesh with her family, stated, "I have a 75-day-old baby and have to take care of two other children. It is difficult and we are grateful to these people. They are providing us rice, pulses, vegetables, eggs and occasionally meat. They also gave us warm clothes and medicine. They have said that this will continue until my husband earns enough for us. We feel safe here than anywhere else".

The youth among them are employed as labourers and the children are being sent to the local madrasas to study. Hussain Gaji revealed that his Desh Bachao Samajik Committee coordinated with "people in Bangladesh" (which he had visited once) and other Rohingyas in Delhi to bring these families to Kulari. He added that Chief Minister Mamata Banerjee was "sympathetic to the cause of the Rohingya and has said that they will not be driven out. A number of Muslim and human rights organisations in Bengal have joined hands. Soon, we will start a campaign for granting citizenship to Rohingya refugees". Momena's husband Sahidul Islam admitted, "I worked as a daily labourer in Bangladesh before paying a tout some money to help us enter Bengal. Then, we went to Delhi. A few months later, we were offered this home by this organisation and we came here to stay". The organisations helping the Rohingya include Bangiya Imam Parishad, Biswa Manab Kalyan Islamic Trust, Bandi Mukti Committee and All Bengal Minority Youth Federation.

Jammu

The growth of Rohingya settlements in the Hindu-dominated Jammu and Samba districts, including sensitive spots like Army camps, has raised concerns that this may be part of a "bigger conspiracy to strengthen the Muslims who are in a minority in the region".[30] The terror attack on the Sunjwan army camp in February 2018, in which six soldiers and one civilian died, has increased demands for their deportation before they "inflict a major damage on the state." Rohingya refugees settled in the vicinity of the camp are the main suspects in the incident. Former DGP, J&K Police, M.M. Khajooria, said, "They have set up consultation camps on the border near Myanmar. These camps direct the refugees to settle at a particular place or city. In the first place, they are directed to Jammu because it is safe and secure for them to stay in a Muslim-majority state, besides it is also located close to Pakistan. They are also told to help in strengthening the Muslim minority in Jammu". Khajooria warned that some NGOs have been tasked with the responsibility to settle the Rohingyas in Jammu and, "they have full backing of the Kashmir-centric government".[31] The onus is on the Centre to understand that Jammu and Kashmir is a conflict-riven zone and Rohingya presence poses a grave security threat. In an ominous admission in the Legislative Assembly in 2017, the State Government admitted that the number of Rohingya illegals might be over 10,000 in Jammu.

Rohingyas have been unable to explain why they feel that Jammu, which is thousands of kilometres from Myanmar, is the "safest place" for them; the reason of course is the backing of Kashmir-based political outfits. As a result, they received all amenities, including illegal power and water connections, from the then dominant PDP, for living in Hindu-dominated areas. Journalists visiting the Narwal settlement saw the extent of government support for Rohingyas in Jammu in the newly built 100-odd hutments with illegal electricity and water connections. Some had even purchased land on the outskirts of the city by fraudulently securing permanent residence certificates (PRCs), Aadhaar and ration cards, none of which is possible without complicity at the very top. More tellingly, Rohingyas in the camp were instructed not to talk to outsiders and to leave all interaction to the "Maulana sahib" of the 10-room madrassa in the Narwal colony. In fact, Rohingyas have been fearlessly setting up shops without any hindrance from the authorities. A "Burmese" market has sprung up close to Karyani Talab, and a host of shops sell items of daily use while blithely running fans, coolers, refrigerators, television sets, etc.

In Vidhata Nagar and Bathindi areas, several empty plots were occupied by small groups of Rohingyas who planned to build houses.

Article 370 is a highly adjustable statute if one has the right religious affiliation, as witnessed when Sheikh Abdullah bestowed citizenship rights on Uighur Muslims from China in 1952 to help them escape the wrath of the Communist regime; similarly, Bakshi Ghulam Mohammad gave citizenship to Tibetan Muslims in 1959 after the Chinese annexation of Tibet.[32] Both Abdullah and Bakshi Ghulam Mohammad gave the cold shoulder to Hindus driven out of West Pakistan, and settled their respective protégés in the Eidgah area of Srinagar, where they can readily be distinguished from the Kashmiri population.[33] Historian Hari Om observed, "That the Kashmiri leadership would settle in Srinagar the Uyghur and Tibetan Muslims with full citizenship rights and make unjust, invidious and humiliating distinctions between them and the non-Muslim refugees from West Pakistan, establishes that its whole approach was communally motivated".[34]

Another reason for local resentment against Rohingyas is their association with crime. In February 2018, a Rohingya, Noor Gul Ameen, gang leader of a trafficking racket, was arrested and two minor girls recovered.[35] Jammu SSP Vivek Gupta stated that Ameen revealed that the gang brought girls every Friday and hunted for buyers after the community namaz. They had sold girls as far as Ramban and Kishtwar districts for prices ranging from Rs 40,000 to Rs 50,000. On the directions of the Union Home Ministry, the State Government set up a high-level Group of Ministers (GoM) to monitor the illegal settlements of foreigners in Jammu and Samba districts in May 2017.[36] The GoM was empowered to examine the settlement of illegal migrants from Myanmar and Bangladesh in totality, but was little more than a formality. The BJP kept demanding removal of illegal immigrants from both districts, but the PDP covertly protected them. The only substantial outcome was that the State submitted details of NGOs that were funding the stay of Rohingyas in Jammu and Samba districts.

Return

External Affairs Minister Sushma Swaraj conveyed to Myanmar's President U Win Myint and State Counsellor and Foreign Minister Aung San Suu Kyi that India wanted the safe, speedy, and sustainable return of the Rohingyas to Rakhine State.[37] During a two-day visit to Naypyidaw in May 2018, Swaraj assured help in tackling issues related to Rakhine State and observed that under the aegis of the bilateral Rakhine State Development Programme, India is already implementing various projects to cater to the needs of different sections of the people, such as construction of prefabricated housing for displaced persons. After initially condemning the terrorist attacks of August 25, 2017, in which Myanmar security forces lost their lives, New Delhi included the displaced Rohingyas in its worldview at a nudge from Dhaka that was shouldering the burden of a massive refugee influx, comparable to India's burden prior to the liberation of then East Pakistan in 1971. By the time the then Foreign Secretary S. Jaishankar visited Myanmar in December 2017, India was committed to the restoration of normalcy in Rakhine State and to "enable the return of displaced persons".

Faced with intense international opprobrium, Myanmar's National Security Adviser Thaung Tun expressed willingness to take back all 7 lakh Rohingya Muslims who had fled to Bangladesh, if they agreed to return.[38] Speaking at the Shangri-La Dialogue, Thaung Tun denied accusations of ethnic cleansing and said, "If you can send back 700,000 on a voluntary basis, we are willing to receive them. Can this be called ethnic cleansing?" Myanmar and Bangladesh, in January 2018, agreed to complete the voluntary repatriation of the refugees within 2 years. In June, Myanmar signed an agreement with the UN to allow Rohingyas in Bangladesh to return safely and voluntarily. India also needs to take up with Myanmar the expeditious return of its citizens who have been sneaking into India over the years, using the services of dubious touts and other agencies whose sources of funds deserve official scrutiny. Myanmar has agreed to set up an independent commission to investigate "the violation of human rights and related issues" in Rakhine State after the army retaliated to the attacks by Rohingya insurgents. Many members of the UN assert that the military action after the attack by ARSA terrorists was tantamount to "ethnic cleansing", but Myanmar has stoutly denied the charge. Thaung Tun was forthright "Myanmar does not deny that what is unfolding in northern Rakhine is a humanitarian crisis. There is no denying that the Muslim community in Rakhine has suffered. The Buddhist Rakhine, Hindu and other ethnic minorities have suffered no less".

Relieved at Myanmar's deference to international pressure, the Union Ministry of Home Affairs directed the authorities in Jammu and Kashmir to prevent illegal migrants from entering the state, including Rohingyas from Myanmar. Regarding foreigners who are illegally residing in the country and the state, the ministry said, "Such illegal migration poses serious challenges and has security implications since some of the migrants have been found to have indulged in illegal activities and are vulnerable to radicalization".[39] New Delhi has outlined five measures to be taken against Rohingyas/foreigners who have entered and are staying in India illegally, beginning with confining them to specified identified locations and strictly monitoring their activities and movements. Second, identify each person by personal details (name, date of birth, sex, place of birth, father/mother names, address in Myanmar/some other country, nationality, etc.) and have this signed by such illegal migrant or his/her guardian. Third, take the biometrics of illegal migrants, including Rohingyas, to ensure unique identification/de-duplication and to prevent impersonation in future. The Foreigners Registration Office (FRO) has been directed to coordinate with the Unique Identification Authority of India to ensure that no Aadhaar card or other identity documents are issued to Rohingya immigrants, which can be used by them later to claim to be Indian citizens. Fourth, personal forms/identity documents of such Rohingyas/foreigners must be shared with the Government of Myanmar through the Ministry of External Affairs for their nationality verification, issue of travel documents and repatriation to Myanmar. And finally, states must monitor the movement and activities of the outsiders and ensure their speedy repatriation/deportation as per law, policy and instructions.

Despite the Union Home Ministry directing all states with a Rohingya presence to collect personal details of each entrant and monitor their movements and activities in September 2017, which was reiterated in June 2018, the Jammu district administration claimed to be unaware of the directives,[40] a clear indication of the intent of the People's Democratic Party to defer action on the issue. Ten months after the instructions were given, the regime did not order confinement of the Rohingya illegal migrants to pre-defined locations.

Interestingly, Indian Islamic scholar Maulana Wahiduddin Khan rejected the narrative of Rohingya victimhood:

> Since 1966, my opinion on the Rohingyas is only one and that is: The case of the Rohingya Muslims is not one of "oppression", but rather, it is the outcome of ill-judged political activities instigated by unwise leaders. If the whole picture were to be seen, one would arrive at the conclusion that the Rohingya Muslims are not victims of oppression, but are rather paying the price for their own unrealistic actions carried out under the influence of misguided leaders. Such a separatist movement would be unacceptable to any country, even if it were given the euphemistic name of "self-

determinism". The solution to the problem of the Rohingya Muslims is only one – that is, they must disavow their insurgency and militant activities. They should make it known that they are a larger part of the Myanmar nation. He added, "The separatist movement has only caused a deterioration of the condition of the Rohingyas to the point of ruination, although prior to this they were living prosperously in Myanmar. Indeed, the best interests of the Rohingya Muslims lie not in wanting a separate land, but rather, in living as part of the state of Myanmar. This is true both in the religious and secular sense".[41]

*

NOTES

1 Rohingya militants massacred civilians in Myanmar: Amnesty Report, Jon Emont, *The Wall Street Journal*, May 22, 2018. https://www.wsj.com/articles/report-alleges-massacres-committed-by-rohingya-militants-against-civilians-1526992514?mod=e2tw.

2 Briefing: Attacks by the Arakan Rohingya Salvation Army (ARSA) on Hindus in northern Rakhine State. https://www.amnesty.org/en/latest/news/2018/05/myanmar-new-evidence-reveals-rohingya-armed-group-massacred-scores-in-rakhine-state/

3 Myanmar: New evidence reveals Rohingya armed group massacred scores in Rakhine State, 22 May 2018. https://www.amnesty.org/en/latest/news/2018/05/myanmar-new-evidence-reveals-rohingya-armed-group-massacred-scores-in-rakhine-state/.

4 Stop ignoring the ethnic cleansing of Rohingya Hindus, Rachel Avraham, September 26, 2017. http://www.jpost.com/printarticle.aspx?id=506058.

5 India's concerns over Rohingya justified as Saudi Arabia, Pakistan links could make them easy conduits of terrorism, Prakash Katoch, Sept. 27, 2017. http://www.firstpost.com/india/indias-security-concerns-over-rohingya-justified-as-saudi-arabia-pakistan-links-make-them-easy-conduits-of-terrorism-4087475.html.

6 SIMI (Students' Islamic Movement of India); DGFI (Director General of Forces Intelligence); BDR (Bangladesh Rifles).

7 Arakan Rohingya army denies links with al-Qaeda, IS, banglanews24.com, Sept. 15, 2017. http://www.banglanews24.com/english/international/article/63661/Arakan-Rohingya-army-denies-links-with-al-Qaeda-IS.

8 Pak Rohingya leaders rope in JuD to take up their cause, Bharti Jain, Dec. 11, 2017. https://timesofindia.indiatimes.com/india/pak-rohingya-leaders-rope-in-jud-to-take-up-their-cause/articleshow/62014696.cms.

9 UN-listed terror group found collecting donations for Rohingya in Pakistan, Ayesha Tanzeem, Sept 26, 2017. https://www.voanews.com/a/terror-group-found-collecting-donations-rohingya-pakistan/4045507.html.

10 Lashkar recruiting Rohingyas for terror ops in India, Abhinandan Mishra, April 25, 2018. https://www.sundayguardianlive.com/news/11021-lashkar-recruiting-rohingyas-terror-ops-india.

11 How JuD's 7-tier team trains youths for war against India, Rohan Dua, May 28, 2018. https://timesofindia.indiatimes.com/india/how-juds-7-tier-team-trains-youths-for-war-against-india/articleshow/64346786.cms.

12 Militant killed in south Kashmir was of Burmese origin: Police, Oct. 8, 2015. http://www.tribuneindia.com/news/jammu-kashmir/community/militant-killed-in-south-kashmir-was-of-burmese-origin-police/143514.html.

13 Rohingyas' long history of jihadism must be acknowledged, Brahma Chellaney, Sept. 30, 2017. http://www.atimes.com/article/rohingyas-long-history-jihadism-must-acknowledged/.

14 Rohingya militancy poses a regional threat, Brahma Chellaney, Nov. 28, 2017. https://www.japantimes.co.jp/opinion/2017/11/28/commentary/world-commentary/rohingya-militancy-poses-regional-threat/?utm_content=buffer6f69d&utm_ medium= social&utm_source=twitter.com&utm_campaign=buffer#.Wh7QMLrTTcd

15 They who belong to the earth, Gautam Mukhopadhyaya, Sept. 25, 2017 https://www.outlookindia.com/magazine/story/they-who-belong-to-the-earth/299316.

16 36,000 Rohingyas in India, terror links cannot be ruled out, says BSF, *PTI*, Nov. 29, 2017. http://www.hindustantimes.com/india-news/36-000-rohingyas-in-india-terror-links-cannot-be-ruled-out-says-bsf/story-TnJ99GRYIb8cAjh4ebfy6N.html.

17 UNHCR tells Rohingyas Jammu may not be safe, offers relocation funds, *IANS*, Dec. 3, 2017. https://economictimes.indiatimes.com/news/politics-and-nation/unhcr-tells-rohingyas-jammu-may-not-be-safe-offers-relocation-funds/articleshow/61901854.cms.

18 MLC flays forced admission of foreign immigrants children in Govt school, May 14, 2017. http://news.statetimes.in/mlc-flays-forced-admission-foreign-immigrants-children-govt-school/

19 Forged IDs make Rohingya "Indians", Bharti Jain, Dec. 6, 2017. https://timesofindia.indiatimes.com/india/forged-ids-make-rohingya-indians/articleshow/61939561.cms.

20 Jammu: Police seize Rs 30 lakh from Rohingya settlements near Army Camp, suspect funding by terrorists, *Swarajya* Aug. 09, 2018. https://swarajyamag.com/insta/jammu-police-seize-rs-30-lakh-from-rohingya-settlements-near-army-camp-suspect-funding-by-terrorists..

21 Watch: How Rohingyas are entering West Bengal by paying Rs 25000; *DNA Web Team*, Jan. 15, 2018. http://www.dnaindia.com/india/report-rohingya-crisis-now-rs-25k-to-illegally-cross-over-the-border-into-west-bengal-2575603.

22 Confine illegal Rohingya to designated camps: Centre to states, *TNN*, Jun 4, 2018. https://timesofindia.indiatimes.com/india/confine-illegal-rohingya-to-designated-camps-centre-to-states/articleshow/64441862.cms.

23 SC to hear pleas on deportation of Rohingyas in January, *PTI*, Dec. 5, 2017. http://indiatoday.intoday.in/story/sc-to-hear-pleas-on-deportation-of-rohingyas-in-january/1/1103706.html.

24 Rohingya crisis: Northeastern states wary of free movement pact with Myanmar, Rahul Karmakar, Sept. 20, 2017. https://www.hindustantimes.com/india-news/rohingya-crisis-northeastern-states-wary-of-free-movement-pact-with-myanmar/story-zefaEAJKuaXxuvvuQcA5LI.html.

25 Around 400 Arakan refugees have entered Mizoram: Minister, *PTI*, Nov. 15, 2017. http://indiatoday.intoday.in/story/around-400-arakan-refugees-have-entered-mizoram-minister/1/1090047.html.

26 Six Rohingya minors apprehended from railway station in Tripura, *HT*, Jan. 15, 2018.

http://www.hindustantimes.com/india-news/six-rohingya-minors-apprehended-from-railway-station-in-tripura/story-34rQ1lM9bVFKKfCbvxVB4J.html.

27 Rohingyas being settled in Darjeeling to render Gorkhas homeless: Bimal Gurung, *New Indian Express*, Apr. 27, 2018. http://www.newindianexpress.com/nation/2018/apr/27/rohingyas-being-settled-in-darjeeling-to-render-gorkhas-homeless-bimal-gurung-1807205.html.

28 Mamata govt settling Rohingyas in Darjeeling hills, alleges BJP minister, Pramod Giri, May 9, 2018. https://www.hindustantimes.com/india-news/mamata-govt-settling-rohingyas-in-darjeeling-hills-alleges-bjp-minister/story-G6KKS1XG5dUUZB0WR7ZUPM.html.

29 Eight Rohingya families, grateful for being settled in West Bengal, Ravik Bhattacharya, Jan. 12, 2018. http://indianexpress.com/article/india/kulari-south-24-parganas-eight-rohingya-families-grateful-for-being-settled-in-west-bengal-5021161/.

30 "Deport Rohingya" clamour gets shriller, *Tribune News Service*, Apr. 8, 2018. http://www.tribuneindia.com/news/jammu-kashmir/-deport-rohingya-clamour-gets-shriller/570736.html.

31 The BJP pulled out of the coalition government on June 19, 2018.

32 Uyghur, Tibetan Muslims were granted citizenship rights, *Early Times Report*, June 3, 2018. http://www.earlytimes.in/m/newsdet.aspx?q=187254.

33 India's forgotten nationals, *The Pioneer*, July 22, 2013. https://www.dailypioneer.com/2013/columnists/indias-forgotten-nationals.html.

34 Ibid.

35 Rohingyas operating girls' trafficking racket in Jammu; kingpin arrested, Vivek Sharma, Feb. 17, 2018. http://news.statetimes.in/rohingyas-operating-girls-trafficking-racket-in-jammu-kingpin-arrested/.

36 Govt acts on Rohingyas: GoM set up, first meeting today, Sanjeev Pargal, May 10, 2017. http://www.dailyexcelsior.com/govt-acts-on-rohingyas-gom-set-up-first-meeting-today/

37 India makes Rohingya stand clear to Myanmar: "Want their safe, speedy, sustainable return", Shubhajit Roy, May 12, 2018. http://indianexpress.com/article/india/india-makes-rohingya-stand-clear-to-myanmar-want-their-safe-speedy-sustainable-return-5173352/.

38 Myanmar says willing to take back all Rohingya refugees, *Reuters*, June 2, 2018. https://www.reuters.com/article/us-asia-security-myanmar/myanmar-says-willing-to-take-back-all-rohingya-refugees-idUSKCN1IY0AS.

39 Centre tells J-K Govt. to prevent Rohingyas entry, *ANI*, Jun 2, 2018. https://www.aninews.in/news/national/general-news/centre-tells-j-k-govt-to-prevent-rohingyas-entry201806022058180001/.

40 State govt. yet to act on Centre's direction on Rohingya refugees, Jammu, June 6, 2018. http://www.tribuneindia.com/news/jammu-kashmir/state-govt-yet-to-act-on-centre-s-direction-on-rohingya-refugees/600734.html.

41 Rohingya Muslims: Editorial by Maulana Wahiduddin Khan, Sept. 16, 2017. http://www.speakingtree.in/article/rohingya-muslims.

CHAPTER THREE

Rassana: India's Most Exploited Crime Story

Sarjana Sharma

Through the month of March 2018, the national and international media and social media were abuzz with stories of the Kathua incident – the alleged rape and murder of an 8-year-old girl – with a flood of Twitter and Facebook posts. Thereafter, this crime in the nondescript village Rassana was the toast of the mainstream media. In a blatant violation of India's victim-sensitive laws such as section 228A of Indian Penal Code (IPC) and the Protection of Children from Sexual Offences Act (POCSO Act), the name, religion and photographs of the victim and also the accused were splashed across newspapers, television channels, Twitter, and even hoardings in some cities. The media, activists (NGOs) and even women's organisations and the legal fraternity, which is supposed to be mindful of the law, revealed a rare but concerted insensitivity in this case. One has only to recall that to this day, the media has not taken the name of the victim of Delhi's "Nirbhaya" case, despite her mother publicly pleading for recognition of her dead daughter, because the media then abided by the law and exercised exemplary restraint.

The generally somnolent hamlet of Rassana was suddenly in sharp focus. The murder (and alleged gang rape) of the Gujjar-Bakarwal (nomad) child was the subject of heated discussions and impassioned debates. What made the tragic event even more repulsive was the media claim that the crime took place in a sacred site of the Hindu community. Some "activists" claimed to be ashamed of being born Hindus. Accusations were hurled all around. It was a free for all. The shrill and sustained brouhaha over the Kathua case intrigued us, members of a group of professional women and social activists, particularly the speed with which this one case was singled out for so much media attention, nationally and internationally. We wondered if there was some motive behind the manner in which so much information about the deceased and the alleged "accused" was made public – Google, Wikipedia, YouTube, BBC and a host of other sources are still readily accessible on the internet – and if there was a deliberate attempt to discredit the Hindu community and its places of worship as the crime scene was described as a "temple" (it was actually a *Devsthan*, an equally sacred space).

Disturbed by these issues, we felt that some of us should visit Kathua to learn firsthand about the events that had transpired there and prepare a fact-based narrative from ground zero.[1] We studied all available reportage on the case and made tentative lists of people to meet and interview in Rassana, Kathua, and Jammu city. In this respect, we were fortunate to be able to meet Ms. Mehbooba Mufti, the then Chief Minister of Jammu and Kashmir,[2] in Jammu, among other persons. We landed at Jammu airport on the morning of April 23, 2018. Rassana is an otherwise sleepy hamlet of 14 houses in tehsil Hiranagar of district Kathua in the Jammu region, about 60 km from Jammu city. The journey by road took around 90 minutes.

As we neared the village, we came across a group of women from Rassana and adjoining villages sitting on a relay hunger strike on Kootah Mod on the National Highway. They expressed lack of faith in the investigation carried out by the local police and Crime Branch, and wanted an impartial investigation by the Central Bureau of Investigation (CBI), which, they were convinced, would clear the fair name of their village. The protesters included Madhu, elder daughter of the main accused Sanjhi Ram Jangotra (also known as Sanjhi Ram or Sanjhi Ram Patwari) and Tripta Devi, mother of a minor adolescent boy who was the first to be arrested in the case. We decided to proceed to the village and conduct our own investigation first and then meet with the protesters. Tiny Rassana is bisected by a narrow, metalled road. On both sides of the road are well-constructed pucca houses. Most men in the village have retired from the armed forces, a fact that explains the comparative affluence witnessed in the construction of the houses. As we entered the village, we saw the beautiful temple (distinct from the much maligned Devsthan) on the left. Behind the temple is a pond with steps descending into it; beyond sprawls a thick jungle.

We first visited the cowshed where the deceased child was allegedly held hostage (in the first version of the story). The 15-year-old juvenile who was first arrested for the crime allegedly stated in his confessional statement (police version) that he had kept the girl in this cowshed from January 10 to 17, 2018. Later, the police themselves trashed this theory. The cowshed belongs to the main accused Sanjhi Ram Jangotra. It is located at a spot surrounded by houses on both sides. The cowshed is an open compound where on the right is a room with a low entrance that is used as storage for cattle-feed and on the left is a shed that has now been locked by the Crime Branch. There were calves tied on the left portion of this shed. This is frequented by women of the village who ritually feed the cows and calves here. We surmised that it would have been extremely difficult, if not downright impossible, for a hostage to be kept there without attracting notice.

Crossing the village, we entered the Devsthan that has been under media glare and has been wrongly called a temple or *Devi-sthan* by the media as well as the Crime Branch charge sheet. According to media reports, it was here that the deceased child was allegedly confined for 6 days, gang raped, and murdered. The *sarpanchs* (heads) of Rassana and some neighbouring villages informed us that the Devsthan is not a traditional temple consecrated to popular Hindu divinities. It is a shrine that houses the *Kul-devatas* (family/clan deities) of Rassana and the neighbouring villages of Damiyal, Kootah and Patta. These devatas (Baba Kali Veer, Raja Mandalik, Baba Birfa Nath, Sargal Nag Devata, Mata Mal Devi) are not gods and goddesses of the classical Hindu pantheon. They are folk heroes and guardian spirits of the area and are revered and worshipped by the local populace, in addition to the Vedic pantheon. Outside the devsthan is the *sthan* of Peer Baba who is held in high reverence and is worshipped along with the Kul-devatas.

The devsthan is a small, humble structure approximately 20 × 35 feet, it has three doors, three windows and four ventilators. The windows have no panes of any sort, just iron grills. There are *chowkies* (simple, unadorned shrines) symbolizing the presence of the Kul-devatas and a picture of Mal Mata. Anyone standing outside can see what is going on inside the structure. The *garbhgriha* (sanctum sanctorum) where the gang rape allegedly took place is nowhere in sight. It does not exist, for this is not a traditional temple. Following local tradition, *bhandara* (free public feeding) is held here from time to time. So some containers and pots and pans are also kept here. There is a small table adjacent to the large window to the left. It is said to be the table under which the child, concealed in a *durrie* (rug), was hidden. But there is a mismatch:

how can one hide a girl with a height of 4 feet under a table only 3½ feet long? How is it possible to hide a girl in this room with three doors and three windows with only grills and no panes – glass or otherwise?

According to the charge sheet, the child was drugged and gang raped on January 10, 11, 12 and 13. On the night of January 14, she was strangulated. Local residents trash the police version, "On 13, 14 and 15 January 2018, on the days when the Crime Branch charge sheet states that the victim was kept in captivity at the Devsthan, there were many people around. The place was not empty. January 13 was Lohri, January 14 was Makar Sankranti, a major festival again … and on January 15 there was a *yagya* and *bhandara* at the Devsthan. How could anyone not have noticed something amiss?" Also, apart from the set of keys in the possession of Sanjhi Ram, at least four other sets of keys are with persons from the adjacent villages of Damiyal, Kootah and Patta. Anyone could walk in any time. Why would anyone choose such a place to commit a crime?" The villagers have questions of their own. Uneasy questions nobody is willing to answer, or even listen to. They feel there is a conspiracy to sow seeds of discord in this traditionally peaceful area, "What happened to the little Bakarwal child is terrible. She was a daughter to us all. We here revere girls as the Virgin Goddess incarnate. This incident is a blemish on our name. It can be cleaned only when the real culprits are caught and brought to justice", they said in unison.

We took the same short, narrow kuccha path that leads from the Devsthan to the back of the house of Sanjhi Ram; the deceased child's body was found barely a hundred metres from the house. On this path is also the pole under which, according to the Crime Branch charge sheet, the accused juvenile hid tablets of Epitril 0.05. Why would a murderer dump a body so close to his own house? There are a number of safer sites in the jungle; a small *nullah* nearby would have been the logical site for dumping a dead body. Sanjhi Ram is held in high esteem by his neighbours. The residents told us,

> He is as a rule a very decent man, but he is nobody's fool and does stand up for his rights. The police claim that he has spent hundreds of thousands of rupees to pay bribes to cover up for himself and his son. If he is that resourceful and "smart" why would he dump the body right behind his own house, at a spot on the path which leads to the devsthan and for that reason sees heavy footfalls? It was winter, the deceased was only a child, he could easily have carried her body to a better, safer spot. And would an elderly father ask his son to miss his exam and come home to rape a child? He has better sense than that.

Residents of the village shared crucial information about the background of the deceased child. According to them, Yusuf, the child's adoptive father, had been bringing his animals to the village for decades. His wife's brother, Mohammed Akhter, gave him his daughter a few years ago when Yusuf lost his daughters in an accident. Instead of going to school like other chidden of her age (including Yusuf's two sons), the 8-year-old child used to take her family's animals to the jungle to graze. Mohammed Akhter resented this and had been asking for his daughter to be returned to him. Yusuf often got into altercations with two other Gujjars, Ashraf Ali and Mumtaz Ali. The duo had even burnt his house down in the past.

We went to Sanjhi Ram's house to speak with the family members. There we met Monika, younger daughter of Sanjhi Ram, her brother Lovelytosh who works with the Indian Navy, and an elderly aunt. Her mother and elder sister, Madhu, were at the sit-in at Kootah Mod, demanding a CBI probe into the case. Madhu and Monika are married and live in nearby Charwal; both sisters came back to be with their parents in their hour of crisis. Initially, Monika seemed composed. She did not mention the travails of her family, "We want justice for the dead girl. We want the real culprits to be caught. Only then will her soul rest in peace. The innocent must not be pilloried; the spreading of canards must stop. We have no faith in the J&K Crime Branch; we want the CBI to investigate the case. We have no quarrel with Yusuf; he does not live close to our house. We allow the Gaddis from Himachal to graze their sheep on our land, we don't allow the Bakarwals. It's our land and we have a right to decide who gets to graze on it". Punching holes in the "rape and murder in devsthan" theory, she said, "There are multiple sets of keys to the three doors of the devsthan, apart from my father, Bishandas Sharma from our village and a few men from other villages have them. Anyone could come there anytime. Every evening the women perform *kirtan* there. On Lohri (January 13, 2018) devotees had been visiting the shrine throughout the day, on the 15th, there was a *bhandara*. The room was cleaned in the evening. Had the child been there, wouldn't someone have noticed her presence?"

Shuddering at her family's name being dragged into this crime, she says, "The truth is the child never was in the *devsthan*. It is a sacred space. Only people from this area know what our *Kul-devatas* mean to us. An outsider can have no idea... . How could my father and brother commit such a terrible sin in the *devsthan*? This whole thing is a tissue of lies. Our family's name has been tarnished! We are being branded sinners! We too have many questions. Who will answer those?" Monika defends Sanjhi Ram,

> My father has six sisters, two daughters. He has been a respected government employee ... retired as *patwari* (revenue official) from the J&K Department of Irrigation on November 30, 2017. My older brother, Lovelytosh, is in the Indian Navy and the younger, Vishal, who is falsely implicated in this case, studies at Meerut. The records from his college prove his innocence. My cousin S----- is only 14; he was taken away by the police without any warrant. The police came, spoke with him and went away. Then they returned and asked my mother to send him with them for a couple of minutes as they needed to ask a few questions. He has not been returned to us to this day. He had been expelled/suspended from school for smoking, so my father made him come here ... who knew such a terrible fate was to befall us.

She continued,

> "The deceased child was last seen by our neighbour, Veena Sharma, on January 10, 2018. She had been inquiring about her horses. The police say the child was kept in the cowshed, you can see yourself how improbable that would be – the cowshed is surrounded by family homes, people come at all hours to feed the *peda* (customary lump of dough) to the cows. We too go there several times a day to feed and water and milk the cows. How could anyone be held a hostage there and go unnoticed?"

Nodding towards her brother, she said,

> "Lovelytosh works for the Indian Navy so he has been spared. He was home on leave for Papa's retirement and returned to duty afterwards. He was on the high seas from December 23, 2017 to March 20, 2018 or they would have implicated him too. Even our neighbour, P----- Sharma, was not spared. He was forced to make a statement to the effect that he witnessed Sanjhi Ram commit the crime".

Anger, frustration and helplessness tinged her voice at this point, "We don't know who to appeal to. We have no faith in the J&K police but are confident that the [Centre] would get us justice. We are only demanding a fair probe into the matter, death by hanging for the guilty and freedom for the innocent". Monika's restraint gave way and she wept, "I appeal to you. Please present our narrative of events. The media is just not considering our side". The villagers' general complaint was, "the Crime Branch has created an atmosphere of terror in the area. They pick up people randomly, torture them and pressure them into making patently false statements".

We met Ashok Sharma, father of a minor boy who had been picked up by the police. The 17-year-old P----- (aka Mannu) was visiting his aunt when the police "needed to question him". Ashok works in Mumbai; on learning that his son had been taken by the police, he returned to be with his family. Ashok and other villagers said, "The police tortured the boy, made him urinate on a working electric heater, crushed his fingers ... he was intimidated to state that he had seen Sanjhi Ram commit the crime". Ashok is a man of humble means and his family is now in dire financial straits. Ex-serviceman Bishandas Sharma is bitter, "The British rule was better ... compared to what is happening now". The villagers complain, "Thousands of Gujjar-Bakarwals descended on the village for the child's *chautha* (fourth day prayer ceremony). They raised slogans against India, kicked at people's doors and generally intimidated the residents... This is a border area. Of late, there has been a rise in drug trafficking and trafficking of cows. People who protest this are seen as enemies by the Bakarwals". Bishandas's wife laments at the loss of trust between the villagers and the nomads, "The Gujjar women come to our homes regularly to fill drinking water, to recharge their phones and to watch television. We have always had cordial relations with them; now this...". The villagers are angry, "The name of our village has been dragged in the mud ... the culprits must be caught and hanged, the innocent freed".

People reluctantly mention a seemingly unrelated incident, "There is a pond at the edge of the jungle at the upper part of the village. There used to be a holy man's *dera* there. The Gujjars' animals used to dirty the water of the pond. The holy man tried to stop that... . Two years ago he was found murdered". Though it was never conclusively proved who killed the holy man, the needle of suspicion pointed towards the nomadic visitors. Still relations between the residents had remained "cordial". The rape-cum-murder of the girl child has finally soured the brew of "Hindu–Muslim unity".

Residents of the village point to a serious lapse in the investigation: in the evening of January 16, 2018, the transformer in Rassana faulted with a loud bang and the village was plunged in darkness. Around 2.30 a.m., a Bullet bike with two persons huddled in blankets was seen going towards the upper part of the village. Half an hour later, the bike left the village. A few hours later, the body of the deceased child was found lying between the devsthan and Sanjhi Ram's house. Bishandas Sharma confirms this, "Around 2.30 a.m. on the night of January 16, I saw a Bullet bike going towards the upper edge of the village. No one in our village has a Bullet motorbike, but at that point I did not think much about it. After about half an hour the bike left the village. Had I suspected anything amiss I would have blocked its way with logs".

The people of the area were stunned, shocked that a crime was being painted as a deliberate act of communal discord. They felt that some persons, such as the self-styled Gujjar-Bakarwal leader, Talib Hussain, have political ambitions and are trying to encash the opportunity presented by the crime. They pointed out, "Up to the 16th, he suspected no one. A few hours after the body was found, he became active, gave the murder a communal turn... . His role in the case ought to be probed seriously ... his phone and travel records must be scrutinized". Talib Hussain has been registered as a student at the Law Faculty of Jammu University since 2011. In a telephonic conversation, he showed awareness of only the discredited and abandoned cowshed story. This gives rise to several questions that can only be answered by a proper investigation (*see interviews at the end*). Our team tried to visit Yusuf's house, which is situated just above Rassana. He had purchased 10 marlas of land from Harnam of Kootah and built a pucca house. We learnt that he had left Rassana for the summer migration; a police team guarded his house.

Having finished our investigation at Rassana, we left for Kootah Mod where the residents of the area were sitting on a relay hunger strike since January 23, 2018, to demand justice and a CBI probe into the case under the banner of *Hindu Ekta Manch*. The need for this outfit was felt as soon as it became clear that the gruesome murder of the child was becoming a pawn in a larger, sinister game. The Manch was hastily announced by former J&K State BJP secretary, advocate Vijay Kumar Sharma. Members of the Hindu Ekta Manch, namely, Ardiyal sarpanch Jagram Sharma, social activist Rajkumar Sharma, Satoora sarpanch Bhagmal Khajuria, Nonath sarpanch Vijay Tagotra, Tribhuvan Sharma of Gagwal, Shyamsundar Chadwal, and law students Mintoo and Abhinandan Sharma were at Kootah Mod. They explained that they formed the Manch when they felt that nobody was listening to their side of the story – not the political parties, not the police, not the administration, not even the media. The Manch objected strongly to the gang rape theory: "We were shocked when the child's body was found on January 17, 2018. She was a daughter of ours. To us, all girls are *kanjak* (Virgin Goddess), if anyone's foot inadvertently brushes a girl, they touch her feet as a penance for the sin. How could any of us commit such a heinous crime against the little girl? We want the culprits to be brought to book and to be punished; the innocent must not be pilloried for something they did not do". Others lamented, "When the body of the child was found, about 400 Hindu families from the area protested to demand justice for her. The same evening Talib Hussain, the so-called leader of the Gujjar-Bakarwals, began to demand the arrest of Sanjhi Ram. The police arrested anyone named by Talib". That, they said, was truly astonishing.

On January 20, the day of the deceased child's *chautha*, Talib Hussain, Nazakat Khatana and hundreds of their supporters arrived and raised slogans of "Pakistan Zindabad ... Hindustan Murdabad"; "they banged at people's doors, gathered outside Sanjhi Ram's house and swore at him. Ram's teenaged nephew, S----- was picked up by the police under false pretenses, beaten and intimidated into making a 'false' statement. Another teenager of the village, P-----(Mannu), was also picked up and pressured into claiming that he was a witness to Sanjhi Ram's crime. When the boy shared this with the Manch, he was made an accused. The police also harassed Hiranagar chemist Amit and Kootah chemist Rajneesh to state that the medicines used to drug the victim had been bought from them".

Our team was told that Sanjhi Ram's son, Vishal Jangotra, was in Meerut on January 12, 13, 14 and 15. He and three other local boys, Neeraj, Sahil and Sachin, study in Meerut and live in shared accommodation there. The group alleged that the boys were brutalized by the police, "Neeraj, Sahil and Sachin were forced to state that Vishal was not in Meerut on January 12, 13 and 14. When they were brought before the magistrate, they simply stated they had been forced to make that statement by the police". Special police officer Deepak Khajuria was arrested on February 7, just days before his marriage. He had been pressured to turn approver, but had refused. Soon afterwards, special police officer Surendra Verma of Satura was also arrested. The agitated villagers added, "We were terrified and seeking safety in numbers at Hiranagar Ramlila ground. Then on February 28 they imposed Section 144 ... A child waved the tricolour and the incident was mischievously reported as nationalists supporting the perpetrators of the crime. What kind of media attitude is this? Where do we go for a fair hearing?"

The then J&K minister of Forests Lal Singh Chaudhary and Industries minister Chandra Prakash Ganga visited the *dharna* site to hear the grievances of the villagers. But when they supported the demand for a CBI probe into the incident, the Chief Minister forced them to resign from their offices, to the dismay of the villagers. "Is it a crime for an elected representative of the people to stand by his constituents?" they asked, adding that initially, Yusuf, Talib Hussain and Nazakat Khatana also asked for a CBI probe, but retracted later, acting on some invisible command.

The Rassana residents point out that the Gujjar-Bakarwal nomads had been coming to the area for decades and there was never any open animosity. Sometimes their cattle grazed the villagers' crops and Sanjhi Ram often protested against this. But on the whole, relations between the two communities were amicable. The three police stations of the area do not have a single registered complaint of an altercation between the two communities. In fact, it was the Gujjar-Bakarwals who often fought amongst themselves and lodged reports with the local police. Indeed, the police initially picked up a Bakarwal named Ashraf, with whom Yusuf had had serious disagreements in the past, but released him the next day. The Bakarwals traditionally move to the higher slopes between March 31 and April 15. They inform the local police in writing of their migration. They are required to pay a grazing fee so the local tehsildar makes a card for them, which is renewed every year. The villagers strenuously insisted that they never turned away the Bakarwals and that the current case is a deep conspiracy to intimidate the Hindus and force them to migrate. Yusuf had purchased 10 marlas of land above Rassana and built a pucca house and also encroached some surrounding land. The local people alleged that Kashmir-centric communal forces were at work to foment unrest in the region, and that the proposed changes in the Tribal Act and the settling of Rohingyas from Myanmar were parts of this conspiracy.

A problematic issue concerns the manner in which the deceased child's high-resolution photograph was circulated in the media. Who took that photograph, when, why? Her body was found wearing the same clothes in which she disappeared. How could a child who was gang-raped over several days have her shoes and hairband intact? It would seem that the real conspirators are at large and innocents are being framed. The residents are adamant that only a non-partisan probe can reveal the truth. Certainly, the case has had too many unexplained twists and turns. There are wide gaps between the charge sheet and the version of the local residents. The postmortem report is incompatible with alleged gang rape. What is abundantly clear is that the incident was deliberately given a political-communal overtone to kill two birds with one stone: spoil the so far cordial relations between the Gujjar-Bakarwal and Hindu communities within Jammu, and give Hindus and their holy places a bad name.

It is pertinent that in recent times, the orthodox Sunni Muslims of the valley have been trying to win over the Gujjar-Bakarwals whom they had hitherto shunned for their unorthodox ways. The nomad groups were always regarded as culturally inferior. Moreover, the terrorist groups think that the nomads serve as informers for the army and the government. This community raised the alarm over the Kargil intrusions and has often been the target of terrorist attacks in the past.

*

Social and political volatility behind Kathua case

The kidnapping and murder of a child is a heinous crime and the atmosphere was understandably emotionally charged when the body of the child was found 7 days after she went missing. The murder shocked Rassana and adjoining villages, as the simple villagers of this innocuous area were not used to such dramatic events. Unfortunately, the larger volatility in Jammu and Kashmir made it easy to spark off wider tensions in the region. Thus, a kidnapping-cum-murder that occurred in mid-January was manipulated into a full-fledged political-communal episode by April, aided and abetted by the media (both print and electronic), with unseen actors maintaining full control of the narrative, both nationally and internationally. On one side of the dividing line were the Gujjar-Bakarwals, the state government dominated by the People's Democratic Party (PDP) and political parties such as the Congress and the National Conference. On the other side were the Hindu Ekta Manch and the Kathua District and Jammu Bar Associations that demanded a CBI probe to bring out the truth. The Bharatiya Janata Party maintained the coalition government (till June 19, 2018) but expressed itself against certain policies, especially the State Government's cynical move to turn a blind eye to encroachment of forest land in Jammu province.

In the course of our 2-day probe in Jammu and Kathua, we encountered people from a wide cross-section of society. Many softly whispered information and asked and answered questions while lacking the confidence to speak out in public. It was fairly evident that the people of Jammu region had no faith in the state government and the local police. They were especially suspicious of the mainstream media that they believed had stereotyped them as anti-national and pro-rapists, without even trying to hear their version of the events. They viewed this as part of a well-planned conspiracy to change the region's demography. Their suspicions were fuelled by the fact that thousands of Rohingya infiltrators from Myanmar had been settled in Jammu, a region hundreds of miles from Myanmar and utterly alien to them.

The then Minister for Food Supplies and Tribal affairs, Chaudhary Zulfiqar

Asi, strenuously defended the Rohingyas, "These are peaceable people. So far, there have been no instances of violence by them. We have checked their credentials, they are clean. Since the case is pending in the Supreme Court, we can't take any action in this matter. They are getting help from some Delhi NGOs". Chief Minister Mehbooba Mufti repeated this argument and alleged that "Interested parties are manipulating the Kathua case just to improve their political graph". Local leaders, however, disagreed and pointed out, "The army's anti-terrorism operations in the valley have rendered all major terrorist outfits leaderless. This has made Mehbooba unpopular with them. The general public too has been discomfitted by the continuing army operations. In order to regain the lost ground, Mufti has turned a crime into an opportunity to give the Hindus and their shrines a bad name. The case became a stick to beat the Hindu community".

Post-independence developments in Jammu suggest that the fears of the Hindu majority were justified. Even if we set aside the brutal and bloody exodus of Kashmiri Pandits from the valley in early 1990, the absence of a Hindu Chief Minister since the accession of the State in 1947 is convincing evidence for many. From intellectuals to plebians, people from Jammu region are unanimous in the belief that for the last seven decades they have suffered gross injustice in the matter of jobs, opportunities, development of the region, and even distribution of funds allocated by the Centre. They allege that State Census records have been tampered with to establish Hindus as a fast dwindling minority in the state, and assert that no Chief Minister has ever worked for the development of the Hindu-majority Jammu region. In fact, all have exerted themselves to change the region's demography. To substantiate this view, residents point out that Mehr Chand Mahajan was the only Hindu *wazir-e-azam* (the Persian term for prime minister, which was used until March 1965 when, through an amendment in the State's constitution, the then wazir-e-azam Ghulam Muhammed Sadiq was sworn in as the first Chief Minister of Jammu and Kashmir). Mahajan held the post for less than 5 months, 142 days to be exact. Thereafter, only Muslims from the Srinagar valley have been elected as Chief Ministers of the State.

Another bone of contention is the appropriation of all minority benefits by the Muslim community in the Muslim-majority state. According to the 2011 census, the percentage of the Muslim population in the state as a whole is 68.31. Within the valley, Muslims comprise 96.4 percent of the population, 14 percent of whom are Shia; Hindus count for a meagre 2.45 percent, Sikhs

0.98 percent and others 0.17 percent. Advocate Ankur Sharma of the Jammu and Kashmir High Court stated, "The fact is, it is all about efforts to change the demography of the area. The strategy is to intimidate the Hindus of the region to the point where they will migrate voluntarily". Sharma elaborated, "The Census is scam ridden as well ... Census officials are instructed to use pencils while filling the forms which are later tampered with". Arguing that due to Article 370, the rules and parameters of the National Minorities Commission cannot be applied in Jammu and Kashmir, Sharma filed a PIL to challenge the status quo and demand the formation of a Minorities Commission in the state. Hearing the PIL, a three-judge bench headed by the then Chief Justice of India Dipak Misra said, "We have legal difficulties. We cannot direct the legislature to legislate on a particular issue. We just asked them (Centre and state) to deliberate". Attorney General K.K. Venugopal, who appeared for the Centre, informed the court that it was still deliberating the issue. The court said it would take up the matter after 8 weeks. On August 8, the court granted a final opportunity to the Centre and other stakeholders to take a decision in three months on issues raised in the petition; it asked the Centre and the state government to "sit together" and find a solution to "contentious" issues, including whether Muslims in the state could be regarded as a minority to avail of benefits under that category. (The petition was later dismissed by the Supreme Court.)

Another bone of contention is the Roshni Act. The Jammu and Kashmir Legislative Assembly passed the historic Roshni Act in February 2007, to give free-of-cost ownership rights to 16.60 lakh kanals of State land under the occupation of farmers in the State. The State Government described the legislation as revolutionary on the lines of the famous land reforms ushered in by Sheikh Abdullah, inspired by the Leftist school of thought. The then Chief Minister Ghulam Nabi Azad said that a nominal fee of Rs. 100 per kanal had to be paid by occupant farmers for getting mutation in their favour in the revenue records. He said the Bill would go down as yet another revolutionary step in the annals of history in Jammu and Kashmir, second only to the Land to Tiller Act. He termed the Bill a farmer-friendly gesture that would help to boost the farming sector. Describing agriculture as the backbone of the State economy, Azad said that unless the farming community was socially and economically well-off, boosting farm produce to cater to the requirements of the State was not possible; the funds raised under the scheme would be dedicated to improvements in power generation, and hence the term, Roshni.

In practice, however, thousands of acres were transferred to beneficiaries who included top ministers of the regime, former ministers, politicians, police officers and bureaucrats. According to official data, 19,293 kanals of state land was transferred to 10,328 beneficiaries in Kashmir and 2,10,398 kanals to 39,829 beneficiaries in the Jammu region. The report of the Comptroller & Auditor General pointed out that the scheme generated only Rs 78.47 crore instead of the estimated Rs 25,000 crore, thus killing its very purpose. In 2014, the Principal Accountant General (PAG) had expressed similar reservations about the scheme, stating that the state government had lost Rs 25,000 crore under the Roshni Act; it described the Roshni Act as the biggest land scam ever.

Advocate Ankur Sharma challenged this Act in court and acquired a stay, but the state government had more cards up its sleeve. On February 14, 2018, it called a special meeting of the ministers and officers of the state to formulate/introduce an act to grant land rights to the nomadic Gujjar-Bakarwals. The minutes of the meeting got leaked and it became a major issue with people from the Jammu region who saw it as an attempt to legalise the grabbing of State and private lands by one community. Ankur Sharma emphasised, "This is part of the Islamic conspiracy of Greater Kashmir and Pakistan's plan of 'Fall of Jammu, fall of North India'". The sacking (forced resignation) of Lal Singh Chaudhary, then minister for Forest, Environment and Ecology, who was not popular with the nomadic Gujjar-Bakarwals on account of his strict implementation of the forest law, must be seen in this light. Talib Hussain, the man behind the media blitz about the Kathua case, countered, "Chaudhary Lal Singh is anti-Muslim. He was unduly harsh towards the Gujjar-Bakarwals. We marched to his residence with our livestock ... I had forewarned him he would have to go". Talib is originally from the valley but his family had settled in Jammu. He had been making efforts to establish himself as a leader of the nomadic community but was widely perceived as a pawn of the Hurriyat and PDP. Local Gujjar leader Nazakat Khatana raised doubts about Talib's hectic travels to Delhi, Aligarh, Mumbai and Hyderabad in the wake of the Bakarwal child's murder and questioned the source of funds for these trips.

The then Chief Minister Mehbooba Mufti was in an unenviable position. As leader of a coalition comprising parties with diametrically opposite ideologies, she walked a tight rope. Within the state, Mufti had the reputation of being a person who could and did bring the BJP-led Central Government to its knees, as evidenced by the resignations of two BJP ministers who supported the Kathua villagers and the unilateral ceasefire in the valley for the duration of Ramzan. Forced by party discipline to remain tightlipped, BJP leaders in Jammu were extremely unhappy with the way the situation was handled. Former J&K BJP secretary, advocate Vijay Kumar Sharma formed the Hindu Ekta Manch when he felt that the BJP was not willing to come to the aid of those subjected to police atrocities. He was made to resign his party post, but asserted with conviction, "We will continue to fight for the honour of the Dogra people. The coalition government might have its reasons for acting the way it did. We are not bound by those limitations".

The people of the area believe that the Kathua case and its handling by the authorities was aimed at scaring the Hindu populace of the border areas into voluntarily leaving their homes and lands to settle elsewhere. A recent instance of this was the treatment meted out to the accused and the witnesses in the Kathua case and the Hindu police officers of the State police force. Rassana comprises just 14 Brahmin families. Around the village is a vast forest of around 250 acres. Knowledgeable persons alleged that the State Government was preparing to hand over this tract to the Bakarwals. The Bakarwals were also full of anxiety and felt that separatist and communal forces had succeeded in their efforts to fracture their centuries-old bonds of trust and coexistence. The Bakarwals have been staunch nationalists and as such a thorn in the side of the mainly valley-based separatist and communal forces. Valley Muslims consider them culturally inferior and do not trust them. The Kathua case is part of a conspiracy to cut-off the Bakarwals from the nationalist mainstream.

The people from Jammu region are also unhappy with the way they have been treated so far. The general feeling was that nobody had ever tried to look into their problems even as jobs and funds were appropriated by the valley. They pointed out that Jammu region served as an effective buffer against Pakistan for the nation, but the Central Government bowed down to every demand of the vested political groups from the valley. Community leaders in Jammu revealed the sad truth, "People have begun to settle their children in other states ... they are buying property in Chandigarh and elsewhere ... the unprecedented increase in the Muslim share of the population is worrying them... . If the demography of the region continues to change at this rate, we will have a repeat of the valley scenario here... . It is wise to safeguard one's family before that".

Clearly, the Kathua case is a complex tapestry of issues and factors, with separatist forces operating from the valley, Islamic forces operating from foreign shores, NGOs with dubious antecedents stirring the pot, and a demoralised and weakened social fabric, all contributing to a simmering unrest.

*

Ms. Mehbooba Mufti, former Chief Minister, J&K

We met the Chief Minister at her Jammu residence. She sounded worried about the Kathua case being given a communal colour: "I wish the news doing the rounds in certain sections of the media that the child was not raped are true. Such cases are heart-breaking". Mufti said that the case was being politicised because people had their own agendas and aspirations; the Hiranagar assembly seat is to be de-reserved soon and that is a big motive for people to come to the fore. The main accused in the case, Sanjhi Ram, is a "well-connected" man. He absconded for a while, but was eventually arrested. "The ghoulish act of violence perpetrated on a child was given a political and communal colour. First, it was two sarpanchs from the Congress; then two sarpanchs from the BJP joined them. Then the Hindu Ekta Manch was formed and the case turned Hindu vs. Muslim and Kashmir vs. Jammu. Initially, the state police did not highlight the case because the incident happened in a Hindu place of worship".

Ms. Mufti declared she had asked the Hurriyat leadership to maintain silence on the issue so that it did not take a communal turn. The step was deemed necessary and prudent because there are several temples in the Kashmir valley. Expressing her faith in the State Crime Branch, she said the demand for a CBI inquiry in the case is unnecessary, "The people of Jammu are basically secular but vested interests are not allowing them to stop the dharna/sit-in. The land mafia, the police and politicians have joined hands and the case is being heavily politicised". She called the Gujjar-Bakarwals nationalists and helpful to the army, and assured that the State Police would investigate the case fairly.

*

Lal Singh Chaudhary, former minister for Forests and Ecology

Lal Singh Chaudhary left the Congress party and won the Basohli Assembly seat on a BJP ticket in 2014. After he became involved in the Kathua case, he lost his post in the Mehbooba Mufti cabinet and was also expelled from the BJP.

Lal Singh claimed to have made efforts to diffuse the situation in the aftermath of the Kathua case; he spoke with Mehbooba Mufti, the state BJP leadership, and even organised a meeting of the Chief Minister with eight sarpanchs (it eventually did not take place). He visited Rassana, met with Yusuf (adoptive father of the deceased child) and presented his report in the Assembly with an appeal that the case should not be turned into a communal issue. Lal Singh revealed that state BJP president Sat Sharma deputed him to meet the villagers on dharna and then suspended him from the party for anti-party activities. He pointed to the unseemly haste with which Forest Department officials were transferred after his resignation; some were subjected to raids. He did not mince his words: "There are developments which, left unattended, would impact the whole nation in the near future. Mufti has her own agenda. The state government has turned a blind eye to the issue of the Rohingya Muslims. There are flagrant instances of partisanship ... Jammu Smart City and AIIMS Jammu have been put on the back burner. Of the roads being constructed under the Centrally-sponsored scheme, 3,300 km are in the valley and only 700 km in Jammu region. The Hindus of the Jammu region are discriminated against when it comes to government jobs. There is a clear plan underway to isolate Jammu region".

Lal Singh supported the demand for a CBI probe in the Kathua case, "Talib Hussain's role in the affair raises suspicions. He is a pawn of Hurriyat leader Syed Ali Shah Gilani. ... Didn't Ms. Mufti demand a CBI probe in the Shopian case? So why does she have objections now?" He warned, "The Kathua case is being used to kill many birds with one stone. The Hindus of Jammu region are being intimidated, the plan to change the demography of the region is being systematically carried out, and it is working. People are beginning to send their children to places outside the region. Why are Rohingya Muslims being settled in Jammu region? And how were they transported from the Myanmar border to Jammu?"

Lal Singh pointed out,

> Neither the Bakarwals nor the Chief Minister like the idea of removing encroachments from state forest land. On the other hand, Hurriyat and Pakistan are hell-bent upon instigating communal riots in the region. Six months ago, a calf was butchered in Hiranagar. Its head lay at one spot, its torso at another. When I checked with Rakesh Kumar, the man who reported the butchering, how he got the information, he showed me on his cellphone the number from which he had received the call. We called the number; it belonged to a Gujjar-Bakarwal. Clearly, they butcher cows and then spread the information with intent to foment communal discord in the region.

> Muslim nomads are illegally squatting on forest land within Jammu region; by introducing the Tribal Act, Chief Minister Mufti wishes to bestow them with powers that would make it virtually impossible to get the lands vacated. The Hindus of Jammu region have strong objections to the provisions of the Bill/Act proposed on February 14, 2018; if passed, it would render the Hindus of the region landless.

Most importantly, Chaudhary said, "The Kathua murder was deliberately given the name of rape. In the first post-mortem report, Dr. Mukul had denied the possibility of rape. But then the doctors were pressured into revising the report. Sanjhi Ram's family are cultured and educated, he was a big hurdle in the way of the Gujjar-Bakarwals. The man was framed and the case given a communal colour. Why would anyone demand a CBI probe into the case and also a Narco test for himself? Jammu region is at the centre of an international conspiracy. If we do not take timely steps, we will have a repeat of the Kashmir scenario sooner rather than later".

*

Talib Hussain's account

Telephonic conversation on April 28, 29, 2018

Talib Hussain sprang into the limelight due to his high-voltage leadership in the Kathua case. Along with Gujjar leaders Nazakat Khatana and Waqar Bhatti, he led protests and sit-ins to press for a CBI inquiry into the murder of the local Bakarwal girl. Interestingly, he is the person who first named Sanjhi Ram as the culprit, even personally presenting a memorandum to Union Home Minister Rajnath Singh. Later, he did an about-turn and began opposing the CBI probe. Talib Hussain's Facebook page says he is an advocate of the Jammu and Kashmir High Court, and the media has referred to him as a professional advocate. The truth is that he is merely enrolled with the Law Faculty at Jammu University. He is accused of the attempted murder of Jammu University scholar, Kapil Shastri (*State of Jammu & Kashmir v. Talib Hussain*; FIR number 226/2013, registered on September 13, 2013, at Police Station Gandhinagar, Jammu; Sections 307, 147, 148).

Talib Hussain became famous when an audio clip of a conversation between Waqar Bhatti and Nazakat Khatana of the All Tribal Co-ordination Committee (of which Talib is Chairman) went viral on the social media. According to the clip, Talib Hussain had collected funds in the name of justice for the deceased Bakarwal girl. Today, Bhatti and Khatana are suspicious of his motives. Our fact finding team was in Jammu from April 23 to 25, but Talib Hussain was said to be in the valley. However, the author was able to have a telephonic conversation with him on April 28 and 29 when he was in Delhi in connection with the Kathua case hearing in the Supreme Court.

Q: For 6 days after the disappearance of the child, you did not suspect anyone. Then after the corpse was found on January 17, you suddenly named Sanjhi Ram and demanded his arrest. What was the basis of your allegation?

Talib: There is solid evidence against Sanjhi Ram. He is dead against the Gujjar-Bakarwals ... so I named him. I named SPO Deepak Khajuria because I knew he was protecting someone. The child was hidden in Sanjhi Ram's cowshed. Didn't he or his wife go there to care for the cows for 6 days? Didn't they see what was going on? Why did they cover-up the crime?

Q: Your own comrades, Nazakat Khatana and Waqar Bhatti, are suspicious of your role in the case. They have made serious allegations against you, that you have collected hundreds of thousands of rupees in the name of seeking justice for the dead child.

Talib: Nazakat Khatana and Waqar Bhatti are hand in glove with the Hindu Ekta Manch. I never collected funds, not even a paisa. Investigate me. Nazakat Khatana and Waqar Bhatti need to survive within their Gujjar community, so they are spreading rumours about me.

Q: But Nazakat says you are using the case to kill many birds with one stone: sowing discord between Hindus and Muslims in the state, gaining advantage for the PDP, hogging media limelight, establishing yourself as a leader of the Gujjars.

Talib: I am sincerely fighting for justice for the daughter of my community. We (Nazakat, Waqar and I) started a movement to demand justice for the child and we succeeded too. But I am also interested in the case as an advocate.

Q: But you are still a law student, how do you call yourself an advocate? There are also allegations that though the incident happened in Kathua, since January you have been travelling to Delhi, Aligarh, Hyderabad and Mumbai. Where are the funds coming from?

Talib: Yes, I am still studying law because I am involved in agitations and movements for my community from time to time. That is how I miss sitting for my exams. I hope to complete my studies this year (2018). And yes, I did visit Delhi, Aligarh, Hyderabad and Mumbai. And not in connection with the Kathua case. I was in Hyderabad for the All India Student Leader's Meet;

in AMU for the All India Youth Leader Meet; in JNU to deliver a lecture about the incident.

Q: What were the dates of your visits? Who invited you to JNU?

Talib: I don't remember the exact dates. You will find them on my Facebook page though. I don't remember who invited me to JNU or when, but I do remember the audience was mostly J&K students.

Q: There are allegations that you reduced a very sensitive case to a drama on political and religious lines because you have political ambitions and are connected to Hurriyat.

Talib: I avoid politics and communalism. I am fighting for the rights of my community; we are nomads, we don't grab people's lands. At the Center, the BJP's attitude towards the Bakarwals is alright, but the Jammu BJP is gunning for the community... . In the name of the Forest legislation, the former minister for forests, Lal Singh, started throwing our people out of the forests, so we agitated from November 2017 to January 2018. After Chief Minister Mufti's intervention, Lal Singh slowed down... . Call me Hurriyat or whatever, I do not need a certificate from anyone. I firmly believe in the Indian judicial system. I know we will get justice in the Kathua case. My struggle to demand the Forest Act will continue because it is also connected with the Kathua case.

*

Chaudhary Nazakat Khatana

Nazakat Khatana, state president of the Jammu Kashmir Gujjar-Bakarwal Desh Tehrique-i-Insaaf, no longer leads a nomadic life. An activist, he raises issues of his community from time to time. It was he who advised Yusuf to lodge a missing person's report with the Hiranagar police station after the child went missing. He led the protest on January 17, 2018, when the child's body was found, and was one of the first persons to demand a judicial and CBI inquiry into the murder. He refuses to delve into details of the crime, but was conspicuous at the postmortem and burial of the victim.

Khatana said, "More than 5000 persons including the SDM and SSP, Gujjar MLA Qamar Ali, Miyan Altaf Kangan, Congress MLA Indrawal, CPI MLA Yusuf Tarigami, former Congress MLA Rajesh Gupta, former National Conference MLA Surjeet Singh Slathia came to mourn the child's death on her *chautha* in Rassana on January 20th. A large number of Hindu women too came bearing packets of chocolate and snacks as the departed was a child. The crowd inquired of the SSP about the progress in investigation to which he replied it would take time. This agitated them and they sat on the national highway ... when the DC asked us to open one side of the highway, we did so".

On the night of January 20, the police lathi-charged the protesters and Talib Hussain and Nazakat Khatana were injured. Talib was taken to Hiranagar police station and Nazakat was lodged in a Gujjar *kool* (mud-thatch hut). He fell out with Talib Hussain for grabbing the media limelight: "I and Waqar Bhatti did all the leg work in connection with this case and he just walks in and becomes a media hero". After the lathi charge, he needed to be hospitalized for 3 days, but on January 25, Khatana led a candle march in front of Jammu Press Club. Later, he was arrested by the J&K police.

About the grazing situation, Khatana said, "The Gujjar-Bakarwals pay grazing tax. The government allows grazing areas but they have no basic facilities like subsidised food grain, electricity, medical treatment or education. They sat on a hunger strike demanding the enactment of the Forest Act, but it could not be enacted because of dhara 370" (Article 370). Khatana claimed that Sanjhi Ram and Deepak Khajuria were enemies of the Gujjar-Bakarwals; Patwari harassed them and Khajuria was much feared. However, the local villagers are good people and their relations with the nomad visitors have been cordial. He rejected the "rape in the devsthan" theory, saying, "Yusuf's child was everyone's daughter. The temple is very holy to me, the crown on my head ... why would I say the rape took place there? We celebrate festivals with the Hindus ... this is all due to vote-based politics ... a devious plan to tear the Hindu-Muslim unity".

Nazakat Khatana and Talib Hussain together led the march for the forest legislation in 2017, but now distrust each other. Talib accuses Khatana of being a pawn of the BJP-RSS and "advancing their cause in Jammu" whereas the latter accuses Talib of having links with Hurriyat leaders and travelling with them in the valley since January, propagating the PDP as the messiah of the Gujjar community. Khatana said investigators should get details of Talib Hussain's phone calls and air travels. Khatana also questioned the role of Jammu advocate, Deepika Rajawat (since dismissed by the victim's father for neglecting to attend the court proceedings in Pathankot): "She has past links with Talib. When she heard the audio clip of the conversation between me and Waqar, she flew into a blind rage, phoning me and using filthy swear words I can't repeat to you".

*

Dr. Javed Rahi, prominent Gujjar activist

Rahi: The Gujjars are a predominantly nomadic tribe found all over Northern India and parts of Pakistan. We trace our origins to Gujarat and the Gurjara-Pratiharas. Our history has not been recorded properly and is not taught; as a result we are clubbed with the Rajputs. We have a distinct and a glorious history in India.

Q: So are the Gujjars nomadic?

Rahi: You will find three types of Gujjars. One would be the completely nomadic and have no permanent land. The second are semi-nomadic. Yusuf, father of the victim in Kathua, falls in this category. A small miniscule section of these are also elites now with substantial land and money.

Q: Tell us your feelings post this incident.

Rahi: A very unfortunate crime has happened. The child cannot come back now. I would request the Indian government only one thing. Please grant us the same rights as rest of the Tribals in India.

Q: Do the Gujjars feel insecure in Jammu?

Rahi: It is only very recently that this has started happening. The Gujjars migrate annually between Jammu and Kashmir. In Kashmir, we are treated as second class. The Kashmiris are extremely racist. The government led by Kashmiris did not give us any rights till 1991. After that, we were recognised as a Scheduled Tribe. However, we are still not given the complete educational and political rights that the Scheduled Tribes of the rest of India have. In 1989, when the Farooq Abdullah government abandoned Jammu and Kashmir, it was we Gujjars who restored governance. The Gujjar Police was raised and youth from my tribe have taken the brunt of militancy in the valley. We are an extremely nationalist community. Now the situation is that in Kashmir we are called Gujjars, and in Jammu we are branded as Muslims. We have a distinct identity. My tribe converted to Islam only in the 13th century. We maintain our distinct cultural practices. After this incident, many Kashmiris have tried to radicalize us. We do not want to fall into this Hindu–Muslim trap. The government must act before it is too late.

Q: What do you feel about the presence of Rohingyas in Jammu?

Rahi: We have nothing to do with the Rohingyas in Jammu. We also do not understand how they have come all the way to Jammu from the eastern border. Many of them are being radicalized by the *Tablighi Jamaat*. Many are involved in human trafficking. There is no clear indication of their numbers in Jammu. Unofficial estimates are that there are almost 30,000 of them in Jammu.

Q: What is your single message to the Government?

Rahi: We have only one single demand. The Gujjar-Bakarwals and the other nomadic tribes of Jammu and Kashmir should be given the same rights as the tribals in India have been given. We are not concerned about any Tribal Policy that the government of Kashmir is supposed to be preparing. What will a policy do for us? We want concrete legislations. If there had been an SC-ST Commission in Jammu and Kashmir, this particular issue would not have been exploited by vested interests. We would have got justice under the directions of the Commission. I request you to carry this message. If the Gujjars are radicalized, the State of Jammu and Kashmir will be lost to India.

*

Shashipal Advocate, president, Kathua Bar Association

Shashipal Advocate informed us that the fraternity was carrying out a peaceful protest since April 3, 2018, to press for four demands: (1) Rohingya Muslims be removed from the Jammu region; (2) Naoshera be declared a district; (3) Kathua murder case be handed over to the CBI and (4) the proposed law/bill giving the nomadic Gujjar-Bakarwal communities unlimited squatting rights that was presented in the Cabinet meeting on February 14, be rescinded.

Shashipal explained that on April 9, members of the Kathua Bar Association were protesting peacefully when the J&K Crime Branch personnel came at 4.30 p.m., presented the challan (charge sheet) and went back. However, Kathua SSP, Suleiman Chaudhary (a Bakarwal), complained that members of the Kathua Bar Association did not allow the Crime Branch counsels to do their work. The national media turned it into an issue and thus began the media trial of the Kathua Bar Association: "The Hindu community was given a bad name". Expressing unhappiness with the manner in which the matter was handled, he added, "Eventually Suleiman Chaudhary was transferred and Shridhar Patil took charge as SSP Kathua. Never did the Kathua Bar Association hamper any procedure, nor did it stop the J&K Crime Branch personnel from presenting the challan in court".

*

Telephonic conversation with Akhter, father of the deceased child

Q: Hello, namaskar. Akhter ji, could we speak? We have come from Delhi. We need some information from you. Could you tell us if you have filed a case in the High Court, Supreme Court?

Akhter: Yes ma'am.

Q: You had given your daughter to Yusuf, was she being brought up alright? We have heard from people ... Yusuf's both sons studied but your daughter grazed the horses. Is that true?

Akhter: (unclear voice) Yes, that is true, [he] educated his sons, did not educate my daughter, left her to graze the horses ... we did not know much either.

Q: You did not know she grazed horses there?

Akhter: They lived some distance away from us.

Q: OK ... why had you given your daughter to Yusuf?

Akhter: His three children (daughters) died in an accident, so we had given him our daughter, given her for a short time, no formal *panchayatnama*; he had been weeping ... (unclear) our case must proceed... .

Q: OK. Did you all demand a CBI inquiry?

Akhter: Oh no no no! We are not demanding CBI inquiry ... (unclear sound ... talking about case in Supreme Court).

Q: Alright. Do you believe the inquiry underway is going in the right direction?

Akhter: Yes, it's alright.

Q: You are saying it is alright. Yusuf has made a statement he wants a CBI inquiry into the matter.

Akhter: That I do not know. My daughter must get justice; that's all we want.

Q: OK. Several (compensation packages) have been announced by now ... have you received any compensation, any money so far?

Akhter: No, no. We have not received anything till now.

Q: Has Yusuf received any money?

Akhter: That we know nothing about. All we have said is, we want justice. Our girl needs justice.

Q: The whole country is with you. The child must get justice.

Akhter: The wrong that has been done to my child must be punished. This is what must happen.

Q: Certainly! The wrong must be punished.

*

NOTES

1 Members of the fact-finding team of the Group of Intellectuals and Academicians included Smt. Meera Khadakkar, retired district judge, Nagpur; Smt. Monika Arora, advocate, Supreme Court of India and Delhi High Court; Ms. Sarjana Sharma, senior journalist; Ms. Sonali Chitalkar, assistant professor, Miranda House, University of Delhi; Smt. Monicca Agarwal, entrepreneur and social activist. They visited the area from during April 23-25, 2018.

2 The BJP pulled out of the coalition government on June 19, 2018.

CHAPTER FOUR

Kathua: Crime, Demography, and Politics

Sandhya Jain

When a missing nomad girl child was found dead in Rassana village in Hiranagar tehsil, district Kathua, few could have imagined that the incident would soon be catapulted to national and even international notoriety, shake the foundations of the uneasy coalition government in the State, and reignite the debate over illegal immigrants in the region. Add a deliberate attempt to scandalize one community and stir passions in another, and you have all the ingredients of a political potboiler. Only, being a poorly contrived script, it fell apart sooner than its authors could have anticipated.

One positive fallout of the murder (and alleged rape) case was that the Supreme Court firmly asserted jurisdiction over the "exceptional" State of Jammu and Kashmir and shifted the trial to Pathankot in neighbouring Punjab, a step that led to a kind of meltdown even as the trial was progressing (and is still going on at the time of this writing). This was a setback for Chief Minister Mehbooba Mufti[1] as it was the victim's biological father, Mohammad Akhter, and not the accused, who demanded transfer of the case outside Kathua through lawyers led by Indira Jaising. In murder cases, the State is the prosecutor, and both parties (State and victim family) were ranged on the *same* side against the alleged killers. But Jaising wanted to move the case out of Kathua because the principal accused persons enjoyed social eminence there, as evidenced by the local movement that sprang up in their defence to demand an impartial inquiry by the Central Bureau of Investigation (CBI) as the villagers felt that the accused were being framed for extraneous (read political) reasons.

Jaising, a senior advocate, simply followed a script perfected by well-connected activists after the Gujarat riots of 2002. But in her haste to get the case shifted from the Kathua district court, Jaising put Mehbooba Mufti in an awkward position as transferring a case outside a State is proof that the Government has been deemed unfit to ensure an environment conducive to a free and fair trial. Once the Supreme Court (Bench comprising Chief Justice of India Dipak Misra and Justices D.Y. Chandrachud and Indu Malhotra) admitted the petition, the People's Democratic Party (PDP)–dominated government proposed Ramban, a Muslim majority district, as alternate venue. Jaising suggested the Union Territory of Chandigarh. It was inconceivable that the Supreme Court would transfer such a sensitive case to a district handpicked by the regime in power, where the accused persons and witnesses might feel nervous and intimidated. It selected Pathankot due to its proximity to Kathua (barely 30 km).

In its order of May 7, 2018, the Supreme Court directed the District & Sessions Judge, Pathankot, to conduct the trial expeditiously, on a daily basis. This was to ensure that the case did not linger indefinitely, as the State Crime Branch had adduced a list of 221 witnesses,[2] and adjournments could easily drag the case for several years in the trial court itself. The possibility of exhausting the accused persons mentally and financially was nixed by the Court, which is monitoring the case on a regular basis. After a hue and cry raised by lawyers for the accused over delay in transferring the case, the case was formally transferred to Pathankot on May 23; the concerned files were compiled and sent to the Pathankot court on May 30, and the first hearing held on May 31, 2018. In the opening days of the trial itself, the State government was seriously embarrassed when, on June 9, 2018, all prosecution witnesses summoned to give evidence in the case failed to show up in court,[3] ultimately, the prosecution closed its case after examining only 114 witnesses.

The Supreme Court has left open the question of a CBI inquiry into the Kathua murder, which relatives of the accused persons claimed was necessary to unravel the larger conspiracy behind the incident. This could happen at a later stage, should the prosecution case collapse in the Pathankot court. More importantly, whenever the Court hears petitions regarding the concerted settlement of Rohingyas from distant Myanmar in Jammu province, its decision will have a far-reaching impact on the State and could also affect the illegal settlement of Bangladeshis in Jammu. Though these issues are not directly the subject matter of the murder trial, they form the larger background to the case and the current turmoil in Jammu province. In fact, the subject has gathered greater salience after the publication of the first draft of the Assam National Register of Citizens on July 30, 2018, and the Centre's reassertion that Rohingya infiltrators would not be allowed to settle in India.

Cause célèbre

The case of *Mohd. Akhter v. The State of Jammu and Kashmir* [Writ Petition (Criminal) No. 85/2018] is now being heard *in camera* by the District & Sessions Judge, Pathankot. Given the importance of the case, we may note the directions given by the Supreme Court before discussing the larger issues involved in Kathua in particular, and Jammu in general. It is important to understand how certain forces made the murder of a girl child a national *cause célèbre*, and even managed to secure international opprobrium against the central government, which had no role in the affair. Stephane Dujarric, spokesperson for UN secretary general Antonio Guterres, called the murder "horrific" and said, "We very much hope that the authorities will bring the perpetrators to justice so they can be held accountable for the murder of this young girl".[4] The International Monetary Fund (IMF) chief Christine Lagarde urged the Prime Minister "to pay more attention" to the women in the country.[5] These interventions are astonishing in view of the fact that Europe is currently being swamped by illegal immigrants who are raping women and girls with unsettling impunity, yet neither the UN Secretary General nor the IMF chief has considered it necessary to address an issue that is tormenting European society so painfully.

These unwarranted statements can be credited to India's West-centric media-activist circuit that pulled its impressive international strings with lightning speed as part of its agenda to humiliate the ruling (ideologically opposed) Bharatiya Janata Party (BJP) regime in the global arena. Neither the BJP as a member in the State coalition nor as ruling party at the Centre had any involvement in the said crime, nor was this alleged. Yet an insidious attempt was made to link the crime to the community of the victim and the community of the accused, and implicate others by association. The contrived nature of the activists' indignation was evident from their silence over similar or more gruesome rapes and murders of children of both genders that have been reported across the country with grim frequency. In Jammu province itself, soon after the Rassana murder, a seven-year-old girl was raped at a madrasa in Katal Battal on March 12, 2018.[6] But the activists kept their selective outrage focussed on Rassana, thus lending credence to suspicions that a carefully calibrated communal polarisation was being whipped up to serve a larger political agenda, and the victim could have been a pawn in this cynical paradigm.

The decisive orders of the Supreme Court for day-to-day hearings shook the complacency of the prosecution by ensuring that witnesses were examined and cross-examined in a continuous manner and "for no reasons whatsoever the same shall be deferred". The State Government was permitted to appoint a Public Prosecutor of its choice, and the trial held *in camera* so that "the witnesses feel protected and the accused persons feel safe". The Supreme Court declared that "As this Court is monitoring the matter, no court shall entertain any petition pertaining to this case". It mandated "all special care and protection as per the command of the law" for the juvenile accused in the case. The transferee court was directed to try the case under the Ranbir Penal Code that applies to the State of Jammu and Kashmir. The statements of the witnesses that were recorded in Urdu were to be translated to English so that the transferee court does not face any difficulty in conducting the trial; the State of Jammu and Kashmir was directed to provide the requisite number of interpreters as directed by the District & Sessions Judge, Pathankot, so that the deposition of the witnesses could be properly recorded and translated copies thereof could be provided to the accused persons. The State of Jammu and Kashmir was entrusted with the duty to transport the witnesses to Pathankot and provide all other necessary facilities, including food, etc. so that the witnesses did not face any difficulty. The court directed that the accused persons be treated similarly "so that they do not feel that solely because they are accused persons, they are presumed to be guilty, for it is the settled principle that they are innocent till they are found guilty".

Lawyers for the accused persons were satisfied with the transfer of the case to a less charged environment. At the Kathua district court on April 16, 2018, the judge had lambasted the State Crime Branch for filing an incomplete challan (charge sheet) on April 9, 2018. This was inexplicable and inexcusable as the murder occurred in January and investigations (in which investigators changed rapidly at Srinagar's whims) were conducted over months. Thereafter, an elaborate theory of rape-cum-murder was constructed and circulated to all media and social media, along with a high resolution colour photograph of the victim and details of her real father (Mohd. Akhter) and adopted father (Mohd. Yusuf, from whose house she went missing). Hence, there was no legitimate excuse for an incomplete challan. A startling and irregular aspect of the charge sheet was that it was written in English instead of Urdu, which is the official language of the State and administration. This is probably the only charge sheet written in English, dated January 17, 2018, the day the child's body was found. This deviation suggests that an invisible hand was pulling strings in the case from the very beginning. The Kathua magistrate berated the Crime Branch for not giving copies of the charge sheet to lawyers for the accused. At the hearing, all the accused persons pleaded for an investigation by the CBI and to be subjected to a Narco-test,[7] which is a powerful sign of innocence. A few days later, lawyers for the accused complained in the media that jail authorities were not permitting them to meet their clients, a serious breach of their right to counsel.[8]

These petty harassments ended with Governor's rule.

The crime

We may now examine the "facts" of the case: the child, belonging to a Bakarwal family, went missing on January 10 after taking the family horses for grazing in the jungle at the back of the village. Her adopted father informed the police on January 11, and an FIR (No. 10 of 2018) was registered at Hiranagar police station, Kathua, on January 12. Joint searches by the Police and villagers failed to find the child, until her body was discovered in bushes close to the most frequented spot in the village, on the morning of January 17, 2018.

A 15-year-old boy was arrested the next day, and the then Minister for Revenue & Parliamentary Affairs, Abdul Rehman Veeri, informed the legislative assembly that the accused had confessed to the crime.[9] Veeri also claimed that the investigation by the Special Investigation Team (SIT) headed by the Sub-Divisional Police Officer (Border) Chadwal had revealed that the accused had kidnapped the child and put her in a cowshed in the village, where he attempted to rape her; when she resisted, he strangled her. However, if the child was strangled in the cowshed, there would be no reason to move her body to a more public place and risk detection while doing so. The cattle shed theory was later abandoned, though the adolescent remains an accused and is still in custody. His case was also transferred to Pathankot, and the Supreme Court ordered the State Government to ensure his physical safety.

However, if this narrative were true, the missing child was logically killed on January 10 or 11, in which case the corpse should have shown signs of decomposition by January 17, despite the cold weather. Reports suggest the body was still warm when found. The original postmortem report of January

17, 2018, clearly stated that rigor mortis was "partially present in upper and lower limbs".[10] It mentioned a "deep lacerated wound behind right ear" and abrasions elsewhere, but there was no mention of injuries consistent with rape, especially gang rape, of a child of such tender age (as alleged later). There was no injury to the neck. The viscera and vaginal smears were handed over to the police, and in the column, "Opinion as to cause of death", it stated, "Opinion kept reserved".

The first postmortem report described the stomach as "empty" and intestines as "filled – digested materials". The postmortem report, along with the original reports from Government Medical College Jammu/ Histopathology/Forensic Science Laboratory, Srinagar, and J&K Forensic Science Laboratory, Jammu, was sent with a covering letter by Dr Suresh Kumar, medical superintendent, Govt. District Hospital Kathua, to the State Health Minister and other officials on March 23, 2018. The J&K Forensic Science Laboratory, Jammu report (February 17) noted the presence of Clonazepam, an anti-convulsant drug, in the viscera[11] this is the chemical salt in Epitril (brand name). However, the report of the J&K Forensic Science Laboratory, Srinagar, dated January 30, 2018, by Mushtaq Ahmad Bhat, Sc. Officer, Head Bio/Serology Division, ruled out sexual abuse (No Spermatozoa Were Detected on the Exhibit No. M-01-2018).[12]

A second postmortem report, also dated January 17, 2018, was attached to the same charge sheet, but was clearly prepared after the laboratory results had been received.[13] It reported the stomach as "empty" but "NAD" (no abnormal development) for the intestines – an anomaly that calls for an explanation.[14] Even this report made no mention of rape (or gang rape) and concluded, "After conducting the autopsy we are of the opinion that the deceased died because of asphyxia leading to cardiopulmonary arrest". This was signed by a board comprising Dr Jyoti, Dr Madhu and Dr Mukul, on March 19, 2018.[15]

Meanwhile, in Rassana, the investigating team was changed thrice in a span of 10 days, and claims of rape and even multiple rapes were included among the charges and the list of accused widened. However, the new theory – that the child was drugged and kept under a small table in a corner of the *Devsthan* – was equally implausible. During the time that the child was missing, the festivals of Lohri (January 13) and Makar Sankranti (January 14) caused crowds from three villages to gather at the Devsthan; the celebrations concluded with a huge feast (*bhandara*) on January 15. It is inconceivable that a child could have remained undetected in those small confines for three whole days when the place was inhabited virtually round-the-clock. Moreover, if the child was kept on a cold stone floor in the Devsthan, with just two durries to conceal her, she would have died of the winter cold. It will be a challenge for the Crime Branch officers to show how the girl was given food and water and fresh doses of sedatives on these three days, where and how she performed her ablutions, and so on. When the body was found on January 17, her clothes did not stink or bear traces of urine or faecal matter.

Mehbooba Mufti

The then Chief Minister Mehbooba Mufti treated the murder as a political issue, and when two BJP ministers in the coalition government, Chandra Parkash Ganga and Lal Singh Chaudhary, supported the families of the accused in demanding a CBI probe, she forced the party to make them resign. A fortnight later, the BJP changed its members in the cabinet entirely, but the coalition became even more fragile; the government finally collapsed on June 19, 2018, when the BJP abruptly pulled its members out of the state cabinet.

The resignations brought the simmering tensions in Jammu province to the fore. These related to separate but converging issues regarding concerted moves to change the demography of the Hindu-dominated Jammu province that has suffered sustained discrimination since 1947, and whose problems increased after the forced exodus of Kashmiri Pandits in 1989-90, especially in recent years. An issue seriously agitating Jammuites pertains to the planned and well-funded manner in which Rohingya Muslims from distant Myanmar came and settled in different parts of the province rather than with their co-religionists in Kashmir province. The Rohingyas occupied public lands with impunity and built houses without obstruction, opened well-stocked shops, and triggered the flight of Hindus in several villages.

Another issue that inflamed passions was the PDP-dominated government's decision to encourage Muslim tribal and nomadic communities (Gujjar and Bakarwal) to grab Jammu forest lands with a view to changing the region's demography. At a meeting chaired by the then Chief Minister on February 14, 2018, the Tribal Affairs Department was directed not to act against Gujjar–Bakarwal encroachers and the Police was directed not to help any official agencies in evicting such settlers. When the minutes of the meeting became public, there was considerable tension in the coalition. At a meeting on April 15, soon after the resignations of Chandra Parkash Ganga and Lal Singh

Chaudhary, BJP leaders urged Mehbooba Mufti to withdraw the directive to the police to ignore anti-encroachment drives against nomads without the prior approval of the Tribal Affairs Department that had been told to maintain status quo. She did not relent, despite repeated reminders. An equally vexing issue was the sharp increase in bovine smuggling from Jammu.

The Chief Minister continued to affront Jammu society. At the sixth convocation of Shri Mata Vaishno Devi University on April 18, 2018, in the presence of President Ram Nath Kovind, she said, "it is very shocking that such a heinous crime was committed with a female child considered as 'the living form of *mata*' inside a temple", in a city where girls are worshipped as an incarnation of Goddess Durga.[16] Mehbooba Mufti was referring to the Crime Branch (packed with officers from Kashmir province) version of events in Rassana, which soon proved to be quite porous. Her highly irresponsible statement put an entire community in the dock. It also pinned down the Devsthan (abode of clan deities Baba Kali Veer, Raja Mandalik, Baba Birfa Nath, Sargal Nag Devta, and Mata Mal Devi) in the village as the place where the child was held for at least six days, allegedly raped by several persons according to the charge sheet, before her dead body was left among bushes close to the beaten pathway (*pakh-dandi*) roughly equidistant from the alleged crime scene and the home of principal accused, Sanjhi Ram, a retired revenue official (*Patwari*). Some media channels – ignorant of the meaning of Devsthan – broadcast reports stating that the child was held in the basement of the village "temple" (which is at a different location).

Mehbooba Mufti's speech targetting the Devsthan, a simple one-room structure housing the *Kul-devatas* of three villages, enraged the villagers, who quickly debunked this narrative with video clips shot on mobile phones to show that the Devsthan did not have a basement, as was being alleged.[17] Instead, it has grilled, open windows without panes, which make everything inside visible to all. Keys to the main door are held by persons in three villages and the place is accessed by all as per convenience.

The third SIT team claimed to have found a single strand of the victim's hair at the alleged crime scene, but no traces of blood were detected, which seems odd if a victim of such tender age was raped. Somehow, the investigation was expanded to include the adolescent accused's 62-year-old uncle, Sanjhi Ram; the latter's 21-year-old son, Vishal Jangotra; friend P – alias Mannu (said to be a minor); Special Police Officers Deepak Khajuria and Surender Verma; and Assistant Sub-Inspector Anand Dutta and Head Constable Tilak

Raj (both Anand Dutta and Tilak Raj were quickly dismissed from service). Anand Dutta and Deepak Khajuria thereafter approached the J&K High Court to demand a CBI probe, alleging that the Crime Branch had compromised the crime scene: "The photographs have also been fiddled with and matter of the fact that the vital evidence available in the shape of clothes and body of the victim being dipped with sand and earth would have negated the theory that she could have been kept at the Devsthan which had cemented pucca floor", the petition said.[18] They also alleged manufacturing of evidence.

Sanjhi Ram

Sanjhi Ram Jangotra, a retired revenue official (Patwari) emerged as the key figure in the politico-demographic dynamics of Kathua. He had taken the lead in raising a local movement to persuade Jammu residents not to sell their property to outsiders and not to abandon their ancestral homes under demographic pressure, as incidents were being reported from various parts of the province for the past few years. After the Chief Minister's directive to Police and State officials not to evict illegal settlers from Jammu forests became public, Sanjhi Ram urged the villagers not to permit the nomads to graze their cattle on their fields.

When Sanjhi Ram's son, Vishal Jangotra, was made an accused in the crime, he countered that at the time of the alleged rape he was appearing for his B.Sc. Part I exam at KK Jain College, Khatauli, Muzaffarnagar, UP. At this, a biased media alleged that a proxy candidate wrote the exam on his behalf.[19] Subsequently, there were strenuous efforts to "prove" this aspersion. Vishal Jangotra is a student of Akanksha College, Meeranpur, Muzaffarnagar; both colleges are affiliated to the Choudhary Charan Singh University, Meerut, UP. The Meerut Police have established that Jangotra appeared for the exam at the designated centre, namely, KK Jain College. The idea that a boy from a remote village in Kathua district can conspire with the chairman of a University in Uttar Pradesh to falsify records is quite absurd. Since then, television channels have aired footage from a bank ATM booth showing Vishal Jangotra withdrawing money from Muzaffarnagar on January 15, 2018, when the Crime Branch claimed he was in Rassana.[20]

But the clinching evidence came when the J&K Forensic Science Laboratory, Srinagar, in its report dated July 26, 2018, stated that "the Admitted writings and Questioned writings have been written by one and the same person due to the reason that the similarities are observed between the

Questioned and Admitted writings in the individual writing habits and some of the general writing habits of movement, skill and alignment".[21]

Bar Association Jammu

The name of Talib Hussain, who claimed to be a lawyer and a social worker, first cropped up in public when the Supreme Court directed the Bar Council of India (BCI) to visit Jammu and investigate the strike by the J&K High Court Bar Association, Jammu (henceforth Bar Association Jammu), which had been projected in the media as an attempt to obstruct justice and protect the alleged rapists and murderers in the Rassana-Kathua case. The Bar Association Jammu played a key role in protesting against some of the perceived injustices against the province, particularly the burgeoning settlements of illegal infiltrators from Myanmar and bovine smuggling that is prohibited in the State under the Ranbir Penal Code.

The representatives of the BCI visited Rassana village on April 19, 2018, and Jammu city on April 20. This was a high-powered delegation chaired by Justice Tarun Agarwala, former Chief Justice of Meghalaya; S. Prabakaran, senior advocate and co-chairman BCI; Ramesh Chander G. Shah, co-chairman, BCI; Naresh Dixit, advocate, Patna High Court; and Mrs. Razia Beg, advocate, member, State Bar Council of Uttarakhand. The Bar Association Jammu apprised the committee of the facts behind the unrest and urged an investigation into the credentials of Talib Hussain who, it alleged, was leading the opposition to the CBI probe and communalising the situation in the State.[22] Bar president B.S. Slathia explained that the demand for a CBI probe in the Rassana murder case was mooted when, after the FIR was lodged, the Chief Minister *suo moto* declared the incident to be one of rape and murder, though the medical board had not even prepared the postmortem (autopsy) report. Moreover, the medical board was constituted twice and the SIT, including officers from the Crime Branch, was reconstituted thrice, each time headed by a different officer. This fact had unnerved even the victim's family, and her biological father approached the High Court of J&K (OWP No. 259/2018 titled *Mohd. Akhter v. State and Other*) through advocate Deepika Rajawat and expressed dissatisfaction with the Crime Branch.

These developments convinced the Bar Association Jammu that the victim family would not get justice without a CBI investigation. It felt that since the investigating agency was portraying a Hindu sacred place as site of a heinous crime and accusing it of destruction of evidence, a potential communal divide could be averted through an impartial probe by the CBI. The Bar Association also pointed out that three young men – Neeraj Sharma, Sachin Sharma and Sahil Sharma – had been tortured by the Crime Branch to make false statements against their classmate, Vishal Jangotra, and had complained of the same before the Magistrate, which was recorded under section 164-A Ranbir Penal Code. The Supreme Court later directed that these three witnesses were to be accompanied by family members if called for further questioning by the J&K Police, and permitted them to approach the J&K High Court with their grievances[23] (they have since approached the High Court in the matter).

As these developments were unfolding, the Bar Association with the legal fraternity and civil society associations in Jammu decided to suspend work from April 4 to 7 in support of the Kathua victim and the demographic challenge, including occupation of state forest land by illegal settlers. They held a protest rally in Jammu city on April 6 and decided on a *Jammu Bandh* and *Chakka Jam* on April 11, 2018. All agitations by the Bar Association Jammu are supported by all District and Mofussil Bar Associations in the province. However, just prior to the bandh, the J&K Crime Branch filed a charge sheet in the court of the Chief Judicial Magistrate, Kathua, on April 9, 2018. Kathua is nearly 100 km from Jammu. However, acting on an unknown command, the national media launched a concerted campaign and alleged that the Bar Association Jammu had obstructed the filing of the charge sheet in the Kathua magistrate's court. In reality, the charge sheet was filed the same day.

Once the case was admitted, the Bar Association Jammu decided to limit the Jammu Bandh to the deportation of Rohingyas and Bangladeshis from Jammu to any other place in India, and withdrawal of the directions on nomadic settlers given in the meeting of February 14, 2018, that was chaired by the Chief Minister. But the frenzied campaign by some television channels compelled the Supreme Court of India to take cognisance of the Rassana case and issue notices to the office bearers of the District Court Bar Association Kathua, Bar Association Jammu, BCI, and J&K Bar Council, to explain the alleged obstruction in the filing of the charge sheet and to lawyers representing the victim's family. To cool temperatures, the Bar Association Jammu decided to resume work.

The J&K High Court Bar Association Jammu in its reply to the Supreme Court (April 24, 2018) asserted that it was fighting a very grave menace – another Kashmir-like situation to force the exodus of one community from the province. Responding to Suo Moto Writ Petition, Criminal, No. 1 of 2018, it asserted that advocate Deepika Rajawat was neither threatened nor obstructed from appearing in the High Court on behalf of the victim family by any office bearer or member of the Association. The Bar Association informed the Supreme Court that since the forced exodus of Kashmiri Pandits from the Kashmir Valley in 1989-90, organised State-sponsored attempts have been made from time to time to create a Kashmir-like situation by instigating demographic change in Jammu region. It pointed out that the illegal settlement of Rohingyas and Bangladeshis at strategic locations in Jammu, and the State Government's directions to Deputy Commissioners and Inspector General of Police Jammu to promote demographic changes and tolerance of bovine smuggling, thus subverting the rule of law, were issues of State and national importance.

First, legislation such as the J&K State Lands (vesting of ownership to occupants) Act, 2001 was enacted after nearly 20 lakh kanals of State and Forest land was found to be illegally occupied by farmers. Their cases were processed for conferring ownership rights by virtue of having illegal possession of Government and Forest land (squatter's rights). In reality, large chunks of land were appropriated by politicians and bureaucrats, causing an estimated loss of around Rs. 25,000 crore to the exchequer. Secondly, at a meeting presided over by Chief Minister Mehbooba Mufti on February 14, 2018, illegal decisions were made whereby no member belonging to the tribal population who encroached upon State land could be evicted under law. Furthermore, the provisions of Section 188 of the Ranbir Penal Code with regard to bovine smuggling and illegal settlements of Rohingyas and Bangladeshi infiltrators were given short shrift by the administration in Srinagar. The Bar Association Jammu expressed apprehensions that members of the Association "feel grave threat to their security, life and property in the given circumstances where the State has miserably failed to perform its constitutional duty". It said that the State Government's acts of omission and commission have had the effect of "encouraging certain forces that are hell-bent to change the Jammu's demography so that the people living in Jammu region are made to feel insecure and toe the line of anti-national forces which are duly encouraged and patronised by foreign powers, especially Pakistan". It claimed that the Association was persevering against all odds to defeat the anti-India forces operating in the State, using all constitutional measures, including peaceful agitation.

Coming to the facts of the case, the Bar Association stated that the Rassana victim family had approached the High Court of J&K (OWP No. 259/2018, *Mohd. Akhter v. State and Other*) through Deepika Rajawat, and expressed unhappiness with the investigation conducted by the police agency and the Crime Branch. The people of Hiranagar tehsil, Kathua, were also dissatisfied with the Crime Branch investigation. The Akhter petition was listed for the first time on February 9, 2018, and the Court issued notice to the respondents. The interim orders passed in the petition clearly establish that Deepika Rajawat appeared in OWP No. 259/2018. The J&K High Court was monitoring the investigation on each and every date fixed in the case, namely, February 9, 19, 21; March 9, 14; and April 9. On April 11, the petition was disposed of as the charge sheet had been filed in the court of the Chief Judicial Magistrate, Kathua.

The BCI, in its report to the Supreme Court (April 22, 2018) accepted the explanation of the Jammu Bar Association. It observed that the "media has misreported the entire episode, especially relating to the conduct of the advocates of Kathua Bar Association and Jammu and Kashmir High Court Bar Association"; the media had wrongly reported that the Kathua Bar Association and J&K High Court Bar Association "are siding with the accused" and failed to report the press release given by the J&K High Court Bar Association that they were demanding a "fair investigation by CBI". Finally, it concluded that "the demand for a CBI inquiry by the public, members of the Civil Society, Jammu, and by the Kathua Bar Association & J&K High Court Bar Association appears to be justifiable".

Questions and Loopholes

The more we look at the Kathua murder, the less the crime makes sense, unless one gives serious consideration to the larger political-demographic struggle that has been joined in Jammu province. To begin with, since the victim belonged to a nomad family that regularly came down the hills for winter pasturing its flock in this village, there has till date been no credible explanation why she grazed her family's horses in the jungle alone. Members of nomad families generally mind the flocks jointly. What did the adults in the family do; where did her family's herd of sheep graze; certainly there were no other animals with her. Was she the sole child in the community; why didn't other Bakarwal children accompany her, including the two sons of her adopted father? Why didn't she go to school like her elder cousins?

The police account was distrusted almost universally. Since they had made up their minds about the case and its culprits, they did not think it worthwhile to follow other leads. As mentioned earlier, the team investigating the murder was changed thrice within a span of 10 days, from January 12, 2018, when the first missing person's report was registered. From January 12 to 18, the investigation was led by the SHO, Hiranagar. Then, on January 19 and 20, it was with ASP Samba. But from January 23 onwards, the case was with the Crime Branch Jammu, though packed with officers from Kashmir province. The first postmortem report made no mention of assault or rape; the second gave the cause of death as "asphyxia leading to cardio-pulmonary arrest" and did not even hint at strangulation. This is extremely odd, and in these circumstances, given the number of arrests made and number of witnesses adduced (triple the total population of tiny Rassana), the demand by the villagers for an impartial probe by the CBI seems legitimate. If justice is to be done to the murdered child, the guilty must be identified and punished and the innocent exonerated.

Sanjhi Ram is alleged to have bribed some local policemen to cover the crime, but no money was recovered from the homes of the accused policemen. However, a supplementary charge sheet filed on July 30 claimed to have uncovered a trail of withdrawals from his bank accounts. The claims have yet to stand scrutiny in court. The Crime Branch reportedly fiddled with the crime scene, but the sequence of events in this regard is not clear. The clothes and body of the victim were covered in mud at the time of recovery; the postmortem report states, "sand and mud present over frock".[24] This is crucial evidence that the child was not kept at the Devsthan that has a cement floor and is washed thrice daily. Normally, after the postmortem, the body should have been handed over to the family for burial. However, it is claimed that the police officers later arrested in the case had washed and dried the clothes to destroy evidence. The questions arise: why did the forensic laboratory not seize and seal the clothes as material evidence in a murder case? Did the laboratory hand back the child's body without clothes, in a sheet, and hand over the clothes separately to the police? Where was the need for the police to wash the clothes if the body and clothes were returned? Where are the clothes now?

The case is riddled with similar discrepancies. The alleged finding of a single hair of the victim in the Devsthan one month after the alleged crime lacks credibility. This hair (which became four hairs during the trial) also disappeared in the opening days of the trial at Pathankot.[25]

The State Government is viewed with suspicion because of the officers assigned to the case. The Crime Branch team is currently headed by Naveed Peerzada, SSP Crime Branch Kashmir. Sub-Inspector Irfan Wani, one of the SIT members, was arrested in 2007 for the alleged murder of one Rishi Kumar, and alleged rape of the latter's sister, in Doda, in 2007 (he was acquitted in 2011). Another investigating officer, Dy. Superintendent Nissar Hussain Shah, was accused of destroying crucial evidences in a case during his tenure in the State Vigilance Organization; he was suspended and withdrawn from the investigation (FIR no. 20/2005) under the Prevention of Corruption Act, registered with Police Station Vigilance Organization Jammu; he has since been exonerated. Another Dy. SP Crime Branch Jammu, Shwetambari Sharma, is the investigating officer who reportedly found the single strand of hair from the Devsthan (now vanished); Tariq Ahmed, ASI, Crime Branch Kashmir, is a Kashmiri.

There has been no attempt to investigate the communalisation of the case. By all accounts, the Hindu villagers helped the Bakarwal family to search for the girl, and attended the *chautha* prayer meet on January 20.[26] But by the time the ceremony was over, hundreds of outsiders, including people from Kashmir, were swarming all over the place, raising pro-Pakistan slogans and rampaging through the village, banging doors and terrorising the villagers. Justice for the deceased was given the go-by; another agenda was clearly in play. Neither the police nor the administration tried to probe the origins of nearly 2,000 protesters who blocked the national highway and demanded the arrest of Sanjhi Ram and special police officer Deepak Khajuria. How were these two persons named as accused even before the investigations had begun? They were named by Talib Hussain who took the lead in instigating the mob. However, Talib Hussain's credibility was seriously dented when Samba district police arrested him for the alleged rape of a married woman on August 1, 2018. Previously, his wife, Nusrat Begam, had accused him of torturing her and demanding dowry after she gave birth to a girl child (June 30, 2018). Since the Crime Branch seemed to have been following Talib Hussain's lead – quickly arresting persons named by him and framing charges accordingly – it remains to be seen how his denouement will affect the case. But the high-profile lawyer Indira Jaising and her team dissociated from Talib Hussain in October 2018 (he joined the PDP on April 1, 2019).

From the beginning of the case, there was deep resentment at the manner in which the Crime Branch conducted itself. Sensing a deeper conspiracy, the people of Kathua and Jammu quickly formed the *Hindu Ekta Manch* to protest against the fast-unfolding events. Sanjhi Ram and special police officer Deepak Khajuria were arrested between January 23 and 25, 2018, when the case was taken over by the Kashmir-centric Crime Branch. But even before the charge sheet could be filed, three witnesses produced before the magistrate for recording their testimony complained that they were being coerced to testify against their classmate, Vishal Jangotra.

Any dispassionate scrutiny of the story so far cannot but veer around to the view that the crime is part of a larger conspiracy to frighten the handful of Hindu families to quit this crucial border village (Rassana has merely 14 Brahmin families, total population around 60-65 persons), that is strategically located close to the international border, with just 100 km of thick forest separating India from Pakistan. Terrorising the few Hindu families in this sensitive region could trigger an exodus and enable Pakistan's jihadi foot soldiers to take over the vital Shivalik hills and Shivalik plains of Jammu for anti-India operations, and nibble at chunks of Indian territory unseen. The project to alter the region's demographic profile would accelerate with the State Government enabling tribal Muslims (Gujjar-Bakarwals) to settle in forest lands. With the demographic danger hanging like the Sword of Damocles over their heads, Jammu intellectuals feel that only the establishment of an Army camp in Kathua can checkmate the conspiracy against the territorial integrity of India.

The Government of India has taken a firm stand that the Rohingyas who are being settled in Jammu under a concerted and well-funded plan must be confined in camps as a prelude to repatriation in Myanmar. The decision was resisted by the PDP, then the dominant partner in the coalition with the BJP. We suspect that there was a sinister plan to change the regional demography so quickly that the accession of Jammu and Kashmir to Pakistan became doable. The then Chief Minister Mehbooba Mufti repeatedly called for dialogue with Pakistan; both her late father Mufti Mohammad Saeed and she have publicly stated that the PDP formed a coalition government with the BJP after clearing the matter with the separatist Hurriyat Conference. The game most likely was to significantly alter the religious demography of Jammu province, marginalise the BJP, and pass a resolution in the Jammu & Kashmir Assembly under Article 1 of the UN Charter, calling for the right to self-determination. However unlikely to succeed, it was a risk India could not afford to take.

If this seems far-fetched, one has only to note the astonishing fact that the entire district of Poonch in Jammu province was quietly transferred to Auqaf Islamia Poonch (Wakf) way back in 1985, vide SRO 320 of 1985, issued by the then Secretary Haj and Auqaf.[27] At that time, Ghulam Mohammad Shah, who toppled his brother-in-law Dr Farooq Abdullah, was Chief Minister (July 2, 1984, March 6, 1986). The residents of Poonch learnt of this astonishing order only in March 2017 when the Administrator Auqaf Islamia slapped eviction notices on the District Information Department; Principal, Government Degree College, Poonch; and other government institutions and various private individuals. The case is now before the High Court of Jammu and Kashmir. The stakes are high; Jammu citizens are fighting for the survival and protection of their civilisation in a turbulent frontier region. Kathua was one of the districts attacked in the war of 1947-48. Currently, the Pathankot magistrate's court is a new frontline in this battle.

*

NOTES

1 The BJP pulled out of the coalition government on June 19, 2018.

2 The village population consists of 13 families of around 65-odd persons; most men are employed in the Mumbai dockyard, leaving mainly women and children at home.

3 Kathua case: No witnesses, court summons Jammu SSP, *TNN*, June 9, 2018. https://timesofindia.indiatimes.com/city/chandigarh/no-witnesses-court-summons-jammu-ssp/articleshow/64515529.cms.

4 Guilty must be held accountable: UN chief on Kathua rape, April 14, 2018. https://timesofindia.indiatimes.com/india/hope-authorities-bring-kathua-rape-perpetrators-to-justice-un-chief/articleshow/63758900.cms.

5 Pay more attention to women in India, IMF chief Christine Lagarde tells PM Modi, Apr. 19, 2018. https://www.indiatoday.in/india/story/pm-modi-imf-chief-christine-lagarde-woman-safety-india-kathua-unnao-gangrape-cases-1216013-2018-04-19.

6 Cleric held for raping 7-yr-old at madrasa, *The Tribune*, March 15, 2018. http://www.tribuneindia.com/news/jammu-kashmir/cleric-held-for-raping-7-yr-old-at-madrasa/557858.html.

7 Conundrums of Kathua, Sandhya Jain, *Pgurus*, Apr. 17, 2018, https://www.pgurus.com/conundrums-of-kathua/.

8 Ibid.

9 15-year-old boy accused of murdering Kathua girl arrested: Government, Jan. 19, 2018. http://m.greaterkashmir.com/news/jammu/15-year-old-boy-accused-of-murdering-kathua-girl-arrested-govt/272787.html.

10 See Annexure I: Post mortem report of January 17, 2018.

11 See Annexure II: J&K Forensic Science Laboratory reports (letter '219' written by hand).

12 See Annexure III: J&K Forensic Science Laboratory reports (letters '219' and '220' written by hand).

13 See Annexure IV: Second post mortem report also dated January 17, 2018 (letters '221' written by hand).

14 I am indebted to the fact-finding team of Group of Intellectuals and Academicians for pointing out this anomaly. The team comprised Smt. Meera Khadakkar, retired district judge, Nagpur; Smt. Monika Arora, advocate, Supreme Court of India and Delhi High Court; Ms. Sarjana Sharma, senior journalist; Ms. Sonali Chitalkar, assistant professor, Miranda House, University of Delhi; Smt. Monicca Agarwal, entrepreneur and social activist (April 23-25, 2018).

15 I am grateful to advocate A.K. Sawhney for confirming this reading of the post-mortem reports.

16 Kathua rape case: How can anybody do such heinous act against a living form of Mata?, *Indian Express*, Apr. 18, 2018. http://indianexpress.com/article/india/kathua-rape-and-murder-case-societys-falling-values-reflected-in-such-heinous-act-against-living-form-of-mata-jk-cm-mehbooba-mufti-5142830/.

17 Kathua tall tales unravel, Sandhya Jain, *Pgurus*, Apr. 20, 2018. https://www.pgurus.com/kathua-tall-tales-unraveled/.

18 2 Rassana accused file petition for CBI probe, *Daily Excelsior*, Apr. 24, 2018. http://www.dailyexcelsior.com/2-rassana-accused-file-petition-cbi-probe/.

19 Proxy candidate wrote exam for Kathua accused?, *The Hindu*, Apr. 14, 2018. http://www.thehindu.com/news/national/proxy-candidate-wrote-exam-for-kathua-accused/article23535295.ece.

20 Was Vishal Jangotra framed in the Kathua rape and murder case?, May 1, 2018. http://www.opindia.com/2018/05/was-vishal-jangotra-framed-in-the-kathua-rape-and-murder-case/.

21 See Annexure V: Vishal Jangotra handwriting forensic report, dated July 26, 2018.

22 Demographic threat behind stir: Jammu Bar, Sandhya Jain, Apr. 21, 2018. https://www.pgurus.com/demographic-threat-behind-stir-jammu-bar/#comment-20199.

23 Kathua rape murder case: Supreme Court allows kin to be with students for questioning, *Indian Express*, May 18, 2018. http://indianexpress.com/article/india/kathua-rape-murder-case-supreme-court-allows-kin-to-be-with-students-for-questioning-5180993/.

24 Two rapes: Howling banshees and their silence, Sandhya Jain, *Pgurus*, Apr. 28, 2018. https://www.pgurus.com/two-rapes-howling-banshees-and-their-silence/.

25 Kathua case: Sealed envelope supposed to contain victim's hair turns out empty in court, July 17, 2018. https://www.greaterkashmir.com/news/jammu/kathua-case-sealed-envelope-supposed-to-contain-victim-s-hair-turns-out-empty-in-court/290766.html.

26 Lacunas persist in Kathua story, Sandhya Jain, *Pgurus*, May 5, 2018. https://www.pgurus.com/lacunas-persist-in-kathua-story/.

27 Poonch city transferred to Auqaf; HC issues notices, August 15, 2018. http://news.statetimes.in/poonch-city-transferred-to-auqaf-hc-issues-notices/.

CHAPTER FIVE
The Occupied Territories

Nidhi Bahuguna

A veil of darkness has engulfed Indian consciousness with respect to certain areas of Jammu and Kashmir for decades. These are territories that have been illegally occupied by Pakistan and China and have since been confined to a dark closet of national skeletons. This chapter attempts to shed some light on these territories that are of immense strategic importance, but have, strangely, never been discussed in the mainstream media.

China-Occupied areas

Broadly, three areas constitute China-occupied Jammu and Kashmir, namely, Aksai Chin, Shaksgam Valley (Trans-Karakoram), and the Principality of Minsar. The Office of the United Nations High Commissioner for Human Rights (OHCHR) report of June 14, 2018, observes,

> Following unresolved colonial-era boundary disputes, India and China went to war in 1962, which resulted in China taking control of the largely uninhabited tract of Aksai Chin in the East. As part of a broader boundary agreement, in 1963, Pakistan ceded to China the Shaksgam or Trans-Karakoram tract in the Gilgit-Baltistan area. The agreement includes a provision for renegotiation in case of a change in sovereign authority after the settlement of the Kashmir dispute between Pakistan and India.[1]

Aksai Chin

It is astonishing and instructive that the only reference to Aksai Chin that finds space in the national consciousness is Prime Minister Jawaharlal Nehru's remark in Parliament that "not a blade of grass grows in Aksai Chin" to minimise the adverse impact of China's occupation of the region. A person of Nehru's sharp intelligence could hardly be unaware of the strategic importance of Aksai Chin, which is why Beijing acquired it. In the historical past, the region once hosted two flourishing trade routes connecting Lhasa (in Tibet), Leh (in India) and Kashgar (in China). Historically, armies follow paths carved out by the caravans of traders, or trade follows roads beaten down by armies. China found and occupied the ancient paths frequented by traders; today its New Silk Roads touch many of the important emporia of the old routes.

When news about China's construction of a highway (Karakoram) became public, Nehru instructed the foreign secretary to lodge an informal protest with the Chinese Embassy. On October 18, 1958, the Indian foreign secretary handed over an "informal note" to the Chinese ambassador in New Delhi.[2] But it was only in August 1959 that Nehru dropped the bombshell in Parliament: *The "Tibet-Sinkiang highway" had been built through Indian territory.*

Aksai Chin spans an area of roughly 37,244 km^2, stretching from the lowest point on the Karakash River at about 4,300 m to the snow-clad peaks up to 6,900 m. The region has a number of endorheic basins with many salt or soda lakes. Much of the northern part of Aksai Chin is referred to as the Soda Plains; its largest river, the Karkash, receives melt water from a number of glaciers, crosses the Kunlun range farther northwest in Pishan County and enters the Tarim Basin, where it serves as one of the main sources of water for Karakax and Hotan Counties (Xinjiang, China). The western part of the Aksai Chin region is drained by the Tarim River. The eastern part of the region contains several small endorheic basins, the largest being Aksai Chin Lake, which is fed by a river of the same name. The region as a whole receives little precipitation as the Himalayas and Karakoram block the rains from the Indian monsoon.

Historically, Aksai Chin was the eastern part of Ladakh, located in the northwestern part of the Tibet plateau and south of Kunlun Mountains. It was a very important trade route, connecting Xinjiang and Tibet during the summer months. Owing to its elevation (5,000 m), it had little human significance except as an ancient trade route, which provided a summer pass to caravans of yaks between Xinjiang and Tibet. The region was important for military campaigns as it was on the only route from Tarim Basin to Tibet that was passable all year round. The Dzungar Khanate used it to enter Tibet in 1717.

Some claim that Aksai Chin area was never under the direct rule of any kingdom as it was uninhabited, but documents prove otherwise. The earliest treaty on boundaries signed in 1842 between Gulab Singh and the Tibetans agreed to stick to old agreed boundaries. After the East India Company defeated the Sikh Empire in 1846, the British installed the Raja of Jammu, Gulab Singh, as Maharaja of Jammu and Kashmir; his general Zorawar Singh quickly added Ladakh, Skardu, Gilgit and Baltistan to the empire, thus expanding India's northern frontiers for the first time in several centuries. The British Commissioners fixed the southern boundary at Pangong Lake. The Johnson Line in 1865 put Aksai Chin firmly within Kashmir.

There were two historic trade routes that ended at Shahidulla (Xaidulla), which was a frontier post of the kingdom of Jammu and Kashmir till the end of the 19th century:

(a) Pamzal along the western limits of the Chang Chenmo valley-Shamal Lungpa-Samsung Ling-Dehra Compa-Quila Jilga-Cung Tash-crossing Tag Pass-Chibra valley-Malikshah to Shahidulla.
(b) Pamzal along the eastern boundary of Chang Chenmo valley-Nischu-Linzi Tang-Lake Tsund-Thaldut-Khitai Pass-Haji Langar and along Qara Kash (Karakash) valley to Shahidulla.

Since the establishment of the kingdom of Jammu and Kashmir, the areas up to the frontiers were regularly administered. The check posts on the trade routes were marked on the maps from 1865 onwards. Till 1901, the state authorities included the territory in the wazarat of the Frontier District. It was later divided into the wazarat of Gilgit and Ladakh. The tehsils of Skardu, Kargil and Ladakh formed the wazarat of Ladakh and Aksai Chin and Chang Chenmo valley were parts of the ilaqa of Tankse in Ladakh tehsil.[3] However, in 1890, Shahidulla and the Karkash river was claimed to be part of Xinjiang by China and by 1892 China had erected boundary markers at Karakoram Pass.

The white paper of the Ministry of External Affairs documents the revenue collection by the Maharaja's administration:

> The arrangements made by the Governments of India and Kashmir for the establishment and maintenance of trade routes across Aksai Chin, the provision of facilities such as rest houses and store houses for those using these routes and the regular use of these routes as of right by Indian trading parties – both official and unofficial – constituted powerful evidence of Indian administrative jurisdiction in the 19th century up to the traditional

> boundary claimed by India. The very fact that there were never any disputes about the exercise of such jurisdiction and the use of these routes by Indians as of right showed that there could have been no difference of opinion in those times between the Ladakhis on the one hand and the authorities of Sinkiang and Tibet on the other as to where the boundary lay.

In 1866, on receipt of complaints that trade with Yarkand was suffering due to excessive duties levied by the Kashmir Government, the Government of India entered into negotiations with the Government of Kashmir for developing a new route from Chushul along the Pangong lake and across Lingzi Tang and Aksai Chin to Shahidulla, and creating other facilities. In May 1870, the two parties signed an agreement. Article 1 of this treaty stated:

> "With the consent of the Maharaja, officers of the British Government will be appointed to survey the trade routes through the Maharaja's territories from the British frontier of Lahoul to the territories of the Ruler of Yarkhand, including the route via the Chang Chemoo Valley. The Maharaja will depute an officer of his Government to accompany the surveyors, and will render them all the assistance in his power. A map of the routes surveyed will be made an attested copy of which will be given to the Maharaja".[4]

Further revenue records and maps prove that the area was administered by the Maharaja of Jammu and Kashmir:

> Mangal Mehta, wazir of Ladakh during 1860-65, organized the revenue settlement of the whole area. In the regular revenue assessment reports the names of areas and villages and the amount of revenue collected from each of them, which is now claimed by China as having been under their administrative jurisdiction for centuries, were included. The report of 1908 mentioned 108 villages including Tankse, Demchok and Minsar and mentions Aksai Chin, Lingzi Tang where rights of pastures and salt collection were exercised, as parts of Tankse ilaqa. The preliminary report of Ladakh settlement outlined a revenue and political history of these areas. The boundary question found direct and indirect mention in these reports. The assessment report of Ladakh tehsil of 1909 stated, "There have been no boundary disputes on the Lhasa frontiers and the existing boundary seems to be well understood by the subjects of both the state and the Lhasa Government".[5]

The India–China border problem is a colonial legacy. The British drew various boundary lines on maps at various times, reverting to lines that suited them the most. The boundaries were never demarcated physically and remained on the map. The three boundary lines were Johnson Line (1865), Johnson–Ardagh Line (1897), and Macartney–MacDonald Line (1899).

Johnson Line

William Johnson, a civil servant with the Survey of India, proposed the "Johnson Line" in 1865, which put Aksai Chin in Kashmir. This was the time of the Dungon revolt when China did not control most of Xinxiang, so this line was never presented to the Chinese. Johnson presented this Line to the Maharaja of Jammu and Kashmir, who then claimed the 18,000 km^2 within the Line and the territory further north as far as Sanju Pass in the Kunlun Mountains. The Maharajah constructed a fort at Shahidulla (Xaidulla), and stationed troops there for some years to protect the caravans.

Johnson–Ardagh Line

In 1897, a British military officer, Sir John Ardagh, proposed a boundary line along the crest of the Kunlun Mountains north of the Yarkand River.[6] At the time Britain was concerned at the prospects of Russian expansion as China weakened; Ardagh argued that this line was more defensible. The Ardagh Line was really a modification of the Johnson Line, and became known as the "Johnson–Ardagh Line".

Macartney–MacDonald Line

In 1893, Hung Ta-chen, a senior Chinese official at St. Petersburg, gave maps of the region to George Macartney, British consul general at Kashgar, which coincided in broad details with the Johnson Line. In 1899, London proposed a revised boundary, initially suggested by Macartney and developed by the Governor General of India, Lord Elgin. This boundary placed the Lingzi Tang plains that are south of the Laktsang range in India, and Aksai Chin proper that is north of the Laktsang range in China. This border, along the Karakoram Mountains, was proposed and supported by British officials for several reasons. The Karakoram Mountains formed a natural boundary that would set the British borders up to the Indus River watershed while leaving the Tarim River watershed in Chinese control, and Chinese possession of this tract would form another obstacle to Russian advance in Central Asia. The British presented the Macartney–MacDonald Line to the Chinese in 1899 in a note by Sir Claude MacDonald. The Qing government did not respond to the note, and the British took that as Chinese acquiescence. Although no official boundary had ever been negotiated, China believed that this had been the accepted boundary since 1949 when the People's Republic of China was established.

The Johnson–Ardagh and Macartney–MacDonald Lines were both used on British maps of India. Until at least 1908, the British took the MacDonald Line as the boundary, but in 1911, the Xinhai Revolution resulted in the collapse of central power in China and by the end of World War I, the British officially used the Johnson Line. From 1917 to 1933, the Postal Atlas of China, published by the Government of China in Peking, depicted the boundary in Aksai Chin as per the Johnson Line, which runs along the Kunlun Mountains. The Peking University Atlas, published in 1925, also put Aksai Chin in India. When British officials learned that Soviet officials were surveying Aksai Chin for Sheng Shicai, warlord of Xinjiang in 1940-1941, they again advocated the Johnson Line.

Post-1947

At independence, the Government of India used the Johnson Line as the basis for its official boundary in the west, which included Aksai Chin. From the Karakoram Pass (which is not under dispute), the Indian claim line extends northeast of the Karakoram Mountains through the salt flats of Aksai Chin to set a boundary at the Kunlun Mountains, and incorporating part of the Karakash and Yarkand River watersheds. From there, it runs east along the Kunlun Mountains before turning southwest through the Aksai Chin salt flats, through the Karakoram range, and then to Pangong Lake. On July 1, 1954, Prime Minister Jawaharlal Nehru wrote a memo directing revision of maps of India to show definite boundaries on all frontiers. Hitherto, the boundary in the Aksai Chin sector, based on the Johnson Line, had been described as "undemarcated".

China occupied this region by building China Highway 219 linking Lazi in the Tibet autonomous region to Xinxiang between 1951 and 1957. On October 6, 1957, a Chinese newspaper, *Kuang-Ming Jih Pao*, reported "The Sinkiang-Tibet – the highest highway in the world – has been completed".

CIA notes of the region describe a flourishing trade in 1953, with Tibetan traders carrying tea, incense and veils for sale in Leh, returning with soap, cigarettes, sugar and dried fruit, while traders from Leh carried wheat, flour, barley and eggs to Tibet and returned with wool and silver coins. The trade route ran from Khotan (Hotan) to Sugat Karaul and Shahidulla Mazar and then to Kargilik and Kashgar, while another route passed through Karakoram Pass and the Depsang plain. This is clearly a very strategic territory. Trade ended with the construction of the Aksai Chin highway.[7] Besides Chinese military officials, the only people who move through this area are nomadic groups like Bakarwals. The sole inhabited village is Tielongtan; China has created a military township, Tianshuihai, at 4890 m, with a few restaurants, small lodges and gas stations.

Shaksgam Valley

China occupies more than 20,000 km^2 of Gilgit Baltistan, covering the Shaksgam, Raskam and Aghil valleys. In 1963, Pakistan handed over 5,800 km^2 of Occupied Gilgit Baltistan to China, which belonged to the ruler of Hunza.[8] Official maps of China of 1917, 1919, and 1933 recognise the border of Jammu and Kashmir at the Kunlun mountain range. An earlier map of Xinjiang of 1762, in the reign of Chinese Emperor Chien Lung, acknowledged the southern border of Xinxiang at Kunlun. These maps firmly place Shaksgam, Raskam and Aghil valleys within the Gilgit Baltistan region of Jammu and Kashmir.[9]

The Ministry of External Affairs Report (Part 3) on the Indo-China boundary dispute states,

> At the outset, the Indian side showed that Indian administrative control had also extended up to the alignment west of the Karakoram Pass. The Mir of Hunza had for centuries exercised sovereign jurisdiction and administrative control over the areas south of the Mustagh and Aghil ranges. Official Indian maps had been showing the alignment along these ranges; and official Chinese maps such as that of Hung Ta-chen and the Postal Atlases of China of 1917, 1919 and 1933, had also confirmed it.[10]

The Shaksgam Valley has hoary links with Baltistan, of which the famous camping grounds of Moni Brangsa (residence of musicians), Balti Brangsa (Balti residence) and Balti Pulo (dwellings of Baltis) provide ample evidence. The Raja of Shigar laid out a polo ground south of Shaksgam Valley in the 5th century AD. The ground called Muztaghi Shagaran drew players and musicians during the annual Autumn Harvest Festival.[11]

Though never ruled directly by Jammu and Kashmir, Hunza was a vassal of Jammu and Kashmir from the time of Maharaja Ranbir Singh (mid-1800s). The Mirs of Hunza sent an annual tribute to the royal durbar until 1947, and along with the ruler of Nagar were considered among the Maharaja's most loyal vassals. According to Baroness Emma Nicholson of the UK Conservative Party, "All the evidence points to the fact that Gilgit and Baltistan region were constituent parts of Jammu and Kashmir by 1877". They remained in this princely domain till the date of accession "in its entirety to the new Dominion of India" on October 26, 1947. This was reiterated in the correspondence of Maharaja Hari Singh (October 26, 1947) with Lord Louis Mountbatten, Governor General of India, which states that the state of Jammu and Kashmir has a common boundary with the "Soviet Republic", which *inter alia* alludes to the fact that Gilgit and Kanjut (which includes the Raskam, Hunza Valley and Taghdumbash) are integral parts of Jammu and Kashmir. Jawaharlal Nehru made a similar statement that "Jammu and Kashmir's Northern frontiers, as you are aware, run in common with those of three countries, Afghanistan, the Union of Soviet Socialist Republics and China".[12] Section (4)[26] of the Constitution of Jammu and Kashmir that pertains to the territorial extent of the Indian state of Jammu and Kashmir also unequivocally states that, "The territory of the State shall comprise all the territories which on the fifteenth day of August, 1947 were under the sovereignty or suzerainty of the Ruler of the State".

Following a strategic alliance between China and Pakistan, Foreign Ministers Zulfiqar Ali Bhutto and Cheng Li signed a provisional agreement on March 2, 1963, in Beijing, allowing China to occupy Shaksgam, Raskam, Shimshal and Aghil valleys of Gilgit Baltistan.[13] China quickly built feeder roads eastward through Shaksgam linking Gilgit with Hotan, a military headquarter at the cross section of the Tibet-Xinxiang Highway and Hotan-Golmud Highway. The highway links Xinjiang to Central China and cuts the distance between Gilgit and Golmund to nearly half. Another feeder road across the southern rim of East Turkestan (Xinjiang) connects Gilgit with Aksai Chin. Chinese occupation of Gilgit Baltistan links the military and industrial complexes of northwestern Tibet with Pakistani and Persian ports.

There is ample evidence, since 2012, of China smuggling heavy and precious materials like uranium, gold and copper from Gilgit Baltistan, to support which Pakistani authorities have placed a 10-year ban on local businesses involved in gem extraction and trade. Reports in local newspapers suggest that China has leased Gilgit Baltistan for 50 years.

Principality of Minsar

Minsar, a small enclave in western Tibet, was part of the kingdom of Jammu and Kashmir for centuries; its revenues maintained the Kailash Mansarovar Yatra. It was ceded to the king of Ladakh under a peace treaty signed between Ladakh and Tibet in Tingmosgang in 1684, which stated, "The King of Ladakh reserves to himself the village of Minsar in Ngari-Khor-sum (western Tibet)".[14] In 1748, the 7th Gyalwang Drukpa, who spent 3 months in Minsar noted, "administratively it is established that the immediate village of Minsar and its adjoining areas are ancient Ladakhi territory". When Ladakh was incorporated in Maharaja Gulab Singh's kingdom, it became part of Jammu and Kashmir State. Maharaja Hari Singh's accession made it Indian Territory. In 1950, a special officer, N. Rigzen Ghagil Kalon, was deputed by Jammu and Kashmir State to visit Minsar. His report was forwarded to the Ministry of States on September 13, 1950 (see "Note on Conditions of Kashmir Village in Minsar in Western Tibet"); some weeks later, China invaded Tibet.

The report states,

> In compliance to your orders I left Leh on 22-6-50 and reached village Minsar on 24-7-50. The route lies via Rudok. It is ten days journey from Demjok [Demchok] to Minsar. Demjok is the last boundary of the Tehsil Ladakh from which begins the Chhangthang Plateau of Lhasa Tibet. The route from Demjok to Minsar passes through Gartok which is the headquarters of Garpons (Administrative Officers of Lhasa Government). The village Minsar is situated to east of Gartok and about 32 miles west of Mount Kailasas [Kailash]. It is a broad valley with vast plains in it.
>
> There are 68 families with 271 souls of which 120 are males and the rest females and are all adherents of Buddhism.
>
> The entire population depends on livestock which is the only source of subsistence and deal in the trade of sheep, wool, and pashmina. The economic condition of the people is neither much satisfactory nor so much frustrated.
>
> On my way I interviewed Garpons at Rudok and exchanged my ideas with them regarding taking my Police Constables to Minsar and installation of a Chowki [guardian] there. They told me that it would create some consternation in Minsar and its suburbs, if the whole quota of six constables along with rifles were permitted to accompany me and so two constables were permitted to accompany me and the rifles were kept concealed under our saddles. I directed the other four constables to stay at Demjok. I also came across with the traders of Kulu [in Himachal Pradesh] and Leh there. They came with an application to me saying that Tibetan Officials were demanding Custom Duty for their livestock and goods which was not supported by any Rule or Regulation in this behalf. I accordingly went to see the Tibetan Officials and discussed the point with them. They were fully convinced by my arguments that the practice was illegal and they agreed to stop it in future.

The various passengers who had met me on way had already intimated to the people of the village Minsar about me and had accordingly arranged a Tumboo (tent of Yak hair) for my lodging. The Numberdar [hereditary title for powerful families of zamindars of a village or town] and few distinguished persons of the place received me heartily. On the following day I had a discourse with the inhabitants of the place and we exchanged our ideas. I found there a few Garhwal tradesmen who did a lot of propaganda in my favour among the people telling them that I belonged to the National Government of Jammu and Kashmir which is a part of India. It proved a great help to me. I asked for the recovery of revenue and the people told me that they had not the least hesitation in paying the amount to the State Govt., but they had a few grievances against our Government which despite their several representations made at Leh, were not heeded to and no action was taken. They expressed that this attitude of our Government had extremely disgusted them and they wanted an immediate redress before payment of revenue. The grievances are as follows:-

1] No help was extended to them at the time of the incursion of the Kazaks. The Kazak raid had wholly ravaged their villages and looted and ruined their monasteries. The figures of personal properties of the people leaving aside the monastic wealth were cash Rs. 25000/-, horses 140, yaks 404, and sheep 4889.

2] The people are subjected to the payment of puggur dues (goods sold by the Tibetan Officials to their subjects at exorbitant price) which is a gross injustice of the Tibetan Government on the people. A few days before my arrival there a Tibetan Official called Urkoo had sent goods such as tea etc. worth Rs. 672/- to the village for forced sale for which the villagers had to pay Rs. 1548/- as cost price to Urkoo.

3] An Official from our Government should stay there annually at least for three months in summer who will look after the general situation of the place.

4] The people have to supply free transport to the Tibetan officials. The transport engaged by the Tibetan for other purposes such as carriage of goods etc. are paid at normal wages of three pice for 32 miles per pony.

In respect of items 2 and 4 it is requested that the Tibetan Government be contacted to stop this mal-practice forthwith which will go a long way in mitigating the troubles and the people will welcome our Government and do whatever we ask them to do.

I contacted the Urkoo who had sent his goods to Minsar and told him to postpone the sale of goods to people for the present till I submit my report to my Government and the requisite orders whether the sale of goods should be made or not are conveyed to his Government by my Government.

> I saw on my way orders of the Tibetan Government affixed on all stages to the effect that no Puggur dues and free transport should be demanded. On my return journey I discussed this point with the high Garpon at Gartok and asked him as to how these mal-practices were in vogue in contravention to the clear and explicit orders in this behalf. Garpon told me in reply that as Minsar virtually formed a part of Government of Lhasa and so the Tibetan Officials were right to enforce their laws in the said territory. He also said that Kashmir Government was only to collect revenue annually from the village as done heretofore and for all other administrative purposes the village constitutes a part of Lhasa Government. I asked him to give it in writing to which he showed reluctance and I could easily infer that he had no such document with him by which he was justifying his action.
>
> From the foregoing observations it transpires that our Government has not so far taken any steps in setting up our administration there. It is submitted that speedy measures may please be taken to alleviate the trouble and miseries of the people of this forgotten place which will assure the loyalty of subjects.
>
> No other political condition worth mention needs to be incorporated in the report.

In 1853, the Wazir of Ladakh, Mehta Basti Ram collected Rs 56 as revenue from Minsar; the collection rose to Rs 297 by 1905. According to Indian censuses 1911 and 1921, Minsar had 44 houses comprising 87 men and 73 women. The final settlement report of J&K in 1958 showed Minsar among the 110 villages in Ladakh Tehsil. Local records suggest that J&K authorities stopped collecting annual revenue from Minsar after the India–Pakistan War of 1965.[15]

In 1953, in pursuit of his doctrine of Panchsheel, Nehru unilaterally abandoned all Indian rights on Minsar, as a goodwill gesture to China. In 1954, Minsar and the Bhutanese enclaves were not discussed at all, which means the issue of Minsar has never been settled or negotiated. As British historian John Bray observed, "The status of Minsar is no more than a minor footnote to these concerns, but one that has still to be cleared up".[16] Currently, Minsar is called Men-Shi and is located at the southern end of Gar (Gartok) on national highway 219 in Ngari prefecture. The nearest points in India are Malari and Niti Pass in Uttarakhand.

Pakistan-occupied J&K

The occupied areas retained by Pakistan were divided into two: (1) Azad Jammu and Kashmir (AJK), a 400-km-long narrow strip with a width varying from

16 to 64 km, and (2) Gilgit-Baltistan (called Northern Areas) that spans an area of 72,496 km^2. The OHCHR report of June 14, 2018, observed, "In 1948, UNCIP acknowledged the existence of 'local authorities' (as distinct from the Government of Pakistan) on the Pakistani side of the ceasefire line in Jammu and Kashmir. These two administrative regions have remained distinct 'territories' since then and have not been formally incorporated into Pakistan as they are considered to be part of the disputed state of Jammu and Kashmir".[17] We may, however, note that even though AJK comprises mainly occupied territories of Jammu province, it includes occupied areas of Kashmir province, namely, Neelum Valley (home to the ancient Sharada Peeth) and parts of Gurez Valley. Gilgit Baltistan province, which mainly consists of Occupied Gilgit and Ladakh province, also includes Astore region of Kashmir province. Astore that once connected Kashmir to Central Asia from Dawar in Gurez (Indian side) to Gilgit, was designated a province in Gilgit Baltistan amidst protests by the region's ethnic residents.

Gilgit Baltistan

Gilgit Baltistan, a constitutional and legal part of India, came under illegal occupation of Pakistan in 1947-48 during the invasion of Jammu and Kashmir under the guise of a tribal attack. On November 4, 1947, Major William Scott, British commander of Gilgit Scouts, declared its accession to Pakistan.[18]

Gilgit Baltistan is an area of surpassing beauty, with three majestic mountain ranges, the Karakoram, Hindu Kush and Himalayas. It shares borders with China's Uyghur autonomous region of Xinxiang, the Wakhan corridor of Afghanistan, Chitral district of Khyber Pakhtoonkhwa, and the remaining parts of Jammu and Kashmir State. It comprises three subdivisions, namely, Gilgit (Gilgit, Ghizer, Hunza, and Nagar districts), Diamer (Diamer and Astore districts), and Baltistan (Skardu, Shigar, Kharmang and Ganche districts). The people of Baltistan have an ethnic affinity with the Ladakh region of Jammu and Kashmir; the Dardi people and those in the Kashmir valley have ancient ties. The Shina of Gilgit also inhabit the Gurez valley of the Indian side of Jammu and Kashmir. The people are peaceful and non-violent; Pakistani occupation has brought strife to the land, with sectarian violence becoming a recurring phenomenon.

The principal reason for friction in the region is Zulfiqar Ali Bhutto's abolition of State Subject Rule in 1974, which opened the floodgates for the demographic invasion of Gilgit Baltistan, as did the Karakoram Highway that was completed in 1970. The Census of 2011 established the veracity of demographic invasion of the region, with population increasing 119 per cent in Diamer district, and 76.6 per cent in Gilgit, between 1998 and 2011. The outsiders, mainly from Khyber Pakhtunkhwa, came via the Karakoram Highway. The demographic invasion has posed a serious threat to the cultural and linguistic identity of the ethnic population, especially to the ethnic languages. The people of Baltistan, once part of Ladakh wazarat, are now making special efforts to preserve the Balti script, language, dress and culture. The Baltistan Students Federation has made the Yung Drung (swastika), the ancient Bon symbol of prosperity, its logo.

Religious militants began to frequent the region after Pakistan's involvement in the Afghan war, and President Zia ul-Haq's support to the spread of Sunni Wahhabism in the area, putting the ethnic population under extreme pressure. The constitutional limbo has aggravated the woes of the people, as it is legally "disputed territory" under various UN resolutions. Thus, though under Pakistani control, the people lack parliamentary representation and access to any High Court or the Supreme Court of Pakistan. For long, Pakistan retained the notorious colonial era Frontier Crimes Regulation (till 1974) that denied rights and dignity to the people. Political parties are banned and the region is deprived of development. Initially, it was called Northern Areas to deny its link with Jammu and Kashmir.

Zia ul-Haq's attempts to insinuate Sunni Deobandi Islam into the region provoked fierce riots in May 1988, as groups like Sipah-e-Sahaba targetted Shias and Ismailis, provoking a violent reaction from the Shias; in retaliation, Sunnis descended in hordes and destroyed crops and houses, and lynched and burnt hundreds to death. Riots again erupted a decade later in Gilgit Baltistan on Zia's death anniversary (August 17, 1993) after the Pakistani Army accused Shias of amassing weapons from Iran in their mosques. Shias objected to Pakistan's policy of Islamiyat as well as Urdu textbooks in 2003-2004, leading to a closure of schools for a full year until April 2005. Through Imam Aga Ziauddin's mediation, the issue was resolved by removing the offending portions in the textbooks, but on January 8, 2005, the Imam's car was attacked by gunmen; he succumbed to his injuries. The incident triggered large-scale riots and sectarian killings in the region.

The Taliban also established itself in Gilgit Baltistan and its collusion with Sunni extremists reignited the sectarian conflict with the assassination of deputy speaker, Syed Asad Zaidi, on April 20, 2009. Bomb blasts in Gilgit on

September 26, 2009, incited fresh riots. Jundallah terrorists shot dead at least 16 Shia pilgrims in Kohistan in February 2012, while they were returning to Gilgit Baltistan. These incidents have made the Karakoram Highway dangerous for Shias from Gilgit and Baltistan, leading to demands for opening the Skardu-Kargil road for safe access in and out of the region. Terrorists from Junood ul Haifa, a wing of the Tehrik-e-Taliban Pakistan (TTP), killed 10 foreign tourists and their local Shia cook at the base camp of Nanga Parbat on June 23, 2013.[19]

Pakistan was keen to incorporate Gilgit Baltistan as part of its territory, from the beginning. The first political agent, Sardar Mohammad Alam Khan, arrived in Gilgit on November 16, 1947. The Karachi Agreement, signed on April 28, 1949, between representatives of "Azad Kashmir", Muslim Conference and Government of Pakistan, attempted to formalise links between Gilgit Baltistan and Pakistan. Azad Kashmir surrendered all rights on this region and all power to administer Gilgit was given to the Pakistani political agent. According to Christopher Snedden, the agreement deprived the native people of significant powers and responsibilities.[20] Prime Minister Liaquat Ali Khan decided in 1950 to keep Gilgit and Baltistan constitutionally separate from Pakistan and ruled directly from Karachi via the Ministry of Kashmir Affairs; it was rechristened Northern Areas. The administration was placed under the Resident of Gilgit Baltistan and the rulers of Hunza and Nagar co-opted in the administration.

Two decades later, in 1972, the legislative assembly of Azad Kashmir passed a resolution seeking the return of Gilgit Baltistan to Azad Kashmir, to which Islamabad has not responded, till date. However, in August 1972, major administrative reforms were instituted, abolishing jagirdari, abolishing the princely status of Hunza and Nagar and converting them into districts, designating Gilgit and Baltistan as a state, and annexing Chitral and merging it with the North West Frontier Province. Bhutto promulgated the Northern Areas Legal Framework in October 1974, abolished the Frontier Crimes Regulation and bought the region under the purview of the Pakistani penal code; he also abolished Maharaja Hari Singh's State Subject Rule. The Northern Areas Council was expanded and renamed the Northern Areas Legislative Council, after the Supreme Court of Pakistan directed the government on May 28, 1999, to ensure local participation in governance. But the area continued to be under the jurisdiction of the Ministry of Kashmir Affairs and Northern Areas.

Pakistan's attempts to incorporate the region as its fifth province have not succeeded so far. The "Supreme Court" of AJK in March 1994 held that Gilgit-Baltistan was part of "Jammu and Kashmir".[21] The region was renamed Gilgit Baltistan with the passing of the Gilgit Baltistan Order (Empowerment and Self-governance) 2009 and the Gilgit Baltistan legislative assembly headed by a chief minister set-up.[22] This was perceived as a step towards amalgamation. Nawaz Sharif as Prime Minister suggested converting the region into a fifth province in 2017, but the British Parliament passed a resolution on March 23, 2017, declaring that Gilgit Baltistan was a part of Kashmir, and designating the China Pakistan Economic Corridor as illegal: "Gilgit Baltistan is a legal and constitutional part of the state of J&K, India, which is illegally occupied by Pakistan since 1947".[23]

The Gilgit Baltistan Order 2018[24] made the Prime Minister of Pakistan chief executive of the region with the sole authority to legislate on 68 subjects. The move was driven by the need to protect the China Pakistan Economic Corridor by establishing firm control over the region, but was fiercely resented by the native residents who demanded that the order be revoked.[25] Curiously, the Gilgit Baltistan Order 2018 was not passed by the Federal Cabinet, and may have been a "feeler" to gauge international reaction. The ruling party also refused to amend Articles 51, 57, 59 of the Constitution to facilitate the region becoming its fifth province.[26] The insurmountable obstacle is the UN resolution of 1948 directing Pakistan to vacate Gilgit Baltistan. Another stumbling block is that India will not amend Article 1 of its Constitution to amend the borders of Jammu and Kashmir. To confound the confusion, AJK is also opposed to making Gilgit Baltistan a Pakistani province, and passed two resolutions to this effect in 2016.

The OHRCR report of June 14, 2018 states,

> Known as the Northern Areas until 2009, Gilgit-Baltistan (G-B) is another part of the former princely state of Jammu and Kashmir, which was on the Pakistani side of the Line of Control in 1949. Under the 1949 Karachi Agreement between the Government of Pakistan and representatives of AJK and the All Jammu and Kashmir Muslim Conference, Pakistan's administrative control over the Northern Areas was ratified. However, the Northern Areas was neither incorporated into Pakistan, nor was it given notional autonomy like AJK. In 1999, the Supreme Court of Pakistan directed Islamabad to extend fundamental freedoms to the Northern Areas within six months. The EU Parliament Rapporteur's report in August 2007 identified "a total absence of constitutional identity or civil rights ... people are kept in poverty, illiteracy and backwardness". When Pakistani authorities

promulgated the Gilgit-Baltistan Empowerment and Self-Governance Order 2009, the Government of Pakistan reportedly argued that this would establish full internal autonomy. According to the prominent national NGO, the Human Rights Commission of Pakistan (HRCP), despite the 2009 Order superior courts in G-B cannot annul laws that violate fundamental rights, unlike in Pakistan. G-B's highest court, the Supreme Appellate Court, does not have powers to act under suo moto jurisdiction unlike the Supreme Court of Pakistan. According to HRCP, the 2009 order does not guarantee the right to a fair trial, protection against double punishment and self-incrimination, right to information and right to education. HRCP found that the constitutional article that guarantees equal protection before the law does not prohibit discrimination on the basis of sex. The 2009 Order does not guarantee dignity of a person and residents of G-B are not guaranteed the right to preserve their language, script or culture.

According to international NGOs, the ban on political parties that do not support the eventual accession of Jammu and Kashmir to Pakistan has in effect silenced all kinds of dissent, including demands for greater transparency and accountability. Moreover, they allege that those who protest Pakistan's position face threats and travel bans, and are subject to imprisonment and torture... .

The Gilgit-Baltistan Empowerment and Self-Governance Order 2009 imposes similar restrictions on freedom of expression and association of people under its jurisdiction. Article 9(2) under the fundamental rights section states, "No person or political party in the area comprising Gilgit-Baltistan shall propagate against, or take part in activities prejudicial or detrimental to the ideology of Pakistan".

According to HRCP, there has been "rampant misuse" of Pakistan's Anti-Terrorism Act, 1997 (ATA) by G-B authorities particularly against young activists... .

Several communities in G-B have been raising concerns about the impact of CPEC on their lives. HRCP was informed that G-B authorities had forcibly evicted locals in Maqpoon Das area, while the Chief Secretary of G-B had allocated the same land to state authorities for the CPEC. The displaced claimed they had not received compensation or relocation from the authorities. OHCHR has received information that indigenous people in G-B have complained of not being properly informed or consulted on decisions affecting them and their livelihoods. Additional work may be needed to verify these allegations.[27]

Azad Jammu and Kashmir

This seemingly free region occupied by Pakistan includes the Jammu districts of Mirpur, Kotli, and Poonch, and the Kashmir district of Muzaffarabad. AJK comprises 15 per cent of the territory of Pakistan-occupied J&K (POJK, 13,297 km^2) but is densely populated, with about 70 per cent of the population. It shares a border with Gilgit Baltistan to the north, Pakistan's Punjab province to the south and Khyber Pakhtunkhwa province to the west. To the east, the Line of Control (LoC) separates it from the State of Jammu and Kashmir. The lower Himalayas span the northern part of AJK, and the Jhelum and Leepa rivers make the land very fertile.

An uprising against Maharaja Hari Singh broke out in Poonch in the spring of 1947, ostensibly on account of punitive taxes levied on the peasantry by the Maharaja's administration. The rebels were mainly soldiers demobilised after World War II, who quickly gained control of almost the entire district. Thereafter, the pro-Pakistan chieftains of the western districts of Muzaffarabad, Poonch, and Mirpur proclaimed a provisional AJK government in Rawalpindi on October 3, 1947. Acting under the assumed name of "Mr Anwar", Ghulam Nabi Gilkar issued a proclamation in the name of the provisional government at Muzaffarabad. However, this government quickly fizzled out with the arrest of "Anwar" in Srinagar. On October 24, a second provisional government of Azad Kashmir was established at Palandri under the leadership of Sardar Ibrahim Khan. By this time, from October 21/22, thousands of Pashtun tribesmen from the North West Frontier Province were pouring into Jammu and Kashmir to "liberate" it from the Maharaja's rule. They were led by experienced military officers and equipped with modern arms. The Maharaja's forces were ill-equipped to withstand the onslaught and the raiders rapidly captured the towns of Muzaffarabad, Mirpur, Kotli, and Poonch. Thousands of local residents were massacred, property looted, and thousands of Hindus fled from these towns towards Jammu for refuge. The besieged Maharaja Hari Singh signed the instrument of accession on October 26, 1947, and India sent its army to defend its new State, but Pakistan remained in occupation of the territory seized by it even after the UN-mandated ceasefire. This region was designated as Azad Jammu and Kashmir.

The Karachi Agreement, which separated Gilgit Baltistan and AJK, was signed on April 28, 1949, by Mushtaq Ahmed Gurmani, Pakistan's Minister without Portfolio and in-charge of Kashmir Affairs; Sardar Mohammed Ibrahim Khan, president of Azad Kashmir; and Chaudhry Ghulam Abbas, leader of the All Jammu and Kashmir Muslim Conference, and was kept secret up to the 1990s. It was not reported in local newspapers of 1949, the memoirs of Sardar M. Ibrahim Khan, or any other sources, and was revealed for the first time in the Verdict on Gilgit and Baltistan (Northern Area) by the High Court of Azad Kashmir in the 1990s, wherein it was mentioned that the agreement "appears to have been executed on 28 April 1949". Later, it was published as Appendix XVII of the Constitution of AJK by Justice Syed Manzoor Hussain Gilani in 2008.[28]

AJK is a "self-governing" state under Pakistani control. The administration is divided into three divisions, namely, Mirpur (Mirpur, Kotli, Bhimber districts), Muzaffarabad (Muzaffarabad, Jhelum Valley, Neelam Valley districts), and Poonch (Poonch, Haveli, Bagh, Sudhanoti districts). Officially, the area has a parliamentary system with a prime minister, an autonomous government, and a president as constitutional head of state, but has always been controlled by the Government of Pakistan. The "Azad Jammu and Kashmir Adaptation of Laws Act, 1988" adapts and enforces most Pakistani laws in the region, but AJK does not send any delegates to the National Assembly. This drew the ire of the European Parliament Committee on Foreign Affairs Rapporteur, whose 2007 report noted Pakistan's failure to fulfil its obligations to introduce meaningful and representative democratic structures in AJK.[29]

According to the AJK Interim Constitution Act 1974,[30] the AJK Council has most powers, including legislative and taxation. The Chairperson of the Council is the Prime Minister of Pakistan, who nominates six Pakistani Ministers/MPs and six members are elected by the AJK assembly. The Pakistani-majority Council is not accountable to the assembly; its decisions are final and not subject to judicial review. At administrative level, virtually all key officers of the AJK Government are deputed from Pakistan, including the Chief Secretary, Inspector General of Police, Finance Secretary, Home Secretary, Health Secretary and Accountant-General, Auditor General and Chief Election Commissioner. They exercise the real authority within AJK and maintain a check on the elected government.

AJK enjoyed a brief period of limited autonomy between 1970 and 1974, being otherwise firmly under the control of the federal government. Even the AJK Council, though headed by the prime minister with the power to override laws passed by AJK's elected legislature, has very little authority in practice as the military exercises almost complete control over the territory.[31]

Maharaja Hari Singh's State Subject Rule is still applicable in AJK; hence the increase of population has been only 22 per cent from 1998 to 2017. The people are almost entirely Muslim, but take their identity from diverse tribal clans (*biradari*) and are culturally and linguistically closer to the Indian side of Punjab than the Kashmir valley. The territory is not ethnically homogenous. Gujjars, numbering close to 800,000, are possibly the largest group. The two most influential biradaris are the Sudhans from the southeast (mainly Bagh district and Rawalakot subdivision of Poonch district) and the Rajputs who are spread out across the territory; both number roughly half a million each. Almost all of Azad Kashmir's politicians and leaders come from one of these two groups. The 300,000-strong Mirpuri Jats hail mainly from Mirpur, Bhimber and Kotli. Though Mirpuris are the closest geographical and cultural relatives of the Potohari Punjabis, in recent decades they have begun to define themselves as Kashmiris. Mirpuris have migrated to the United Kingdom in large numbers and constitute the "Kashmiri presence" in that country.[32] Other groups include the Awans, Abbasis and ethnic Kashmiris of the Neelam and Leepa Valleys.

The OHCHR[33] in its report of June 14, 2018 stated,

> According to the United Nations Country Team in its submission to Pakistan's 2012 Universal Periodic Review, G-B and AJK "spell out additional challenges with less stable constitutional and legislative framework". The Committee on the Elimination of Racial Discrimination noted with concern that the laws of Pakistan are not applicable in these provinces to the same extent as in the other parts of the territory. In fact, Pakistan's prime minister, the federal minister for Kashmir Affairs and Gilgit-Baltistan and the federal civil service reportedly have full control over all government operations in both AJK and G-B. According to an international NGO, federal intelligence agencies are deployed across the two regions and have "considerable powers over local elected representatives and officials".
>
> The interim constitution of AJK has placed several restrictions on anyone criticizing AJK's accession to Pakistan, in contravention to international standards on the rights to freedoms of expression and opinion, assembly and association. It explicitly states, "No person or political party in Azad Jammu and Kashmir shall be permitted to propagate against or take part in activities prejudicial or detrimental to the ideology of the State's accession to Pakistan". The AJK electoral law expands on this, disqualifying anyone running for elected office for propagating any opinion or acting contrary to "the ideology of the State's accession to Pakistan". No person can be appointed to a government position unless they take an oath of office, which includes that they "will remain loyal to the country and the cause of accession of the state of Jammu & Kashmir to Pakistan".

> According to international NGOs, the ban on political parties that do not support the eventual accession of Jammu and Kashmir to Pakistan has in effect silenced all kinds of dissent, including demands for greater transparency and accountability. Moreover, they allege that those who protest Pakistan's position face threats and travel bans, and are subject to imprisonment and torture.
>
> Human rights groups report that publishers of books or periodicals are also required to make a declaration of loyalty to accession to Pakistan. A number of books supporting Kashmiri independence were also reportedly banned by a government order in February 2016.
>
> To publish within AJK, media owners have to obtain permission from Government of Pakistan's Kashmir Council and the Ministry of Kashmir Affairs.
>
> Similar to the Constitution of Pakistan, AJK's Interim Constitution also defines who may be considered to be a Muslim. This definition is used to declare members of the Ahmadiyya community as non-Muslims and is the basis of institutional discrimination against them. On 6 February 2018, the AJK Legislative Assembly passed a constitutional amendment that declared the Ahmadiyya to be non-Muslims.
>
> Pakistan's blasphemy provisions are also reportedly in force in AJK. They have been criticized by several international Treaty Bodies and experts as they violate a range of international human rights principles and embolden those who instigate violence against religious minorities.

The World Bank and Asian Development Bank funded the Mangla Dam built across the Jhelum River in Mirpur district, and the Government of Pakistan agreed to pay royalties to the Government of AJK for use of the water and electricity generated by the dam that submerged over 280 villages and Mirpur and Dadyal towns, displacing over 110,000 people.[34] However, the dam provides water and power to the Punjab province, leaving residents of AJK to battle water and power shortages. In August 2018, the Neelum river dried up even during the monsoons, triggering widespread protests. The Neelum river between India and Pakistan meets the Jhelum in the Pakistani city of Muzaffarabad; there are claims that Pakistan is diverting the water to Punjab province. Three additional hydro projects (Kohala, Karot and Mahal) planned under the CPEC are agitating the civilian population.

Pakistan's ISI has set up terror camps in AJK. In 1989-1991, hundreds of Kashmiri youth crossed the LoC for arms training and returned to run insurgencies against India in Kashmir. In 1994, the ISI organised 13 groups operating in Kashmir into the Muttahida Jihad Council. By 1999, the effective groups were Lashkar-e-Toiba, Hizbul Mujahideen, Al Badr, and Harkat-ul-Mujahedin. Throughout the 1990s, Azad Kashmir was dotted with militant groups operating under the supervision of the Pakistani military, but after the United States launched its global war on terror (GWOT), most groups went underground and changed their names.[35]

The local inhabitants are uneasy at the terror camps being run in close proximity to highly populated civilian areas, which they believe is intended to keep a close watch on the population and ensure political compliance and control. After the 2005 earthquake in the region, only militant groups were allowed to disburse relief material. It is believed that the earthquake destroyed scores of terror camps, but this was never acknowledged by the Pakistani government as they were secret camps. India has often submitted proofs of terror camps running in AJK by the Pakistan Army. In July 2018, General Officer Commanding of Srinagar-based 15 Corps, Lt. Gen. Satish Dua, asserted, "As per our intelligence inputs, there are about 17 terrorist training camps in Pakistan and PoK put together. Out of that, nine are opposite the 15 Corps zone, four each in Manshera which is in Pakistan and Muzaffarabad. Total strength of terrorists in these camps is anything between 1000 to 1150". Dua said there are 23 different launch pads on the other side closer to the LoC, having a strength of 315 to 325 militants waiting for opportunity to sneak in.[36]

In June 2018, a joint sitting of the AJK Legislative Assembly and AJK Council, at Muzaffarabad, moved the 13th Amendment Act 2018, to confer more powers on the State Government. This drew a strong protest from India,[37] which stated,

> The Government of India has conveyed a strong protest through diplomatic channel today against the so-called Azad Jammu and Kashmir Interim Constitution (13th Amendment) Act 2018.
>
> It was clearly conveyed that the entire State of Jammu and Kashmir, which also includes the so-called "Azad Jammu and Kashmir" is an integral part of India by virtue of its accession in 1947. Any action to alter the status of any part of the territory under forcible and illegal occupation of Pakistan has no legal basis whatsoever, and is completely unacceptable. Instead of seeking to alter the status of the occupied territories, Pakistan should immediately vacate all areas under its illegal occupation.

Relationship of AJK with Gilgit Baltistan

The people of Gilgit Baltistan and AJK are at odds in defining the relationship of Gilgit Baltistan with the former princely state of Jammu and Kashmir. Some sections in Gilgit Baltistan favour merger with Pakistan; others favour independence and want Pakistan to abide by the UN resolution and vacate the area. Azad Jammu Kashmir was created to sever Gilgit Baltistan as a territory of Jammu and Kashmir and weaken the latter's claim on it. The Karachi agreement of April 28, 1949, between representatives of AJK, Pakistan, and Agent of Gilgit Baltistan sought to achieve this objective, but lapsed after the promulgation of the 1970 Act by President Yahya Khan. Thereafter, in 1972, the legislative assembly of AJK passed a resolution asking Pakistan to return the Northern Areas; Pakistan responded with silence. This was followed up with a resolution in 1982 that reaffirmed that Gilgit and Baltistan were part of Jammu and Kashmir and should be united with AJK. Interestingly, till this day there is no road link between AJK and Gilgit Baltistan.

Pakistan's constitution is completely silent on the status of Occupied Jammu and Kashmir. Article 257, which reiterates identical provisions in the 1956 and 1962 constitutions, refers only to the future status of the state: "When the people of the State of Jammu and Kashmir decide to accede to Pakistan, the relationship between Pakistan and that State shall be determined in accordance with the wishes of the people of that State". Pakistan has been unable to remove the ambiguities in its position regarding the constitutional status of POJK because it would not like to do anything that could compromise its demand for a plebiscite in accordance with UN resolutions. Hence, it has been careful to refrain from actions that could expose it to the charge that it altered the basic conditions under which those resolutions were adopted and thus impeded their implementation. Secondly, Pakistan has been cautious not to take steps that could imply that it accepts the current territorial status quo dividing the state into two parts as a permanent solution.[38]

In 1993, the AJK high court ruled that Gilgit Baltistan is part of AJK, but the order was set aside by the AJK Supreme Court in 1994, which ruled that the region was part of Jammu and Kashmir. The residents of AJK, often considered the voice of the separatist movement in Indian Kashmir, regard Gilgit Baltistan an integral part of Kashmir and vehemently oppose its merger with Pakistan. In India, both the pro-Pakistan Kashmiri leadership and the separatists (pro-Azad Kashmir) claim Gilgit Baltistan is part of Kashmir. Maulvi Umar Farooq, leader of the separatist Hurriyat Conference, has reiterated

Kashmir's claim over Gilgit Baltistan, and similar assertions have been made by political and religious leaders in Diamer in Gilgit Baltistan, including members of the Gilgit Baltistan National Alliance.

Pakistan's federal institutions, including the Supreme Court, Office of the President, Office of the Prime Minister, cabinet members, chiefs of the armed forces, and heads of different parliamentary committees, maintain that Gilgit Baltistan is an UN-declared disputed area and its residents cannot be declared citizens of Pakistan until India and Pakistan resolve the issue of accession of Jammu and Kashmir. To secure permanent control over Gilgit Baltistan, Pakistan will have to get the issue withdrawn from the UN and amend its constitution to redefine the international boundary between the two countries, something that is highly unlikely.[39]

Given its total control over the region, Islamabad would have been behind the AJK Assembly resolution demanding return of Gilgit Baltistan in 1972. The resolution was followed by Pakistan removing the State Subject Rule in Gilgit Baltistan in 1974 and facilitating large-scale migration of Pakistanis into the region. A decade later, the AJK Assembly again passed a resolution that Gilgit Baltistan was part of Kashmir and should be returned to AJK. In 1993, the AJK High Court ordered Gilgit Baltistan to be annexed to AJK as it was a part of Kashmir, but this was set aside by the AJK Supreme Court in 1994. The same year, Pakistan granted partial empowerment to Gilgit Baltistan. In 2016, the AJK Assembly again passed two resolutions claiming Gilgit Baltistan was a part of AJK and opposing attempts to make it a fifth province. The 2016 resolutions were followed by Pakistan attempting to declare Gilgit Baltistan its fifth province[40] that analysts believe are part of an attempt to keep the separatist fires burning in Indian Jammu and Kashmir.

The timing of the resolutions and court orders seems linked to the rise of terror camps in AJK after 1989, when scores of brainwashed youth from the Indian side crossed the LoC for arms training. In Srinagar valley, Azadi slogans were blared from mosques and chorused by mobs that drove the Kashmiri Pandit community into exile. In the international arena, as Pakistan supported the call for an independent Kashmir, the High Court order was seen to legitimise the claims of one "Azad" Kashmir. Reading the AJK High Court judgement of March 8, 1993, is like reading the Pakistani view on Jammu and Kashmir.[41]

Pakistan planned to table a resolution in the UN Human Rights Council in Geneva regarding alleged human rights violations in the Indian side of

Jammu and Kashmir, in 1994. However, India smartly pre-empted this with a unanimous resolution of both Houses of Parliament on February 22, 1994, declaring that the occupied areas of AJK and Gilgit Baltistan are parts of Jammu and Kashmir State of India and India is committed to get these areas back.[42] This put Pakistan on the back foot and forced it to withdraw its resolution on March 9, 1994.

The farcical AJK assembly resolutions and Pakistani attempts to declare Gilgit Baltistan as the fifth province are clearly attempts to keep all stakeholders in the Jammu and Kashmir issue happy. Pakistan regularly raises UN resolutions at international forums where it reiterates its claim over the erstwhile kingdom of Maharaja Hari Singh, knowing well that it cannot incorporate Gilgit Baltistan unless it withdraws from all occupied territories as mandated by the UN resolutions, prior to a plebiscite. In an embarrassing reversal for Islamabad, however, PoK human rights activist Jamil Maqsood intervened during the 38th Session of the UN Human Rights Council in June 2018 and denounced attempts to engineer demographic changes in Gilgit Baltistan, denial of State Subject Rule, and claimed that locals were "forcefully evicted from their land and property".[43] There have been instances of land grabbing in Bagh and Kotli districts and the people of Gilgit Baltistan are crushed under the Pakistan National Action Plan. There have been large-scale violations of human rights throughout the region, dissent is being muffled under anti-terror laws, while banned outfits continue to operate with impunity. From India's perspective, the strategically important area of the erstwhile kingdom of Jammu and Kashmir, that was India's gateway to Afghanistan, Central Asia and Europe, is restless under the vice-like grip of China and Pakistan. It is time to rescue the area from the veil of darkness and silence shrouding it for decades.

*

NOTES

1 Office of the United Nations High Commissioner for Human Rights (OHCHR), Report on the Situation of Human Rights in Kashmir: Developments in the Indian State of Jammu and Kashmir from June 2016 to April 2018, and General Human Rights Concerns in Azad Jammu and Kashmir and Gilgit-Baltistan, June 14, 2018, p. 9. https://www.ohchr.org/Documents/Countries/IN/DevelopmentsInKashmirJune2016ToApril2018.pdf.

2 Arpi, Claude, Nehru's Aksai Chin Blunder, Rediff.co, Feb. 3, 2017. https://www.rediff.com/news/column/nehrus-aksai-chin-blunder/20170203.htm.

3 Verma, Virendra Sahai, Sino-Indian Border Dispute at Aksai Chin: A Middle Path for Resolution, May 2010. https://chinaindiaborderdispute.files.wordpress.com/2010/07/virendravermapaperborderdispute.pdf.

4 Report of the Officials of the Governments of India and People's Republic of China on the Boundary Question (Part 3), Ministry of External Affairs, pp. 7, 8. http://www.archieve.claudearpi.net/maintenance/uploaded_pics/OR_Part_3.pdf

5 Verma, op. cit.

6 Woodman, Dorothy, *Himalayan Frontiers: A Political Review of British, Chinese, Indian and Russian Rivalries*, London: Barrie & Jenkins, 1969, pp. 101, 360.

7 Arpi, op. cit.

8 Sering, Senge, China's Interests in Shaksgam Valley, Oct. 10, 2013. https://www.sharnoffsglobalviews.com/china-shaksgam-valley-191/

9 Ibid.

10 Report of the Officials, op. cit., p. 26.

11 Sering, op. cit.

12 Excerpts of telegram dated October 26, 1947, from Jawaharlal Nehru to the British Prime Minister, Clement Attlee. https://www.mtholyoke.edu/acad/intrel/kasnehru.htm.

13 The Boundary Agreement between China and Pakistan, 1963. http://people.unica.it/annamariabaldussi/files/2015/04/China-Pakistan-1963.pdf.

14 Arpi, Claude, Minsar, an Indian Principality in Tibet, March 1, 2015. http://claudearpi.blogspot.com/2015/03/what-about-minsar-indian-principality.html.

15 Stobdan, P., *Resituating Menser and Darchen-Labrang in the Boundary Negotiations with China*, February 16, 2018. https://idsa.in/policybrief/resituating-menser-darchen-labrang-in-boundary-negotiations-china-pstobdan-160218.

16 Ibid.

17 Office of the United Nations High Commissioner for Human Rights, op. cit., p. 41.

18 Bansal, Alok, *Gilgit Baltistan and Its Saga of Unending Human Rights Violation*, New Delhi: Pentagon Press, 2018, p. 27.

19. Ibid., pp. 111-117.

20 Snedden, Christopher, *The Untold Story of the People of Azad Kashmir*, New York: Oxford University Press, 2011, p. 90.

21 Singh, Priyanka, Gilgit Baltistan: Between Hope and Despair, IDSA Monograph No. 14, 2013. https://idsa.in/monograph/GilgitBaltistan_psingh.

22 Bansal, op. cit., pp. 79-90.

23 Five points about UK parliament resolution on Gilgit-Baltistan, March 27, 2017. https://www.governancenow.com/news/regular-story/-five-points-uk-parliament-resolution-gilgitbaltistan.

24 Gilgit-Baltistan Government Order 2018. https://www.scribd.com/document/378073496/Gilgit-Baltistan-Government-Order-2018.

25 Explainer: Why GB's opposition parties oppose new order, June 1, 2018. https://www.dawn.com/news/1411321.

26 Cabinet refuses to give provisional status to Gilgit Baltistan, December 6, 2018. https://www.pakistantoday.com.pk/2018/12/06/cabinet-refuses-to-give-provisional-province-status-to-gb/amp/?__twitter_impression=true.

27 Office of the United Nations High Commissioner for Human Rights, op. cit., p. 44.

28 AJK Interim Constitution Act 1974 by Asif Raja. https://www.scribd.com/doc/2505469/AJK-Interim-Constitution-Act-1974-by-Asif-Raja.

29 Office of the United Nations High Commissioner for Human Rights, op. cit., p. 42.
30 Ibid
31 An Appraisal of Constitutional, Financial and Administrative Arrangements between the Governments of Pakistan and Azad Jammu and Kashmir, Centre for Peace, Development and Reforms (CPDR), Azad Jammu and Kashmir, June 2011. http://www.cpdr.org.pk/images/publications/2011_CPDR_Kashmir_Report.pdf.
32 "With friends like these: Human rights violations in Azad Kashmir", *Human Rights Watch*, September 2006, Volume 18, No. 12(C). https://www.hrw.org/reports/2006/pakistan0906/index.htm.
33 Office of the United Nations High Commissioner for Human Rights, op. cit., p. 43.
34 Terminski, Bogumil, *Development-Induced Displacement and Resettlement: Theoretical Frameworks and Current Challenges*, Indiana University, 2013. http://dlc.dlib.indiana.edu/dlc/handle/10535/8833?show=full.
35 "With friends like these, op. cit.
36 Around 1150 militants in training camps in Pakistan, PoK: Army, July 13, 2018. https://economictimes.indiatimes.com/news/defence/around-1150-militants-in-training-camps-in-pakistan-pok-army/articleshow/49062099.cms.
37 India protests to Pakistan against so-called "Azad Jammu and Kashmir Interim Constitution (13th Amendment) Act 2018", Press Release, Ministry of External Affairs, New Delhi, June 11, 2018. https://www.mea.gov.in/press-releases.htm?dtl/29972/India+protests+ to+Pakistan+against+socalled+Azad+Jammu+and+Kashmir+Interim+Constitution+ 13th+ Amendment +Act+2018.
38 Kashmir's legal status, July 16, 2009. https //www.thenews.com.pk/archive/print/186528.
39 Sering, Senge, What is the Kashmir and Gilgit-Baltistan Dispute about?, March 26, 2013. https://www.sharnoffsglobalviews.com/the-kashmir-and-gilgit-batistan-dispute/.
40 Explainer, op. cit.
41 High Court of Judicature, Azad Jammu and Kashmir, Verdict on Gilgit and Baltistan, March 8, 1993. I am indebted to the Jammu Kashmir Study Centre, Delhi, for this document.
42 Parliament Resolution on Jammu and Kashmir. http://www.satp.org/satporgtp/countries/india/document/papers/parliament_resolution_on_Jammu_and_Kashmir.htm.
43 Pakistan occupied Kashmir Activist Made Intervention During 38th Session of UNHRC, June 29, 2018. https://wokejournal.com/pakistan-occupied-kashmir-activist-made-intervention-during-38th-session-of-unhrc/.

CHAPTER SIX

Kashmiri Pandits: Last Bastion of Nationalism

Shakti Munshi

The original inhabitants of the valley of Kashmir, with a history going back more than five thousand years, were reduced to a powerless minority owing to centuries of decimation at the hands of culturally alien rulers. The establishment of the modern nation state of India did not bring much respite as the region-specific political arrangements that followed independence did not bring equality for all communities living within the erstwhile kingdom of Jammu and Kashmir. In recent decades, the rise of Islamic fundamentalism in the neighborhood (Afghanistan, Pakistan) impacted India's Kashmir province, and in a violent convulsion, the tiny ethnic minority of Kashmiri Pandits was subjected to a swift and shrill campaign of violence and intimidation that forced it to flee from its ancestral home and hearth.

Medieval era

According to the recorded history of Kashmir, Sultan Mehmood of Ghazni made an unsuccessful attempt to conquer this region in the 11th century AD. Kalhan's *Rajatarangini* (written between 1147-50 AD) narrates the history of Kashmir's most celebrated ruler, Raja Lalitaditya, who became king in 719 AD, whose kingdom stretched to the Cauvery basin in the south, Assam in the east, and up to the Caspian Sea, north of Iran. The ruins of the imposing Martanda (sun) temple attest to the grandeur of his reign. Another famous and progressive ruler was Raja Avantivarman, who founded the Utpal dynasty and ruled from 855 to 883 AD.

During the reign of Raja Suhadeva (AD 1301-1320), Kashmir was visited by the missionary Bulbul Shah, Shahmir (AD 1313) and Lhachan Gualbu Rinchan, a Buddhist prince from Ladakh. Shahmir arrived with a large family from the Swat valley, land of Panini, and now in the North West Frontier Province of Pakistan. Raja Suhadeva gave Shahmir a jagir in a village near Baramulla and his prime minister, Ramachandra, employed Rinchan and gave him jagir in a village in the Lar Valley. After a period of turmoil following a Mongolian invasion of the region, first Ramachandra and then Rinchan seized the throne. Rinchan now expressed a desire to embrace the Hindu faith of Kashmir, but was shunned by narrow-minded leaders of the community. In anger, he turned to the missionary, Bulbul Shah, and converted to Islam. Thereafter, Shahmir and Rinchan established Muslim rule in Kashmir and initiated the process of converting the population to Islam, a process recorded in the *Baharistan-i-Shahi*. Hindus suffered much persecution in the centuries that followed, eventually becoming a minority group in the Kashmir Valley. The rise of the Sikh Empire (1819-1846) and Dogra rule (1846-1947) afforded some respite, but the Kashmiri Pandit population had declined to merely 7 per cent (Census 1941), and currently stands at around 0.1 per cent of the valley's population. This essay briefly encapsulates the community's precipitous decline.

1947

Mohammad Ali Jinnah, founder and first Governor-General of Pakistan, wanted the Muslim-majority kingdom of Jammu and Kashmir to accede to Pakistan but was unsure of Maharaja Hari Singh's intentions. According to authors Larry Collins and Dominique Lapierre (*Freedom at Midnight*, 1975), Prime Minister Liaquat Ali Khan called a select group of collaborators to Lahore in mid-September 1947 to discuss the Kashmir issue. They mulled over three scenarios: outright invasion (war); fomenting internal uprising via supply of arms and money and sending Kabali tribals from the North West Frontier Province to invade the state in the name of *jihad* (religious war). Pakistan opted for the latter course in order to maintain deniability in the event of the plans going awry.

The story of how Maharaja Hari Singh tried to accede to India but was rebuffed by Prime Minister Jawaharlal Nehru and compelled to hand over power to Sheikh Mohammad Abdullah has been written about elsewhere (See *Genesis of the Praja Parishad*). Four precious days of massacre and mayhem by the invaders were lost before the besieged king threw in the towel and appointed Sheikh Abdullah as administrator of the State; only then was he allowed to sign the Instrument of Accession to India on October 26, 1947.

At independence, there was a tacit understanding between Kashmiri Muslims professing Sufi Islam and the mainly Shaivite Pandits. Raising slogans, "*Hamlavar Khabardar, Hum Kashmiri Hai Tayaar*" (Invaders beware, we Kashmiris are ready),[1] the two communities joined hands to resist the Pakistan-backed invaders. Nevertheless, there were some in the valley who wanted the Muslim-majority State to accede to Pakistan. Moreover, an undercurrent of radicalism had already been unleashed by invisible forces in the Jammu region of Poonch-Mirpur in 1947, as evidenced in uprisings against Maharaja Hari Singh, including Sheikh Abdullah's "Dogras Quit Kashmir" (*Dogron Gaddi Chhodo*) agitation in Srinagar 1931. Jawaharlal Nehru's firm backing and manoeuvring to bestow total political power on the untested Sheikh Abdullah led the latter to support accession to India as part of his quest for political lebensraum and to avoid domination by Mohammad Ali Jinnah. By 1949, Sheikh Abdullah's burgeoning ambitions, egged on by external powers, to carve out an independent principality became more overt and created new stresses in the socio-political fabric, and eventually resulted in his split with Nehru in 1953.

Although Pakistan managed to grab critical strategic territory during the war, it remained unwavering in its desire to incorporate the entire erstwhile kingdom of Maharaja Hari Singh into its territory, and spared no efforts to radicalize the population, particularly in the Muslim majority valley of Kashmir. Around the late 1960s, a militant outfit named Al Fatah, led by Ghulam Rasool Zehgeer, a Plebiscite Front activist, plotted to achieve independence from India, a goal opposed by Pakistan that wanted Jammu and Kashmir to merge with it.[2] The Soviet invasion of Afghanistan (December 1979) provided a unique opportunity as American arms and munificence flowed into Rawalpindi and the coffers of the ubiquitous Inter-Services Intelligence (ISI); the Kashmir border went "live" as hundreds of youth crossed the border for arms training before returning to perpetrate terror attacks inside the State. This is the backdrop in which the minuscule Kashmiri Pandit community, seen as the bulwark of the Indian nation state and a hindrance to the mission of *nizam-e-mustafa* (rule of Allah) and union with Pakistan (land of the pure), had to be removed from the valley. The ensuing decade saw a grim escalation of Islamic terror in the valley, culminating in the exodus of the terrorised community in the bitter winter of 1989-90. We shall briefly examine the events that led to this tragic dénouement.

Sheikh Abdullah

Sheikh Abdullah succeeded in getting Article 370 (introduced as Article 306A during the Constituent Assembly debates) incorporated into the Indian Constitution on October 17, 1949. Introduced during the course of the war, the statute was projected as one that would fully integrate Jammu and Kashmir State with the rest of India once hostilities ended. In reality, it became a tool by which Abdullah and his successors exploited, blackmailed and manipulated the national government and the local population, encouraging the growth of communalism and separatism. The demographic denigration of the Kashmiri Pandit populace began under Sheikh Abdullah from 1947 itself, most notably under the guise of land reforms, and continued under successive regimes, depriving Pandits opportunities for higher education in State institutions, making it difficult for Pandit youth to avail of Central or State scholarships, and systematically eroding employment opportunities for them in the State Government. *Kashmiriyat* or Kashmiri particularism gradually became coterminous with the welfare of one community, to the exclusion of all others.

J&K Big Landed Estates Abolition Act, 1950

Agriculture was the major source of livelihood in Kashmir when Sheikh Abdullah introduced the J&K Big Landed Estates Abolition Act 1950, on October 17, 1950, with the aim of depriving Kashmiri Pandits of their land, without compensation, an early instance of the use of Article 370 for sectarian ends. Thus, land in excess of 182 kanals per family or institution was confiscated and given to Muslim tillers for free. Under the law, 188,775 acres of land was confiscated from Pandit families. The Pandits tried to get justice through the legal route, but when tribunal after tribunal proved farcical, they realized the adamancy of the administration and gave up the fight.

Abdullah's next move was to nationalise industry and create a licensing system that again victimised Hindus and favoured Muslims, with the result that Muslim entrepreneurs soon monopolised all businesses in the valley. Many Pandits had to go outside the state to earn a living, which suited the Sheikh's agenda.

Wahhabism

From ancient times, Kashmir was the abode of *rishis* and sages who came to meditate in the serenity of the Himalayan caves and valleys. When Islam entered the valley, these deep cultural moorings drove the converts to seek a softer version of Islam, namely, Sufism, which emphasised bonds of love with and surrender to the almighty. The concept of *ziyarat* at a rishi's burial place, anathema to fundamentalists as a form of idolatry, became an accepted practice because of the Hindu heritage of the converts. But from the mid-1970s, Saudi petrodollars and Pakistani interventions saw Wahhabi Islam make inroads into the State, and local youth were instigated against the "kafir" minority.

Political downsizing

Kashmiri Hindus were a peaceful crime-free community with a high literacy rate of over 90 per cent. The community comprised the best educationists, doctors, judges and engineers who made a sterling contribution to Kashmir's progress. They were not interested in politics and lacked the numbers for politicians to be interested in them. However, Pandits were numerically significant and could influence the electoral results in three constituencies – Habba Kadal, Baramulla and Anantnag (Sham Lal Saraf was elected from Habba Kadal in the Constituent Assembly of 1951). Thereafter, delimitation was conducted in a manner that ensured that all constituencies in the valley had a Muslim majority population, leaving Kashmiri Pandits without any representation in State politics.[3]

Education

Kashmiri Pandits have always valued education and were academically bright. Successive governments in the State manoeuvred to deprive Pandit children from availing of higher education in the State by prescribing limits according to percentage of population in the valley. In Jammu region, where Hindus comprised the majority, the criterion was changed to backwardness and economic status. In Ladakh, the Buddhists were completely deprived of all reservations. As a result, only a minuscule 2 per cent Pandits managed to get admission for higher studies in the State. Among Kashmiri Muslim students who got admission into higher education institutions in the State, only 31 per cent secured more than 60 per cent in the qualifying exams, whereas 63 per cent Kashmiri Pandit applicants secured more than 60 per cent in the qualifying exams. Despite their better scores, the Pandits were denied admission in higher education institutions in the State. These unfair and partisan policies politicized educational institutions and made them incubators for radicalisation of young Muslim minds even as Pandit youth were compelled to leave the State in droves in search of education and opportunities, eroding their links with their ancestral abode and rupturing ties between Muslim and Pandit youth of the valley. Even grants for studying outside the State were made difficult for Pandit students.

Employment

Successive governments in Jammu and Kashmir failed to improve the economy and to develop the infrastructure. Article 370 and rampant corruption in the administration inhibited outside investment in industry in the State, thereby limiting employment opportunities to the State Government, Central Government and public sector agencies. Here again, an average 70 per cent of the higher posts benefitted Muslims. With time, even primary and secondary schools, Kashmir University, agricultural university, medical and engineering colleges and hospitals were not spared. So the highly qualified Pandits had no option but to migrate in the quest for employment. In some cases, when the Pandits went to court for justice and received a favourable verdict, the legal decisions would be bypassed. As the recruitment of Kashmiri Hindus fell to merely 1.7 per cent, the radicalisation of the work environment became easy to execute.[4]

Media

With financial support from the ISI, foreign sources and the support of politicians (especially when in opposition) and the radicalised youth, the media also got radicalised. Media in Kashmir valley is controlled by Kashmiri Muslims who own most of the daily newspapers, news journals, weekly news magazines, and other periodicals that carry inflammatory and separatist propaganda, advocating secession and instigating radicalised youth and general Muslim population against the minority population.[5] Previous Governments in Delhi showed complete apathy to the rising radicalisation and Islamisation in the State. Some in the electronic media misinformed the nation about the happenings in the valley. The valley-based family politicians manipulated the situation for personal gains and to hold on to power and further fanned the terrorist fires by giving sound-bytes in favour of terrorists and professional stone-pelters. Instigation by politicians and years of vicious propaganda and brainwashing in schools, madrasas, institutes and other places encouraged the perpetrators to commit the genocide and extermination of the 1990s that reduced the Kashmiri Hindu population from 5 per cent in 1981 to 0.1 per cent.

Valley in 1980s

Armed militancy and terrorism entered the valley during the 1980s on a large scale with the connivance and support of Pakistan. Muslim youth crossed the borders in large numbers from 1984 onwards, and returned with sophisticated arms and ammunition after being trained in sabotage and warfare. The objective was to subvert democracy and secularism and establish an Islamic theocratic State. "Mullahs" from Pakistan, Bihar and UP with Saudi influence were brought to Kashmir to convert the locals to Wahhabi Islam. Some local politicians joined in this activity and others took political benefit as and when it suited them. For the plan to succeed, the minority Hindu community had to be expelled or converted and therefore became the first victim of this enterprise.[66]

In the early 1980's, this exercise was launched with the torching of temples and destruction of properties of Kashmiri Pandits. In February 1986, Ghulam Muhammad Shah (Gul Shah), husband of Farooq Abdullah's sister Khalida Shah, staged a coup against Abdullah and occupied the Chief Minister's chair. He incited Kashmiri Muslims with slogans of *Islam khatrey mein hai* (Islam is in danger); as a result, violence began in South Kashmir where the Pandits were targeted. Although many houses and temples were plundered, destroyed and looted, no Hindu was killed.[7] An investigation into the Anantnag riots later revealed that members of "secular parties" in the State, rather than Islamists, had played a key role in organizing this violence to gain political mileage through religious sentiments.[8] The same year, Gul Shah decided to construct a mosque within the premises of an ancient Hindu temple inside the New Civil Secretariat area in Jammu, and make it available to the Muslim employees for *namaz*.[9] The people of Jammu took to the streets to protest against this decision, which led to a communal clash. Politicians from time to time have fanned communal unrest to suit their interests.

By the late 1980s, Islamisation and radicalisation had taken firm roots in the valley. The Soviet occupation of Afghanistan had ended (February 1989) and large numbers of terrorists and weapons had entered Kashmir through Pakistan. Article 370 had isolated the State from the rest of India, making it easy for secessionist elements to infiltrate the state administration and fuel extremist ideology and terrorism amongst the local Muslims in the valley. Around this time, bus conductors in Lal Chowk could be heard shouting, *Sopore, Hand'wor, Upore* (border towns of Sopore and Handwara across Line of Control). This was clearly meant to entice the youth to cross over the border for arms training and launch a *jihad* against India. On a hill in the Badami Bagh cantonment, someone painted "JKLF" (for Jammu and Kashmir Liberation Front).

The plundering of temples and burning of Pandit property was scaled up with bomb blasts and the abduction of Ms. Rubaiya Sayeed, daughter of the Union Home Minister Mufti Mohammed Sayeed, on December 8, 1989; she was released in exchange for five JKLF terrorist leaders.[10] There were series of bomb blasts against symbols of "Indianness", such as the India Coffee House, Punjab National Bank, Press Trust of India. On June 23, 1989, pamphlets were distributed in Srinagar by an organization called *Hazb-i-Islami*, giving an ultimatum to Muslim women to comply with "Islamic" standards and wear hijab within two days or face "action". Pandit women were asked to put a tilak on their foreheads for identification. Unknown masked men with Kalashnikovs used to force people to reset their time to Pakistan standard time. The tide also turned against wine shops and cinema halls[11] to send the message that Kashmir had turned into an Islamist state.

Despite the repeated attacks on their homes, temples and property throughout the 1980s, Kashmiri Pandits clung to their faith in the democratic republic and stayed put in the valley, living under a pall of perpetual insecurity. Defence expert K. Subrahmanyam cited the existence of a secret Pakistani plan to start a Kashmiri uprising, code-named "Operation Topac", set in motion by late Gen. Zia-ul-Haq.[12] The former Director General of Jammu and Kashmir Police, M. Khajooria later recalled, "The mischief of the summer of 1989 started with serving notice to the prominent members of the minority community of Kashmiri Pandits to quit Kashmir. The letter said, 'we order you to leave Kashmir immediately, otherwise your children will be harmed. We are not scaring you but this land is only for Muslims, and is the land of Allah. Sikhs and Hindus cannot stay here'. The threatening note ended with a warning, 'If you do not obey, we will start with your children. Kashmir Liberation, Zindabad'". This was the bugle cry for the events of January 19, 1990.

January 19, 1990

The Farooq Abdullah Government had long become dysfunctional. Instead of accepting responsibility for the situation in the valley, Abdullah resigned on the pretext that he disapproved of the appointment of Jagmohan as Governor of Jammu and Kashmir. On January 4, 1990, a local Urdu newspaper, *Aftab*, published a press release issued by Hizb-ul-Mujahideen (HuM) asking all Pandits to leave the Valley immediately. Even after January 1990, threats through press releases continued targetting the few Pandits who had not yet left the valley. HuM published in the morning edition of *Aftab* of April 01, 1990, *Kashmiri Pandits responsible for duress against Muslims should leave the Valley within two days*. The headlines of the Urdu daily, *Al Safa*, of April 14, 1990 lauded, "With Kalashnikov in one hand and Quran in the other the Mujahids are openly roaming the streets singing the Tarana-e- Kashmir".

The night of January 19, 1990, was the longest night for Kashmiri Pandits when dawn seemed like a distant dream. Three taped slogans repeatedly played the whole night from mosques: *Kashmir mei agar rehna hai, Allah-O-Akbar kehna hai* (If you want to stay in Kashmir, you have to say Allah-O-Akbar); *Yahan kya chalega, Nizam-e-Mustafa* (What do we want here? Rule of Shariah), and *Asigachchi Pakistan, Bataoroaste batanev san* (We want Pakistan along with Hindu women, but without their men).[13]

And in this manner, the descendants of *Rishi Kashyap* were disinherited and dispossessed from the "paradise on earth". The timing was chosen carefully. JKLF armed cadres and HuM terrorists had prepared for the events of January 19 for months: in villages and towns across the Kashmir valley, terrorist hit lists had been floating about and all names were of Kashmiri Pandits. The walls of schools, hospitals and other public establishments were pasted with posters with threatening messages to all Kashmiris to strictly adhere to Islamic rules, including the Islamic dress code, prohibition on alcohol, cinemas, and video parlors. All offices, buildings, shops, and establishments were coloured green as a sign of Islamic rule. Threatening posters were posted on doors of Hindu homes asking them to leave Kashmir within 24 hours or face death and worse. Some were explicit: *Be one with us, run, or die!*[14]

Curfew notwithstanding, the valley on January 19, 1990, was uncontrollable. As evening set in, Srinagar city reverberated with shouts of *Jihad* from loudspeakers of all mosques. Provocative slogans were shouted, exhorting hysterical mobs with Kalashnikovs to embark on *Jihad* against the "non-believers". Thousands of audiocassettes carrying similar propaganda messages were played at numerous places in the Valley, to instill fear into the already terrified Kashmiri Pandit community. The *Jihad* plan of JKLF armed cadres and HuM terrorists was supported by the Muslim Janbaz Force, Ul Umur, Al Burq, Al Jihad, Ikhwan-ul-Muslim[15] and others. They published advertisements in local dailies proclaiming their intent: "Aim of the present struggle is the supremacy of Islam in Kashmir in all walks of life and nothing else. Anyone who puts a hurdle in our way will be annihilated".

There was a blackout in Srinagar city on the night of January 18-19; electricity was cut off everywhere barring mosques that broadcasted divisive and inflammatory messages asking for a purge of the Pandit community. Those working outside the State could not contact their old parents and other relations in the valley as all telephone lines of Kashmiri Hindus were cut off. Pandits witnessed the assassination of several intelligence operatives, friends and relatives on the streets and at work. The constant bombardment of hysterical slogans in the streets around their homes throughout the day terrorized the Pandits who spent the night huddled together in a single dark room. Many tried to call authorities in Jammu, Srinagar and Delhi for help, but no one came to their rescue. The State Government had shifted to the winter capital of Jammu and the meagre staff left in the valley could not cope with the frenzied mob. Delhi was indifferent to the enveloping crisis.

With the administration virtually non-existent and police nowhere to be seen, many Pandit families with young daughters prepared to emulate the medieval-era *jauhar* concept, keeping cans of kerosene ready for women to immolate themselves. According to Dr Shakti Bhan and Shiben Kishen Tikoo,[16] even elderly women volunteered for this end. As the night wore itself out, despondency gave way to desperation and the exodus began. In just a few days, most Kashmiri Hindus left Kashmir valley and moved to other parts of the country; those without relatives in other parts of the country landed in refugee camps in the Jammu region. This mass exodus occurred in the world's largest democracy: India. The minority community was a helpless victim of terrorism sponsored by outside forces but supported by radicalised members of the majority Muslim community of the valley, with the connivance of the State administration, even as successive Central governments remained mute spectators. By 1992, the locks of most Pandit homes had been broken; many were looted and burnt down.

Run-up to the exodus

March 14, 1989: According to a Jammu and Kashmir police report, the first case of murder of a Kashmiri Pandit was of Prabhavati, a woman from Nawagari, who killed on the Hari Singh High Street. Her killers were not found.[17]

September 14, 1989: The first important killing was of Tika Lal Taploo, an advocate and a prominent leader of the Bharatiya Janata Party, who was gunned down by the JKLF. Later, his funeral procession was stoned by radicals, and Muslims who downed the shutters of their shops as a mark of respect to the martyr were forced to re-open their shops as commands were issued not to mourn the death of a Kafir.

October 31, 1989: Sheela Koul, 47, a housewife, was pumped with bullets at Habba Kadal bridge. She had to be brought home on a hand-cart as the local taxis refused to take her to the hospital and the ambulance failed to arrive despite repeated phone calls to SMHS Hospital, Srinagar. She was ultimately taken to the hospital on a folding bed, but was left unattended. The JKLF is reputed to be behind the killing.

November 4, 1989: Nilkanth Ganjoo, a judge of the Srinagar High Court, who had sentenced Maqbul Bhat (founder of the Jammu Kashmir National Liberation Front) to death, was shot dead by a group of three persons on the Hari Singh Street near the High Court in Srinagar in broad daylight. The killers left a note on his body warning anyone against picking it up.

December 12, 1989: Prem Nath Bhat, a prominent lawyer, was returning home when terrorists pumped bullets straight into his head. His murder was hailed as a triumph of *Nizam-e-Mustafa*. Notwithstanding the curfew, terrorists disrupted the tenth-day rites and planted a bomb in the courtyard of his house during the period of mourning.

February 2, 1990: Satish Tikoo, a young social worker, was murdered near his home in Habba Kadal, Srinagar.

February 13, 1990: Lassa Kaul, station director of Srinagar Doordarshan, was shot dead by militants for his pro-India media policy.

April 19, 1990: Sarla Bhat, a nurse in Soura Medical Institute, was abducted and gang-raped by JKLF militants and eventually killed on April 25.

April 29, 1990: Pandit Sarwanand Premi, an 80-year-old poet and teacher, and his son, were abducted, tortured, their eyes gouged out, and hanged to death. The terrorists entered his home on April 28 and ordered all members of the family to gather in one room along with their ornaments, money, shawls and precious clothes. They offered all their valuables to the killers, who also snatched the ornaments worn by the ladies. Stuffing their booty in a suitcase, they ordered Premi to carry it and follow them for a few words, just a small distance away from his house. His son insisted upon accompanying his old father. Premi was tortured with burning cigarettes, his limbs broken, eyes gouged out. He was hanged from a tree and bullets were fired on him. His son was subjected to the same treatment.

May 2, 1990: Surinder Kumar Raina, an orphan in his early twenties, worked as a lift-man in the Institute of Medical Sciences, Soura. He was kidnapped while performing his duties. His body, riddled with bullets, was left on a road named after the legendary physician, Ali Jan, who despite his brilliance had allowed the Medical Institute, Soura, to be transformed into a snake-pit of bigotry and fanaticism.

May 13, 1990: Veer Ji Bhat, a young man employed as Junior Engineer in the State Irrigation Department at Shopian, was also a social activist. He was sprayed with bullets but managed to catch one of the killers, despite bleeding profusely. Bhat was carried to SMHS Hospital where a doctor operated upon him and declared him out of danger. But thirty minutes later, a man from the operation theatre declared him dead. On removing the white cloth from his face, his relatives found him snow white; it is believed that accomplices of the killers nestling in the hospital had drained out his blood.

May 13, 1990: Ashok Kumar was kidnapped by Hizbul Mujahideen, his hands and feet broken, and taken to the main road crossing where his eyeballs were plucked with iron rods in the presence of hundreds who relished the barbarity. He was then killed with a barrage of bullets even as a spectator sang "Islam is glorious and great".

May 18, 1990: Manmohan Bachloo, in his twenties, was at home when a friend called and took him along for a cup of tea at a tea shop in the heart of Baramulla town. When he entered the tea shop, others waiting fired upon him, killing him on the spot.

May 19, 1990: Dilip Kumar's killers knocked at his door and his mother came out to tell them that Dilip was not at home. Determined, they waited outside for a while and ultimately broke open the door and dragged him out and carried him off. His wailing mother followed the killers who abused the hapless lady. His brother rushed to the nearby police station, but no help came from that quarter. Dilip was tortured, his dentures hammered out and twelve bullets pumped into him; he was hung from a tree with a letter pinned on his chest that warned that whoever dared to lift the body would be paid one lakh. His body was cremated by the police.

June 4, 1990: Girja Tikoo, a teacher from Bandipur, was abducted, raped in a taxi by her colleagues, and when she recognized their voices she was shred to pieces by an electric saw.

June 24, 1990: Ashwani Kumar Garyali, 25, was studying chartered accountancy when five masked men affiliated with JKLF entered his room and accused him of being an informer. They carried him down to the first floor of his own residence and pumped five bullets into his head and abdomen. He was rushed to SMHS Hospital, Srinagar, for surgery but the doctors refused to admit him. He was then carried to the Institute of Medical Sciences, Soura, where doctors did not attend to him and allowed him to die. The body was sent to the Jawahar Lal Nehru Memorial Hospital, Rainawari, for post-mortem, where relatives alleged they had to wait for hours on end and were asked to pay for the procedure.

July 6, 1990: G.K. Muju, lecturer at the Medical College, Srinagar, and working committee member of the Kashmiri Pandit Conference, was told in February 1990 that his name had been seen on hit lists passed by militants in some mosques in the city. The following month, the family went through a number of harrowing incidents: people threw stones at his house, mysterious phone calls were made to the house, and so on. On March 6, Muju, his wife and children left the city, but his 80-year-old father, a retired teacher, and 75-year-old mother stayed behind. On July 6, intruders entered the house and brutally knifed the old couple to death.

July 7, 1990: Chand Ji Kher, a teenager, was called out by friends who shot at him and ran.

July 15/16, 1990: Shiban Kishen Koul, a primary school teacher in Kulgam, Anantnag, taught Muslim students with dedication. He was slaughtered on the uneven pot-holed paths of his native hamlet, and his father slaughtered the next day. The assassins were their own neighbours.

August 24, 1990: Radha Krishen Kaw, a teacher who retired as Tehsil Education Officer, continued to teach even after his retirement. The assassins entered the school where he was teaching, forced him out of the back door, and sprayed him with bullets.

Ashok Kumar Bazaz was in his thirties when he was shot dead by terrorists on grounds of being an informer and an agent of India. His grieving wife asked the killers to massacre the whole family (wife and seven daughters), but was told that they were spared to weep and atone for the sin of carrying Kashmir into the fold of India.

October 7, 1990: Jagar Nath Pandita, a widower, was kidnapped from his home in Bagatpora, Handwara, and taken to the thick groves of his own orchard and strangulated with steel wires.[18]

October 15, 1990: Maheshwar Nath Bhat's killers were making enquiries about his son-in-law, an officer in the Department of Forests. They were told that he had migrated to Jammu, though he had returned on promotion as ACF on assurances from colleagues with whom he had maintained close contact. At the time of the enquiries, the son-in-law hid himself in a bathroom. Frustrated at not getting the prize catch, the killers opened fire, killing Maheshwar Nath on the spot.

January 2, 1991: Omkar Nath Wali, an assistant sub-inspector of police posted at District Police Lines, Anantnag, was kidnapped and shot dead. The family was in Jammu. No last rites were performed, and no FIR was filed. It was alleged that his own colleagues in the Police Lines were responsible for his murder, being hand-in-glove with the JKLF.

October 18/19, 1991: Kanya Lal Peshin, a poor farmer, was abducted from his house at 9 pm. He was found with pins driven into his nails and more than one metre of cloth stuffed into his mouth to stifle him to death.

March 31, 1992: Bimla Braroo from Nai Sarak, Srinagar, and her daughter, Archana, were raped in the presence of her husband, Sohanlal, before all three were killed.

December 5, 1992: Hriday Nath Wanchoo, a trade union leader and human rights activist, was murdered at Bal Garden in Srinagar city. All militants charge sheeted for the crime are out on bail.

*

The above are few instances of the killings and the terror of that chilling time. In the preceding months, 300 Hindu men and women, intellectuals, poets and lawyers, nearly all Kashmiri Pandits, had been slaughtered in a very violent manner. Many women were abducted, raped and murdered, throughout the exodus.[19] During 1990-2010, security forces seized around 35,000 assault rifles, over 25,000 pistols, more than 30,000 kg explosives, about 2500 UMGs and RPGs, from terrorists.[20] Governor Jagmohan wrote a detailed letter to the then Prime Minister, Rajiv Gandhi on April 21, 1990, endorsing the alarming signals.[21] But the Indian leadership was unconcerned and the heinous murder of Pandits continued in the valley.

After the 1990 exodus, there were less than 10,000 Pandits left in the interior villages of Kashmir. In 2010, the Government of Jammu and Kashmir reported that 808 Pandit families were still living in the Valley, many of whom were economically weak. Suman Bhat offered two reasons for his staying back, "We did not migrate because we were not financially well off and we thought that it would be difficult to survive in Jammu. My father had invested almost all his money in land and property here". Some good Muslim neighbours sheltered the Pandits during these troubled times and that was another reason why a few families stayed back. However, the continued *jihadi* agenda of cleansing the valley of Kafirs led to the targetting of the remaining Pandits who had survived the 1990 genocide and were living in interior villages of Kashmir. A few instances may be noted:

July 1, 1990: Four persons killed in Ali Kadal locality, Srinagar.

October 14, 1990: Four gunned down at Rehbab Saib, Srinagar.

June 6, 1991: Four family members shot at home in Malpura of downtown Srinagar.

1991: All 47 houses in remote village Hangalgund were burned.

March 22, 1997: Sangrampora mass killing of a family of seven Pandits. This was the first mass killing that terrorised Pandits still living in remote villages and discouraged those who had fled from returning.

June 15, 1997: Three gunned down in bus at Gool in Udhampur.

January 25, 1998: At Wandhama, 23 Pandits were killed by gunmen dressed as Indian Army soldiers. The sole survivor, Vinod Kumar Dhar, witnessed the massacre and according to his testimony, the gunmen had tea with them while waiting for a radio message indicating that all Pandit families in the village had been covered. After a brief conversation, they rounded up all members of the Hindu households and summarily gunned them down. The Wandhama Massacre has been closed by the government citing un-traceability of the perpetrators.[22]

April 21,1998: Unidentified militants beheaded 26 Hindu villagers, including women and children, in Prankote and Dakikote, Udhampur.[23]

1998:16 Hindus killed in Shana Thakarail village, Doda.

February 5, 2000: Three killed in Telwani, Anantnag.

March 4, 2000: One person killed in Brariangan, Anantnag.

March 6, 2000: One killed in Pethibug, Anantnag.

March 20, 2000: *Chittisinghpura massacre of Sikhs* – The killers came wearing Indian Army fatigues to avoid detection, lined up the Sikhs in front of their Gurdwaras and opened fire, killing 36 persons who were celebrating Holi.

March 23, 2003: In Nadimarg village near Shopian, Pulwama district, terrorists dragged Hindus out from their homes, lined them up and shot them with automatic weapons. At least 24 Hindus, including 11 women and 2 children, were killed. The policemen posted there fled the scene. The killers allegedly disfigured the bodies of the victims, looted their houses and took away ornaments from the bodies of the dead women.[24]

*

In its first report compiled since the outbreak of militancy in the Valley, the Jammu and Kashmir Police said militants killed 209 Kashmiri Pandits since 1989.[25] Charge sheets were filed in 24 cases while the killers in 115 cases remained unidentified or untraced. The police report, according to Muzamil Jaleel of the *Indian Express* (August 8, 2017), stated that 140 cases of killings of Kashmiri Pandits by militants have been registered at police stations across the Valley. The police have booked 31 local militants for the killings in 24 cases in which charge sheets have been filed. All other militants who have been charge sheeted are out on bail.

According to the report, the perpetrators of the Wandhama massacre are still untraced, but Pakistani militants Abu Haris and Abu Khalid have been identified as the culprits behind the Sangrampora killings. Both militants were killed in an encounter at Hewader on March 24, 1997. The police identified and charge sheeted Zai Mustafa alias Abdullah of Rawalkot, Pakistan, in the Nadimarg massacre case. The accused were released on bail for want of credible proof that the State Police did not have or did not want to produce in court.

Terrorists thus released include notorious terrorists of yester years like Yasin Malik, Javaid Mir, Bitta Karate and others. These three alone are responsible for killing more than 50 Kashmiri Pandits. When the designated TADA judge, N.D. Wani, released Bitta Karate,[26] he said, "The court is aware of the fact that the allegations levelled against the accused are of serious nature and carry a punishment of death sentence or life imprisonment, but the fact is that the prosecution has shown total disinterest in arguing the case, which is in complete violation of Article 21 of the Constitution".[27]

According to a Jammu and Kashmir government report,[28] 219 members of the community were killed in the State between 1989 and 2004,[29] but none thereafter. Panun Kashmir Movement's *Kashmir Documentation: Pandits in Exile* lists 319 Kashmiri Hindus killed between 1989 to October 1990, and a total 1,341 Pandits killed since 1990. Kashmiri Pandit Sangharsh Samiti[30] conducted a survey in 2008 and 2009, and concluded that 399 Kashmiri Pandits were killed by insurgents from 1990 to 2011, with 75 per cent of them being killed during the first year of the Kashmiri insurgency. It said that during the last 20 years, about 670 Pandits have been killed in the valley.

UN and ethnic cleansing

The official UN definition of ethnic cleansing is "rendering an area ethnically homogeneous by using force or intimidation to remove from a given area persons of another ethnic or religious group".[31] Ethnic cleansing is a crime against humanity under the Statutes of the International Criminal Court (ICC). Some academics consider genocide as a subset of ethnic cleansing, but what happened in 1990 were both together, as Norman Naimark observes: "literally and figuratively, ethnic cleansing bleeds into genocide, as mass murder is committed in order to rid the land of a people".

Ethnic cleansing is often followed by the removal of physical, cultural, civilizational and ritual evidence of the targeted group. The Jammu and Kashmir Government admitted on the floor of the Assembly in 2010 that 280 temples were destroyed. Pandits believe this is a conservative number. Hindu cremation grounds were encroached. Several landmarks were renamed: Anantnag (Islamabad), Gow Kadal (Madina Chowk), Srinagar (Shere-e-Khas), Hari Parbat (Koh-e-Maran). Furthermore, the tradition of Vichar Nag, where scholars once gathered annually to finalise the Kashmiri *Panchang*, called *Jantari* (*Saptrishi Samvat*), a must in every Pandit home, has been lost. The Jantari is a lunar calendar for time keeping of the days, rituals and festivals. Worse, there is an ongoing effort to erase the memory of Vichar Nag by changing its name to Firdoos.

Life after the Exodus

In 1990, Kashmiri Pandits who had children or relatives outside Jammu and Kashmir received some financial and emotional support and managed to rehabilitate themselves, often quite well. But the vast majority of Pandits who fled the valley in panic had nowhere to go, and have had to live without any amenities in the derelict tented camps erected in the inhospitable terrain and climate of Jammu. Once proud of their rich cultural heritage and life in the lush green and cool environment of the valley, they landed on the outskirts of the hot city of Jammu and were forced to reside in cramped one-room tenements of 110 to 120 sq. ft. Three generations have since lived in this way, even cooking outside the tents as there was no space for this chore inside. They have to use community toilets and baths and are reduced to grovelling poverty, dependent on government doles and charity. Many Pandits living in the camps died because of snakebites, heat stroke, diarrhea and viral fevers. The exodus caused severe psychological problems as many brooded over the painful events of the past, the loss of property, and other related issues.[32]

The high literacy rate of over 90 per cent, of which the Kashmiri Pandits were justly proud, crashed drastically by around 20 per cent in exile, as the resourceless families could not afford to send their children to good schools in Jammu city, and the makeshift schools in the camps were inadequate in terms of infrastructure, staff, libraries, laboratories, and recreational facilities. Students began to drop out until finally, goaded into action from various quarters, the State government and the Central Government took up the issue of education of the displaced students and helped them get admission to various Kendriya Vidyalayas.[33]

Surveys of the displaced children reveal immense harm to their psyche, with a powerful sense of bitterness caused by the deprivations of camp life. There has been a commensurate strain in the pursuit of higher education as all candidates could not gain admission in post-graduate colleges of Jammu University, which have to accommodate local students, and getting admitted to institutions in the Kashmir valley is out of the question. Added to this is the paucity of jobs in Jammu city, which aggravates personality disorders and low self-esteem. A little noticed aspect of the problem is the precipitous decline in the nutritional standards of the refugees, which impacts their performance in school and is also impacting life expectancy. Children Rights and You (CRY), a non-government organisation that conducted a survey in 2007 at one of the largest displaced Kashmiri migrant camps in Purkhoo, 13 km southwest of Jammu city, found "very poor stability in the supply of drinking water in displaced migrants camps", which runs for one hour daily and is grossly insufficient to meet daily requirements. Add to this the regular power cuts that range from 9 to 12 hours every day, making life intolerable in summer, and the children reported that the scarcity of electricity affected their studies.[34]

By 2016, around 1,800 Kashmiri Pandit youths returned to the valley after the UPA government announced a Rs. 1,168-crore rehabilitation package in 2008. They were housed in transit camps in the valley, but after terrorist Burhan Wani was killed in an encounter with security forces in July 2016, the transit camps housing Kashmiri Pandits were attacked by mobs. The inmates fled to the local MLC's residence during the night of July 8, 2016, and asked for protection from the State Government.[35] Posters threatening them and warning them to leave were allegedly put up by the Lashkar-e-Islam. Many left their jobs and quit the valley, once again. So it is back to zero.[36]

This is an appropriate place to lambast the false propaganda that Governor Jagmohan instigated the Kashmiri Pandits to abandon their home and hearth to stare into the abyss. This vicious and motivated lie is repeated ad nauseam by those who know full well that the exodus had been planned long before Jagmohan arrived in Kashmir. The terrorist threats, violence, acts of intimidation were ongoing for many years; Jagmohan took charge on January 19, 1990, the very night the great mass exodus took place. It bears recalling that in the 1990's, mobile phones and social media were non-existent, so how did the newly installed Governor contact 400,000 to 500,000 persons unknown to him and persuade them to leave the valley, and why would they listen to him, a complete stranger? Above all, if the exodus was artificially induced, why did Kashmiri Pandits find it so difficult to return and resume their lives, even with Central Government incentives?

A few words of gratitude are due to Shiv Sena leader, Bal Thackeray, who rose to the occasion and provided reserved seats in engineering colleges in Maharashtra for Kashmiri Pandit students. Other States followed suit later. Successive Central Governments have paid lip service to the return of Kashmiri Pandits to the valley, but have failed to acknowledge that the 1990 massacres led to genocide and ethnic cleansing of Kashmiri Pandits. Since the tragedy, many organisations have sprung up to represent the cause of the displaced community and provide rehabilitation in the valley through peace negotiations, mobilisation of human rights groups and creation of jobs for the Pandits. Some have demanded a separate homeland for the community in southern Kashmir.

Roots in Kashmir, an organisation of activists in Delhi, filed a petition in the Supreme Court of India in 2017, pleading for reopening of 215 cases of more than 700 alleged murders of Kashmiri Pandits, but the Supreme Court dismissed the plea on grounds of delay of 27 years and lack of documentation.[37]

The order caused extreme distress and outrage among the community; the organisation's review petition was also dismissed on October 25, 2017. The bereaved community feels that there is an urgent need for the Centre to set up an impartial Commission to investigate the 1990 genocide and exodus from the valley and give justice in one of the ugliest chapters of forced exodus and ethnic cleansing in India since 1947.

Although the violence against the miniscule Kashmiri Pandit community is often compared with the targetting of the Sikh community in Delhi and some north Indian towns in 1984, the two tragedies differ in very fundamental ways. It is true that the violence against the Sikhs was premeditated, but it did not have the endorsement of the larger Hindu community. Hundreds of Sikh families in middle class colonies were saved by their Hindu neighbours who argued with the mobs and turned them back; Sikhs were mainly killed in colonies where they formed the majority of the populace. More importantly, the Sikhs were not terrorised and asked to leave their home and hearth; they stayed put in the same localities, rebuilt their lives, and fought for justice in the same cities. Kashmiri Pandits did not have this liberty: no one stood up for them in the hamlets, towns and cities of Kashmir and the political elite feigned amnesia about their plight. The few voices that spoke for them were easily brushed aside, pigeonholed as "fundamentalists". However, the sentencing of Delhi Congress leader Sajjan Kumar (most other named perpetrators are long deceased) has given hope to the Pandit community.[38] At the same time, amidst ominous signs that Jammu province is the next target of jihadis, the Government of India must neutralise the terrorists on a war footing.

*

NOTES

1 Pandit, Kashinath, *Contemporary Kashmir Politics: Some Insights* (based on Reshi Dev's Political Dairy), Asian-Eurasian Human Rights Forum, 2008, p. 70.

2 Kashmir: The Al-Fatah Conspiracy, March 1, 2015. https://kashmirglobal.com/2015/03/01/kashmir-the-al-fatah-conspiracy.html.

3 Jammu Kashmir Constituent Assembly debates; Jammu Kashmir Study Centre.

4 S., Jiji Paul, Militancy in Kashmir and the Socio Economic Situations of Pandits, *Thesis Paper*, p. 25. http://shodhganga.inflibnet.ac.in:8080/jspui/handle/10603/4178.

5 For details, see Tikoo, Tej K., *Kashmir: Its Aborigines and Their Exodus*, Atlanta, GA: Lancer Publishers, 2012.

6 The Exodus of Kashmiri Pandits, July 2017, European Foundation for South Asian Studies (EFSAS), Amsterdam. https://www.efsas.org/publications/study-papers/the-exodus-of-kashmiri-pandits/.

7 De, Arindam, *Multiple Versions Of The Truth, Kashmir Observer*, July 16, 2018. https://kashmirobserver.net/2018/opinion/multiple-versions-truth-34153.
8 Pandit, op. cit., p. 113.
9 Verma, P.S., *Jammu and Kashmir at the Political Crossroads*, New Delhi: Vikas Publishing House, 1994, p. 214.
10 We planned to release Rubaiya anyway: JKLF, June 22, 2008. https://www.hindustantimes.com/india/we-planned-to-release-rubaiya-anyway-jklf/story-kfi9K7YJ1nbmwSolWUoYDO.html.
11 Cinema halls remain shut though all residents of the valley have access to television and entertainment through internet.
12 Indian Defense Review, July 1989. See also, Desmond, Edward, *The Insurgency in Kashmir (1989-1991)*, Contemporary South Asia, March 1995, 4(1), p. 8.
13 Jagmohan, *My Frozen Turbulence in Kashmir*, New Delhi: Allied Publishers, 1991, Chapter V, et seq.
14 The Exodus of Kashmiri Pandits, op. cit.
15 Massacre of Kashmiri Pandits, http://ikashmir.net/wailvalley/b2chap8a.html.
16 The longest night: Recalling 19 Jan. 1990; January 27, 2011. https://kashmirblogs.wordpress.com/tag/shiben-kishen-tikoo/.
17 Unless otherwise stated, all instances are from "The Exodus of Kashmiri Pandits", op. cit., Tikoo, op. cit., and ikashmir.net.
18 http://www.ikashmir.net/wailvalley/b2chap8a.html.
19 The Exodus of Kashmiri Pandits, op. cit.
20 Ganjoo, Satish, Satanic Holocaust of Kashmiri Pandits, June 9, 2017. https://www.linkedin.com/pulse/satanic-holocaust-kashmiri-pandits-dr-satish-ganjoo-satish-ganjoo.
21 Jagmohan, Letter to Mr. Rajiv Gandhi, April 21, 1990. http://www.ikashmir.net/jagmohan/jagmohan2rajiv.html.
22 1998 Wandhama Massacre: When 23 Kashmiri Pandits were killed in the dead of night, Jan. 26, 2018. https://www.greaterkashmir.com/news/kashmir/1998-wandhama-massacre-when-23-kashmiri-pandits-were-killed-in-the-dead-of-night/273535.html.
23 "The village resembled a ghost area with beheaded bodies lying scattered", Mukhtar Ahmad, April 20, 1998. https://www.rediff.com/news/1998/apr/20jammu.htm.
24 Swami, Praveen, The Nadimarg outrage, *Frontline*, Vol. 20 (08), 2003. https://frontline.thehindu.com/static/html/fl2008/stories/20030425002903800.htm.
25 "219 Kashmiri Pandits killed by militants since 1989", Shujaat Bukhari, March 24, 2010. https://www.thehindu.com/todays-paper/ldquo219-Kashmiri-Pandits-killed-by-militants-since-1989rdquo/article16006510.ece.
26 Warm reception to Bitta Karate in Srinagar on his release, OneIndia, October 27, 2006. https://www.oneindia.com/2006/10/27/warm-reception-to-bitta-karate-in-srinagar-on-his-release-1161948974.html.
27 Centre to reopen Bitta Karate's case after expose on Pak links, May 25, 2017. http://www.thenorthlines.com/centre-reopen-bitta-karates-case-expose-pak-links/.
28 Bukhari, op. cit.
29 Aiyar, Swaminathan S.A., A tale of two ethnic cleansings in Kashmir, Jan. 18, 2015.

https://timesofindia.indiatimes.com/blogs/Swaminomics/a-tale-of-two-ethnic-cleansings-in-kashmir/.

30 At least 399 Kashmiri Pandits killed in JK since 1990: Survey, June 19, 2011. https://economictimes.indiatimes.com/news/politics-and-nation/at-least-399-kashmiri-pandits-killed-in-jk-since-1990-survey/articleshow/8914441.cms.

31 "Ethnic cleansing" and racial hatred, 89th Plenary Meeting, Dec. 16, 1992. http://www.un.org/documents/ga/res/47/a47r080.htm.

32 S., Jiji Paul, Militancy in Kashmir and the Socio Economic Situations of Pandits, op. cit.

33 Kashinath Pandit, Contemporary Kashmir Politics: Some Insights, op. cit., pp. 132-142.

34 Jammu Kashmir Association of Social Workers, https://www.cry.org/projects/jkasw-jammu-kashmir-association-of-social-workers. See also, Sudan, Falendra K., Social and Economic Implications of Armed Conflicts on Displaced Migrant Children: A Case Study of Purkhoo Camp in Jammu City, 2007. https://www.cry.org/resources/pdf/SudanFK_2007_NCRF_CRY.pdf.

35 Jammu & Kashmir: BJP panel to meet Kashmiri Pandit employees as protest enters 12th day, Jan. 26, 2016. https://indianexpress.com/article/india/india-news-india/jammu-kashmir-bjp-kashmiri-pandit-employees-protest-12th-day-kashmir-valley-jammu-2935545/.

36 Pandits in Kashmir threaten to quit jobs, Jan. 25, 2016. https://www.tribuneindia.com/news/jammu-kashmir/pandits-in-kashmir-threaten-to-quit-jobs/187655.html.

37 Supreme Court refuses to reopen 215 cases In Kashmiri Pandits' killings, July 24, 2017. https://www.ndtv.com/india-news/supreme-court-refuses-to-reopen-215-cases-in-kashmiri-pandits-killings-1728500.

38 Bhat, Sunil, After Sajjan Kumar's conviction, clamour grows for probe in Kashmiri Pandit killings, December 18, 2018. https://www.indiatoday.in/india/story/sajjan-kumar-conviction-1984-riots-kashmiri-pandit-killings-1411685-2018-12-18.

CHAPTER SEVEN

Ladakh: The Quest for Integration

Sandhya Jain

The mystical highlands of Ladakh straddle a vast terrain of over 186,909 km^2, at an average altitude of 3,657 m, and comprise a little over 58 per cent of the total area of Jammu and Kashmir State. The difficult topography keeps important regions such as Zanskar, Dras, Suru, Nubra-Shayok, Indus Valley and Rupsho-Changthang plateau remote from each other. But for its size, Ladakh is almost invisible on the political landscape. Won for Jammu ruler Gulab Singh by the intrepid Zorawar Singh (1842), Ladakh became part of the kingdom of Jammu and Kashmir when the British East India Company made Gulab Singh the Maharaja of Kashmir under the Treaty of Amritsar (1846); it became part of the Republic of India with the accession by Maharaja Hari Singh. The region has suffered untold neglect since independence, largely because Article 370 of the Constitution concentrated power in the hands of valley-centric politicians. Beginning with Sheikh Abdullah, successive regimes have focused on Kashmir province to the detriment of Jammu and Ladakh. As a result, Ladakh has been pushed to the margins, denied development and treated as an exotic anachronism, a land of Lamas and stark natural beauty.

Ladakh is a valuable strategic territory that India can ill-afford to treat as its disremembered Himalayan hinterland. It is the only region that has faced hostilities on two frontiers, with Pakistan and China. It was here that the Indian Army fought to retain the strategic Siachen glacier (always occupied by India and acknowledged in the 1949 ceasefire agreement signed in Karachi), which connects the old caravan route to Kashgar through the Karakoram

Pass. Ladakh is India's gateway to the Tarim Basin and the Tibetan Plateau. For centuries, caravans loaded with textiles and spices from the south, and raw silk, carpets, and dry fruits from the north crisscrossed the rugged landscape of Ladakh as they moved towards the Silk Route cities of Yarkand and Khotan. This bustling commerce came to a sudden end in 1950 when the People's Republic of China brought Tibet and Xinjiang under its control. The trade between Ladakh and Tibet via Demchok was also severed, and the pilgrimage to Kailash-Mansarovar discontinued.

Early experiences

History has generally ignored the fact that the people of Ladakh were among the most politically conscious of Maharaja Hari Singh's subjects; at the time of the Partition of India, they sought to link their fate with India rather than the State of Jammu and Kashmir. Ladakh had seen how Major William A. Brown instigated the Gilgit Scouts to revolt against the Maharaja and annexed the region to Pakistan. They had suffered enormously at the hands of the Pakistani raiders (a largely ignored chapter of history). Hence, when Chhewang Rigzin led a delegation of the Ladakh Buddhist Association (LBA) to Delhi (May 4, 1949), they told Prime Minister Jawaharlal Nehru, "Ladakh is not prepared to go to Pakistan whatever the result of the [UN-mandated] plebiscite may be". The LBA memorandum stated, "We seek the bosom of that gracious mother (India) to receive more nutriments for growth to our full stature in every way. She has given us what we prize above all other things – our religion and culture. The Ashoka wheel on her flag, symbol of goodwill for all humanity, and her concern for her cultural children, calls us irresistibly. Will the great mother refuse to take to her arms one of her weakest and most forlorn and depressed children – a child whom filial love impels to respond to the call?"[1] Ladakhis were immensely proud to see the Ashoka chakra at the centre of the Indian flag, and the Ashokan lions as emblem of the new Republic. But from the accession in 1947, Ladakhis (Ladakhpas) suffered indifference at the hands of the State Government in terms of recruitment to government posts, education facilities, fund allocation for development (especially roads and communication), hospitals, etc. The demand for Union Territory (UT) status has gained momentum in recent years, and virtually all sections of society have united on the issue, which is increasingly being framed in terms of Ladakhi identity.

Disturbed at the disproportionate power vested in Sheikh Mohammad Abdullah, Ladakh submitted a memorandum to the Maharaja of Jammu and

Kashmir and to the Government of India in 1947, urging that (1) the Maharaja should govern Ladakh directly without tagging it on to Kashmir Valley, (2) their homeland be amalgamated with the Hindu-majority Jammu and should form a separate province in which adequate safeguards should be provided for distinctive rights and interests of Ladakhis, or (3) Ladakh should be permitted to join East Punjab.[2] In no circumstances were Ladakhis willing to link their fate with that of Kashmir province. However, Hari Singh was in no position to respond because fast-developing events forced him to make an ignominious exit from the State and surrender his authority to Sheikh Abdullah, who was fully backed by Prime Minister Nehru.

Although Sheikh Abdullah had cast his vote with India at the time, he ensured a unique status and high level of autonomy for Kashmir province within the Union of India, making his case for autonomy on the basis of the 1846 Treaty of Amritsar that Jammu ruler Gulab Singh made with the East India Company. Ladakh leaders asserted that their ties with the erstwhile Dogra rulers were governed by a separate and pre-existing treaty of 1834. Hence, the provisions under which Ladakh submitted to the Dogras effectively ended with the accession to India and so Ladakh should not be bound to the State of Jammu and Kashmir. Kushok Bakula Rinpoche, the monk who became the voice of Ladakh at the instance of Jawaharlal Nehru, quickly realised that the Kashmiri leadership was determined to obstruct the region's development. Meeting Nehru at Teen Murti Bhavan on May 20, 1949, he reiterated the views of the Ladakh Buddhist Association and insisted that Ladakh should not be bound by the outcome of any plebiscite held over the future of Muslim-majority Kashmir. If it favoured Pakistan, Ladakh should be allowed to join Hindu-majority Jammu or East Punjab, and thus remain in India. Bakula Rinpoche emphasised the strategic and commercial importance of Leh as a nerve centre of Central Asian trade and said it was in India's strategic interests to retain it.[3]

Having closely observed the functioning of the Sheikh Abdullah government, Bakula Rinpoche again wrote to Nehru in 1951, stating, "For better or worse, we have decided to stay in India and we remain with Kashmir, subject to certain safeguards which have been specified separately in the memorandum addressed to Sheikh Muhammad Abdullah – as long as Kashmir stays in India. This obviously means that in case the rumoured plebiscite is held for the whole state and not on a regional basis and the result is in favour of Pakistan, our connection with the State will terminate and we shall automatically merge without any intervening link with India. We fervently hope that India will not fail us at this critical juncture of our history".[4]

As per his intimation to Nehru, the Rinpoche sent a similar letter to Sheikh Abdullah on December 19, 1951, wherein he listed the demands of the people of the Ladakh. These included the following:

(1) Zanskar, a part of Kargil Tehsil, be transferred to Leh Tehsil, as should the villages of Darchiks and Garkon.

(2) After this is done, the district should be divided into 15 constituencies at the rate of 5,000 people each. In short, he proposed a Provincial Constituent Assembly that would act much like the state government acted in relation to the national government.

(3) He also requested earmarked seats for higher education and technical training, hoping to better provide the necessary local services with local personnel.

(4) The local legislature would be the only authority competent to make Laws for the province and to control its administration and naturally the Executive Council would be responsible to it. But no motion or Resolution affecting the religious or social system of any community inhabiting the Province would be brought before the Legislature unless so desired by the community concerned.

(5) A governor deputed by the Centre would represent the Central Government and be the connecting link between the Province and the Centre. He would exercise the same functions as the constitutional head of the State would do in the State.[5]

Throughout the 1950s and early 1960s, endless obstacles were created and factional and sectarian divisions fomented within Ladakh to undermine Kushok Bakula's moral authority. The Rinpoche had considered the demand for Union Territory status premature in the early years of independence, but with the passage of time, he began to view direct central rule on the lines of the North Eastern Frontier Area (NEFA) as the only salvation. To cite just one instance, Bakula Rinpoche was stunned when the first budget submitted by the Sheikh Abdullah government in May 1952 did not even mention Ladakh, leave alone provide for development in any sector. In his reply to the budget speech in the State Assembly on May 12, 1952, he stressed,

> The Frontier Scholarships granted to the students of elementary, secondary and college in the district by the erstwhile government [of Maharaja Hari Singh] have been withdrawn with a stroke of a pen by the present

government. The old government had sanctioned grants in aid to three primary schools run by Shias, Sunnis and Buddhists communities, which the present government withdrew. The Bodhi language is being taught in the high schools. But no books have been published for the same and the subject is being taught to the students of middle and high schools without any books. No budget has been provided for preparation and publication of such books. In the schools, Urdu, which is a foreign language for our children, is still the medium of instruction. This unnatural medium of instruction proves to be a great stumbling block in the educational development of our children. But no provision for the development of Bodhi in our area has been made in the Education budget... .

No arrangement for the rehabilitation of the Zanskar refugees has been shown in the budget in spite of the fact that these helpless people have been wandering like beggars in the Kullu Valley. Dozens of these wandering refugees have succumbed to death. Nor is there any mention in the budget about the repairs of the religious places (Gonpas), which have suffered tremendous damage at the hands of the Pakistani tribal raiders. Apathy does not end here. Here I recall that historic event when the Prime Minister of the State of J&K and Mr. Jawaharlal Nehru, Prime Minister of India, had visited us and promised that the Chief Engineer and other engineers would be deputed to our area to see the possibilities of digging canals where the water supply is meagre, making the land cultivable, thereby resolving the troubles of the area. But I regret that this promise remains merely a promise and is yet to be fulfilled. The matter does not end here. The erstwhile, condemned government [of the Maharaja] had undertaken in Kargil a survey of the Khurbathang canal. But so far our own government did not take any effective step towards the digging of the canal. I need not emphasize how profoundly bound with our life is the construction of irrigation canals. In view of this principle, in J&K where there already exist many canals, a provision of Rs. 25 lacs has been made in the budget for construction of new canals. But no mention is made of constructing even small canals for thousands of acres of dry land in Ladakh.

Our area is remote and cut off from other areas of the state and its parts are remote from one another. There being a tremendous paucity of roads in our region, construction of roads is essential for linking this area with other areas and the possibilities of trade may open up... .

There are two posts and telegraph offices in our area at Leh and Kargil towns. In Zanskar, the people get post and telegraph facility only after going to Kargil. But can you estimate as to how far Padum, Zanskar is from Kargil? 150 miles of hilly journey across two high mountain Passes, which are more than 4400 meters high in altitude? ... it seems that our area has been regarded as an occupied territory.[6]

By the mid-1960s, after bitter experiences[7] with Sheikh Abdullah and his successors, Bakula Rinpoche concluded that separation from Jammu and Kashmir was the only way ahead for Ladakh.[8] In a meeting with Prime Minister Lal Bahadur Shastri in September 1964, he warned about the growing frustration in Ladakh. In a letter to Shastri, he explained,

> "The Buddhists of Ladakh who can have a future only in association with India have all along urged the Government of India to take this border district into its direct control. The late lamented Pandit Nehru assured us off and on and that this would be done in the course of time and in the meantime responsible administrative officers for the district would be deputed from the Centre. This was undoubtedly a step in the right direction provided these officers were carefully selected which, I am sorry, does not seem to have been done in the case of the present Deputy Commissioner."

By 1967, the Congress unit in Ladakh also demanded NEFA-style central rule in the region. The demand has since grown in strength.

Zanskar

Hauntingly beautiful Zanskar is a jumble of steep ridges and deep ravines south of the Indus valley, which is cut off from the world during the heavy winter snow. The Chhangthang area, which is a part of the Tibetan plateau, is a great desert with giant lakes, and is renowned for its unique species of sheep and large goats that give the famous pashmina wool. The fertile Nubra valley, gateway to the Siachen glacier and Karakoram ranges, lies north of the Indus valley. The Dras plateau, coldest place in the world after Siberia, is fertile in summer and produces barley, wheat and buckwheat. Ladakh has close cultural and spiritual links with Tibet; its gonpas (monasteries) are repositories of the region's art and culture.[9]

Although Mohammad Ali Jinnah's objective in 1947 was to liberate his "Muslim brothers from the yoke of the Dogras (later replaced by Indians)", the purpose of Operation Sledge, which aimed to take over the Ladakh plateau, was to seize the wealth of the Buddhist gonpas.[10] In February 1948, Brig. L.P. "Bogey" Sen, posted in Srinagar, learnt that around 800 tribal Pathans and some Gilgit Scouts planned to raid Ladakh, which was completely isolated in the winter. Already, there was panic in Ladakh as refugees poured in from the captured Northern Areas and bemoaned the atrocities by the invaders. The Pakistani raiders entered the Skardu region of Gilgit-Baltistan in early 1948, overran the district centre and posed a serious danger to Ladakh.

Reinforcements by land for the small Indian Army garrison at Leh were impossible; airlifts were the only solution, but there were no landing strips in Ladakh; the air routes had not been charted; and the inclement mountain weather made flying extremely risky. The only serviceable airstrip in the area was in Gilgit, which had already fallen. Even ground infrastructure, such as roads and bridges, did not exist, making any kind of military deployment challenging. More crucially, the Pathan raiders were better equipped and more numerous; they soon occupied Taru and upper Phyang, barely 20 km from Leh, and parts of Nubra Valley. In this dire situation, Captain Prithi Chand of Lahaul, Himachal Pradesh, led a small group of men and mules across the treacherous Zoji-la to bring supplies of rifles and ammunition for the garrison at Leh.[11] This heroic action brought some respite, but not much.

Bakula Rinpoche was teaching at Lungnag in the interiors of Zanskar, when the Pakistani raiders suddenly moved south and reached Padum, the main village of Zanskar, plundering Buddhist monasteries and villages along the way. A young monk, Tashi Ngodup, rushed to inform the Rinpoche of the tragedy that had befallen the villagers. Hundreds of families fled Zanskar to neighbouring Kullu and Manali, where they led a life of utter destitution.[12] Rushing to Leh, the Rinpoche urged his friend, Sridhar Kaul Dulloo, a retired school teacher, to alert Srinagar and Delhi about the danger.

Meanwhile, the Indian army was making arrangements to save Ladakh. A landing strip was prepared between Leh and Pethub (Spituk) Monastery, at an altitude of 3,256 m, to handle Dakotas. Maj. Gen. K.S. Thimayya, Divisional Commander, requested air dropping of supplies on May 19, 1948, as Leh was in danger of falling. The Air Officer Commanding No. 1 (Ops) Group, Air Commodore Mehar Singh DSO, rose to the occasion and piloted a Dakota to Leh on May 24, 1948, boosting the morale of troops and civilians (Thimayya was also in the plane). Soldiers of 2/4 Gorkha Rifles landed on June 1, 1948, but even by August 1948, the Indian troops were inadequate to repel the invaders. Bakula Rinpoche called upon the youth of Ladakh to join the Indian forces as volunteers and save their land. The "Nubra Guards", under the dynamic leadership of a young Ladakhi soldier, Chhewang Rinchen,[13] became the nucleus of the resistance against the invaders and helped expel the raiders from the Indus and Nubra valleys.

However, Pakistan still held the critical Zoji-la (Pass), cutting off the land link from Srinagar to Kargil-Dras and Leh, which could now be reached only by air (difficult given the weather) or a 400-km detour via Manali. Concluding that tanks alone could save the day, Maj. Gen. Thimayya decided to lead a squadron of Stuart Mark 6 tanks in secrecy, by night. Though no tanks had ever scaled such heights (11,500 ft), Operation "Bison" began on November 1, 1948, amidst a terrible snowstorm, and was so spectacularly successful that the tricolour flew on the Pass on November 2. Dras was recaptured on November 16, and on November 23, Indian troops entered Kargil and linked the town with Leh the same day. Days later, on January 1, 1949, the UN declared a ceasefire that prevented the Army from recapturing Skardu and the Northern areas,[14] but Ladakh had been rescued in the nick of time.

*

The people of Zanskar deeply resented the fact that despite the havoc wreaked by the Pakistani raiders, their saga of neglect continued. Not a single state official in charge of post-war rehabilitation visited the region for long after the invasion. Nor did the State help repair the damaged monasteries, or compensate the people for their losses. In fact, money sanctioned by Prime Minister Nehru for relief to Zanskar was disbursed to people in Kargil or pocketed by disbursing officials and their local agents. To improve road connectivity, the people proposed a Nyemo-Chiling road linking Zanskar to Leh as the Padum-Kargil road is impassable for most of the year. The Nyemo route would be shorter and almost an all-weather road, but Srinagar did not favour Zanskar forming closer ties with Leh.

In 1979, Sheikh Abdullah (rehabilitated after 11 years of house arrest) made Kargil tehsil a separate district, and included the Buddhist-majority Zanskar as a tehsil of Muslim-majority Kargil. Zanskar continued to suffer neglect in economic development, education, and infrastructure; it is the most backward area of the State. This led to demands that Zanskar be made a separate district, and protests broke out in September 1980. With no response from Srinagar, the struggle continued unabated, and on November 20, 1986, the Rinpoche met Prime Minister Rajiv Gandhi and submitted a detailed report about the situation there. He added that gun-toting Gujjar Bakarwals (shepherds) from Kashmir annually raided the Rangdum pastures with their herds and kept the local Buddhists out. On July 12, 2000, three Buddhist monks of Rangdum Monastery were gunned down, the first incident of its kind in Ladakh; the authorities in Srinagar were indifferent[15] and the culprits were never arrested.

Sensing an opportunity under President's rule, a delegation led by scholar-monk, Dr Lobzang Khatup Gyato, met Governor Satya Pal Malik on January

13, 2019, and urged him to declare Zanskar a separate district with a separate Assembly seat.

Saving the Gonpas

Ladakh's Buddhist legacy was seriously affected by Sheikh Abdullah's landmark legislation, the "Big Landed Estates Abolition Act" of July 13, 1950. Ostensibly, the Act aimed at liberating tenant farmers by ending the dominance of large landlords (*zamindars*) and religious bodies. Thus, land above 182 kanals (about 22 acres) held by a single family or institution would be confiscated by the government and given to landless peasants. In this manner, around 80,000 acres were confiscated, without compensation to the former owners.

In Ladakh, the Act endangered the very existence of the Buddhist monasteries and was perceived as an assault on the faith. The monasteries were the lifeline of the communities and catered to their spiritual and secular needs; they were hubs for education, health care, crafts and even trade. More pertinently, Buddhist monasteries housed large numbers of resident monks and nuns. The agricultural land held by monasteries sustained these ascetics, and without this support, the monastic communities would have to reduce their numbers, which could eventually lead to the decline of Buddhism in Ladakh. As appeals to the State Government fell on deaf ears, the people approached the Centre. Prime Minister Nehru gave the Buddhist delegation a patient hearing and promised to help; on his advice, the delegation also met Union Law Minister, Dr. Bhim Rao Ambedkar. Ultimately, the Abdullah government agreed to exempt monasteries from the purview of the new law.[16]

The Tibet crisis

The crisis enveloping Tibet in the early years of independence merits a brief mention. The Government of India planned a grand celebration of the 2500th Buddha Jayanti in 1956, and deputed Kushok Bakula Rinpoche, then deputy minister for Ladakh Affairs in the government of Jammu and Kashmir, to visit Tibet to personally invite the 14th Dalai Lama and 10th Panchen Lama. The invitation, by Vice President Sarvepalli Radhakrishnan, was sent to the Chinese government in Beijing, and also conveyed to the Dalai Lama by the Crown Prince of Sikkim, Palden Thondup Namgyal, as President of the Mahabodhi Society of India. The Rinpoche toured Tibet from November 1955 to March 1956 and interacted with people while visiting the famous monasteries there, even as China was strengthening its hold over the region.

Bakula Rinpoche attended the first meeting of the Government-sponsored Council of Tibet's Tulkus (high-ranking incarnate lamas) at Lhasa on February 28, 1956. Invited to address the gathering, the Rinpoche made a sharp speech in the presence of high-ranking Chinese officials, expressing consternation at the growing interference of Chinese military authorities in the internal affairs of the monasteries. At this time, Tibet was formally independent and had only given control of its foreign affairs and defence to China in the Seventeen Point Agreement. Internal affairs and religious affairs were supposed to remain with the Tibetan Government. However, the Rinpoche could sense the dread among the people at the steady infringement of their freedom by the Chinese authorities. During the course of his five-month stay in Tibet, he met many old friends and acquaintances (he had studied at the Drepung monastery), and gained first-hand knowledge of the developing situation there.[17]

On his return, he met Prime Minister Nehru and explained that the situation in Tibet was extremely precarious, and the population extremely uneasy. He pointed out that the Chinese had intruded into all areas of Tibetan life and unless something was done to help the latter, the complete takeover of Tibet was imminent. He urged Nehru to discuss matters with the Dalai Lama during his visit to India and prepare a strategy, adding that India should consider giving political asylum to the Dalai Lama and Panchen Lama, if they made any such request. The Rinpoche warned that once China occupied Tibet, India's own frontiers, especially in Ladakh would become vulnerable to invasion.[18] In his report to the government of Jammu and Kashmir, Bakula Rinpoche stated, "There were about 12,000 Chinese all over Tibet, engaged in the construction of roads etc. A few schools for Tibetans where the Chinese language was taught had been opened at Lhasa and Xigatse. One hospital equipped with an x-ray machine had been opened at Lhasa. The Chinese at present do not interfere with the administration of monasteries. For that matter, they are said to have declared that their policy would be not to interfere with the religious affairs of the Tibetans, which is a tall claim keeping in view their deep penetration into Tibet".[19]

The occupation of Tibet, exile of many senior religious leaders, and destruction of much of its ancient culture, rankled deeply. Bakula Rinpoche opposed the Indian Government's policy of recognising China's annexation as endangering India's national security interests by obliterating the buffer zone between India and China. On March 31, 1959, he met Tibet's ex-prime minister, Tsewang Rabten Lukhangwa, then in exile in India, who urged him to help resettle the Tibetan refugees and to save Tibetan culture and heritage in India. Many were settled in Himachal Pradesh and Karnataka and the monastic institutions now set up in different parts of the country helped in the spread of Buddhism to the West. The vestiges of Tibet's freedom vanished with the flight of the Dalai Lama and around 100,000 refugees to India. Nevertheless, India did not anticipate any aggression on its soil and was taken unawares when the Red Army attacked Indian posts in Ladakh and NEFA in October 1962 and occupied thousands of square kilometers of territory, before unilaterally retreating on November 20, 1962. Ladakh stood solidly by the Indian Army; women cooked food and carried loads, helped in road-making, while many youth joined the army. After hostilities ended, India set up a series of small posts from Daulat Beg Oldi in the Karakoram to Demchok in the east.

The Rinpoche repeatedly urged India not to succumb to Beijing, and on February 15, 1968, he stated in Parliament, "India's relations with China cannot improve until the issue of Tibet is settled. India has committed a blunder in its policy by allowing China a free hand in Tibet and for which we had to pay a very heavy price. Regrettably, India did little to help the Tibetans. India did not even try to raise the issue in the United Nations. An ancient Buddhist heritage was burnt and world famous Buddhist monasteries were demolished in order to annihilate Buddhist culture. These have been mentioned in the report of International Jurist's Commission".[20] He continued to warn about India's weakness in Kargil. Speaking in the Lok Sabha on March 29, 1968, he said, "Pakistan, in collaboration with China, wants to endanger our independence. During the Indo-Pak war of 1965, the Indian army had twice cleared the hills from Pakistani forces, but later, following the Tashkent Agreement, our army had to leave those strategic hills. I am not criticizing the Tashkent Agreement, but I would like to warn the Government of the serious consequences of our decision to leave those hills. Pakistan can destroy our airport in minutes. Why does the government leave these places of strategic importance to the defense of our country unattended?"[21]

In this connection, we may briefly mention that Pakistan attacked Kargil in 1999, soon after Prime Minister Atal Bihari Vajpayee took a bus across the border to talk peace with Prime Minister Nawaz Sharif. The goal was to seize National Highway (NH-1) that links Srinagar with Leh via Kargil, and cut off the supply lines to all Indian border posts, including the Siachen Glacier, which Pakistan hoped to annex. The Indian Army, including the Ladakh Scouts, and Air Force, rose to the challenge and under the banner of Operation Vijay, regained the heights by July 26, 1999 (Kargil Vijay Diwas).

Scheduled Tribe Status

The people of Ladakh soon realised that the biggest stumbling block in realising their legitimate aspirations was Article 370, and they did not hesitate to call a spade a spade. During a debate in the Lok Sabha on March 29, 1968, Bakula Rinpoche demanded abrogation of Article 370 and the State's full integration with the Republic of India, so that Ladakh's demand for Union Territory status and recognition under the constitutional "scheduled tribes" could be achieved. Related to these were matters of regional autonomy, divisional status, and equitable allocation and distribution of funds, where Ladakh was always given short shrift. What was especially galling was the fact that the State Government received its plan funds from the Centre on the basis of land area, but disbursed funds to Ladakh on the basis of population (Ladakh has a very low population density).

The people of Ladakh noticed that in the neighbouring tribal districts of Himachal Pradesh and in the Himalayan regions of northeastern India, the local people enjoyed various protections and benefits on account of scheduled tribe (ST) status. This made them clamour for ST status but, as the Rinpoche told the Lok Sabha on March 29, 1968, whenever the demand to include the people of Ladakh on the Backward Class and Scheduled Tribe list was raised, it was rejected on grounds that these laws did not apply to J&K. With time, more and more people became convinced that ST status was imperative; it was felt that a concerted campaign by Buddhists and Muslims could facilitate achievement of the goal. Accordingly, the Ladakh Action Committee (LAC) was set up and it launched a peaceful agitation on January 5, 1981. As expected, the State Government began a dialogue with the Leh district administration and a cabinet sub-committee headed by finance minister D.D. Thakur was deputed to Leh (January 12–15, 1981).

The LAC submitted a draft proposal demanding:

- Greater regional autonomy;
- Divisional status for Ladakh (only Jammu and Kashmir were divisions;
- Fairer allocation of central government plan funds to Ladakhi regions;
- The commissioning of hydroelectric projects in the region;

- Improvements to its communication and road infrastructure;
- Better reservation quotas for Ladakhi students in professional and technical institutions in Jammu and Srinagar;
- Improved marketing facilities for locally produced food and vegetable products;
- An industrial development plan for Ladakh;
- Promotion of tourism;
- Improved transport facilities;
- Implementation of much-needed irrigation projects;
- Promotion and use of Ladakhi language in government offices and institutions; and
- ST status for all the people (Buddhist and Muslim) of Ladakh.

The Ladakh Action Committee withdrew its protest on the basis of assurances given by the cabinet sub-committee, but resumed it when faced with the typical delaying tactics and divisive politics. Public meetings and dharnas (sit-ins) were organised all over Ladakh. The authorities used brute force to break up the movement, forcing a delegation of the LAC led by Bakula Rinpoche and P. Namgyal, MP Lok Sabha, to meet Prime Minister Indira Gandhi and inform her of the situation in Leh. She deputed a team of observers led by P. Venkatasubbiah, Union Minister of State for Home Affairs, to Leh. Police attempts to break up a demonstration on January 24, 1982, resulted in violence, and indiscriminate firing resulted in the deaths of two innocent persons, namely, Ven. Lobzang Tsondus, a senior monk at Likir Monastery, and Tashi Wangchuk, a youth from Saspol. Many others were injured, and the public rage intensified as the days passed. Chief Minister Farooq Abdullah did not accede to demands for a judicial probe into the killings, expressed no sympathy for the bereaved families, and offered no compensation.

However, after hectic negotiations, the Chief Minister announced in Leh on October 14, 1982, that ST status would be given to Ladakh, and he would recommend the same to the Government of India. But there was no forward movement despite appeals to Prime Minister Indira Gandhi, who visited Leh and Kargil on April 14, 1983. In Leh, she offered juice and broke the hunger strike of Sonam Wangyal, Nasir Ali and Tsering Stobdan and assured that the demand of ST status would be considered favourably by the Centre.

But forward movement came only in July 1984, when Ghulam Mohammed Shah overthrew his brother-in-law Farooq Abdullah and formed the government, and forwarded the formal recommendation for ST status for

Ladakh to the Centre. Strangely, nothing moved and the Shah government was dismissed by Governor Jagmohan on March 12, 1986, after communal riots in south Kashmir. In September 1989, the Rinpoche appealed to Prime Minister Rajiv Gandhi, and after prolonged peaceful protests in Ladakh, on October 7, 1989, the presidential notification granting ST status for Ladakh was formally issued.[22] From 1968 to 1989, it was a long journey.

University issue

It took seven decades before the Jammu and Kashmir government, under Governor's rule, finally sanctioned a university for Ladakh in December 2018[23]; it still lacks a medical and engineering college. The university will be a Cluster University[24] covering the existing five degree colleges of Leh and Kargil districts, which have been affiliated to the University of Kashmir, which had established two off-site campuses in Kargil and Leh. However, delays in the conduct of examinations and declaration of results caused a sharp drop in enrolments to these colleges, forcing nearly 30,000 Ladakhi students to take admissions outside the region in order to pursue higher studies. A young student explained the region's sense of deprivation in a letter to the *Daily Excelsior*, "In absence of this university, the student community suffers a lot. Students usually have to go other places like Jammu, Kashmir, Delhi and other parts of the country for higher education. This entails a lot of money, which every aspirant here can't afford".[25]

The lack of higher educational facilities has impacted the region's economic backwardness. Despite its enormous natural and mineral resources, there is not a single industry in Ladakh, which in turn affects job opportunities. Educated youth migrate for jobs, adding to the popular discontent in the region. For such a backward region, however, the literacy rate is impressive: Kargil 71.34 per cent, and Leh 77.20 per cent. The renowned educationist Sonam Wangchuk, founder of the non-traditional school, Students' Educational and Cultural Movement of Ladakh (SECMOL), that helped students to clear exams up to the intermediate level, is also planning to set up a skill-based university near Ladakh Hill.

The absence of educational facilities has been felt since independence. Sustained neglect by the State Government led to the absence of even secondary education, forcing aspiring students to go to Srinagar or Jammu for higher education, especially for medical and engineering courses.[26] Security analyst P. Stobdan argues that given Ladakh's unique geographical location, its university could specialise in Mountain Studies, Environmental Studies, Climate Change Studies, Glacier and Water Studies, Geology, Sustainability and other sciences, and could even attract students and researchers from other countries to study these disciplines. The university could play a key role in the preservation of the environment, mitigation of climate change, conservation of glaciers, and promotion of sustainable tourism industry in the Himalayas.

From the early years of independence, the people of Ladakh have struggled to have the Bhoti (also Bodhi, a dialect of Tibetan) recognised as the official language of the region under the Eighth Schedule of the Indian Constitution. They were agitated that the State Government promoted Urdu as the medium of instruction up to the age of 14 years, and thereafter switched to English medium. The SECMOL movement that began in 1988 campaigned for reforms, and by 1993, the mother tongue began to replace Urdu as the medium of instruction, a trend that intensified after the Ladakh Autonomous Hill Development Council (LAHDC) came into existence in 1995 after the concerned act was passed in the Legislative Assembly. Ladakhis are now hopeful that with President's rule in the State, the Bhoti language could be declared as an official language of the State. Besides the Buddhists of Ladakh, the Baltis of Nubra Valley are also trying to make a daily habit of speaking and writing Bhoti. The Central Institute of Buddhist Studies, Leh, and the monasteries have made a sterling contribution in this regard, holding classes in Leh and Jammu every winter for Ladakhi youth to learn and understand the Bodhi language.

Linked with its aspirations for education and employment, Ladakh has been demanding improvements in government schools, a centre at Leh for candidates appearing for the civil services and other competitive examinations, and B.Ed. colleges. The region also wants a Bench of the State High Court, to save people the expense and inconvenience of travelling to Srinagar or Jammu for justice from the High Court; this would also give employment to local lawyers and others. Given the high levels of unemployment in the region that has some unique natural products such as pashmina goats, wonder berry, sea buckthorn, aromatic and herbal plants, and apricots, the people want the government to help in marketing these products that can generate self-employment for Ladakhis.

Zoji-la tunnel

Ladakh's longstanding demand for an all-weather road connecting it to the outside world came closer to fruition when Prime Minister Narendra Modi inaugurated the Zoji-la tunnel project, Asia's longest bi-directional tunnel, for all-weather connectivity, between Srinagar, Kargil and Leh, on May 19, 2018. This will also be India's longest road tunnel (14.15 km) and will reduce the time taken to cross the Zoji-la from 3.5 hours to 15 minutes; it is expected to be completed within five years. Zoji-la lies at an altitude of 11,578 ft on Srinagar-Kargil-Leh National Highway and shuts down during winters due to heavy snowfall and avalanches, cutting off Ladakh region from Kashmir. Locals hope for employment opportunities from the project.[27] They are also demanding extension of the railways lines from Srinagar to Kargil and from Himachal Pradesh to Leh.

Kailash-Mansarovar route

A longstanding demand of Ladakh is the resurrection of the ancient Demchok (Leh) route to Kailash-Mansarovar.[28] The Kailash Mountain and Mansarovar Lake have immense spiritual significance for Buddhists, Hindus and Jains. Up to the 17th century, Kailash and Mansarovar were part of the Kingdom of Ladakh and the nearby village of Minsar paid revenues to J&K State up to 1960; these revenues maintained the Kailash-Mansarovar Yatra. In fact, in 1954, Kushok Bakula Rinpoche, then a Minister in the State Government, visited Kailash-Mansarovar via Demchok. The Demchok route provides the easiest access because Kailash-Mansarovar is a mere two-day drive from Leh; the journey is reasonably easy as there are no major passes en route. Analyst Claude Arpi opines that if this route is opened, it would give Ladakh a national identity as the shortest and easiest route to the Kailash Yatra.[29] It could stimulate the local economy and overall development of Ladakh as it would add a new dimension to trade and tourism in Ladakh. Demchok village is famous for its hot water spring, and its hydro-therapy centre already attracts people from other parts of Ladakh and can be a huge draw for pilgrims and tourists.

Ladakh leaders have long been keen to boost tourism in the region, especially for foreign tourists, in view of its spectacular natural beauty, high mountains, crystal clear lakes, azure blue rivers, rare species of wildlife, and hoary monasteries. For long, however, security concerns dampened the attempts to promote tourism, until Prime Minister Indira Gandhi agreed to open Ladakh to tourists in 1974. From a meagre 527 adventure seekers that year, Ladakh has become a much coveted destination, providing employment and income for many families. Ladakh also hosts the world's highest motorable road, largest brackish lake in Asia, longest glacier outside the Polar regions, and the highest space observatory.[30] In fact, further growth of the tourism industry is stymied by water shortages in the region.

Ladakh Autonomous Hill Development Council

Ladakh's long struggle for Union Territory has yet to be realised; however, divisional status was granted under President's rule on February 8, 2019.

In July 1989, the mishandling of a local episode resulted in violence and heightened communal tensions, resulting in Section 144 being imposed for a long stretch. To show their resentment, the people began to express their dissent peacefully, by gathering outside Jokhang monastery in legal groups of four. However, some agent provocateurs escalated tensions by getting the state government to withdraw the local police force and Central Reserve Police Force (CRPF) and replace them with the distrusted Kashmir Armed Police (KAP). This enraged the Buddhist youth who felt humiliated by the move. It was apparent that the state government had decided to crush the agitation by force rather than discuss the genuine grievances of the people. On August 27, 1989, when a small group of protestors emerged from the Jokhang temple for a symbolic protest defying Section 144, the police reacted with preplanned and disproportionate force, beating the protestors harshly, causing injury to many, and further inflaming the situation. As violence escalated, the police resorted to firing on the unarmed crowd, in which three persons (Tsewang Dorje, Nawang Rinchen and Tsering Stobdan) were killed and several injured. The police then charged into the Jokhang temple and arrested many devotees, besides desecrating the temple. Leh town and adjoining areas were then handed over to the army, which imposed a curfew in the region. Even power and telephone lines were shut down. The police arrested several prominent Buddhist youth leaders, including LBA president Thupstan Chhewang, and took them to Srinagar.

In support of the youth, the state government employees in Leh went on an indefinite strike on September 2, 1989, thus shutting down the district administration. As leaders appealed for peace and urged the State and Central Governments to intervene, Bakula Rinpoche met Prime Minister Rajiv Gandhi on September 22, 1989, and pressed for addressing the core demand of Union Territory status for Ladakh. He suggested that a Union Minister be deputed to Leh to hold tripartite talks between the central and state governments and Buddhist leaders. He also urged, inter alia, that ST status be declared for all Ladakhis (Buddhist and Muslim) without any further delay, as it had already been recommended by the State Government and Registrar General of India. This finally resulted in the promulgation of the Constitution (J&K) Scheduled Tribes Order 1989 that declared eight tribes of Ladakh as Scheduled Tribes.

Tripartite talks also began at Leh for Union Territory status, on October 29, 1989, under the auspices of Union Home Minister Buta Singh. Eventually, an agreement was signed promising a Hill Council on the lines of the Darjeeling Gurkha Hill Council.[31] The agreement led to the return of normalcy as people hoped for a measure of genuine representation and local autonomy. But talks in this regard did not move smoothly, and the agitation resumed, leading to the arrest of many youth activists and striking government employees. At the Centre, the V.P. Singh government was in a precarious position and successive governments at the Centre fell rapidly, causing further delay in the implementation of Hill Council status for Ladakh. Thus, it was only in October 1993 that the Centre formally notified the formation of the LAHDC, but obstacles remained. Finally the LAHDC Act, 1995 was passed and the 26-member Hill Council of Leh came into being with elections in August 1995. Thupstan Chhewang was elected its first Chairman and Chief Executive Councillor (CEC); the Executive Councillors were Nawang Rigzin Jora, Sonam Dawa, Akbar Ladakhi and Tondup Sonam.

The people of Kargil, who had initially rejected the offer of a Hill Council, eventually saw its benefits; the LAHDC Kargil was set up in 2003 at the instance of Chief Minister Mufti Mohammad Sayeed.[32] However, Zanskar remained electorally marginalized in the new Council and decided to boycott the LAHDC Kargil elections. The Chief Minister was urged to consider making Zanskar a separate district. Thereafter, Zanskar received 3 seats out of a total of 26, in addition to one nominated seat in the LAHDC, Kargil Act.[33] In practice, though the LAHDC gave vast executive powers to the chairman and executive councillors (ministers), the purse strings remained with Srinagar; as such, the fruits of the prolonged agitations were far less than expected.

It was a common experience for the people of Ladakh (and Jammu) that various special assistance packages given by the Centre were cornered by the valley. Both regions suffer from a sense of discrimination, exacerbated by differences of faith; Kargil's Muslim-majority (77 per cent) is mainly Shia, while Leh is 66 per cent Buddhist and 17 per cent Hindu. Ladakh's sense of marginalisation is enhanced by the fact that when the Centre sends interlocutors to discuss the problems of the people in the context of terrorism and separatism, the focus remains Kashmir-centric. In 2010, when a three-member interlocutor group appointed by the Centre recommended separation of Ladakh from Kashmir Division and granting it divisional status,[34] the recommendation was simply ignored.

When the demand to grant Ladakh Division status was escalated under President's rule (December 19, 2018), the People's Democratic Party (PDP) promptly demanded Divisional status for the Pir Panchal area that includes Rajouri-Poonch districts and Chenab Valley that comprises Kishtwar, Doda and Ramban districts of Jammu region. The people of Jammu saw this as a mischievous attempt to fragment the province. Assurances of Union Territory status given to Ladakh in the run up to the parliamentary elections of 2014 could not be realised in view of the obstacles posed by Article 370. In despair over the seemingly endless wait, on November 15, 2018, the sitting Ladakh MP, Thupstan Chhewang, resigned from the Lok Sabha and the Bharatiya Janata Party to protest against the sustained neglect of Ladakh and denial of Union Territory status.[35] In a letter to the Prime Minister, he lamented that even the promise of including the Bhoti (Bodhi) language in the Eighth Schedule of the Constitution was belied and blamed leaders who were in-charge of the State of "repeatedly rubbing salt into the wounds of Ladakh".[36] On November 26, 2018, the Ladakh Buddhist Association organised a mega rally, and Leh town observed a complete bandh to protest against the domination of Kashmir. "The Centre must get involved and talk to Ladakhis to know our demands. We will not accept anything less than UT", the protestors chanted. They denounced the pampering of Kashmir and even questioned the logic of the Zoji-la Tunnel, pointedly stating that Ladakh had no desire to connect with Kashmir. The LBA demanded inclusion of Bhoti language in the Eighth Schedule of the Constitution, declaration of Ladakh as a Tribal Area and establishment of a Central University in Ladakh (the last was approved by the Governor in December 2018; Division status was granted in February 2019).

Writer Stanzin Chosphel argues that if the province is granted Union Territory status, its elected legislature will be more responsive to the needs of the region and will be able to make appropriate laws more proactively. There will be better prospects of employment for locals and the Centre can allocate funds for developmental projects directly; aid can be given for small-scale industries to augment the tourism sector that has the potential to be a big revenue earner for the region, but has not been adequately developed.[37] Union Territory status would certainly help the Government of India to better assert its claim over Demchok and the Pakistan-Occupied territories. Ladakh is a sensitive region as it shares borders with China and Pakistan. It has made sterling contributions in all Indo-Pak wars, the 1962 war with China, and bore the brunt of the aggression in Kargil in the summer of 1999. The people are concerned over the continuing violence in the valley and the ceaseless violations of the Line of Control (LoC) and Line of Actual Control (LAC). Chinese are known to enter border villages to harass or entice the citizens, and often Chinese herders come and occupy the grazing lands. In such situations, the local administration simply absents itself while the State administration remains aloof. Union Territory status would make the Centre responsive to the people's security needs, though there is no immediate danger as the Army 14 Corps is responsible for Ladakh's defence. All in all, many believe that the time has come to revisit the valley-centric policies of the Centre and give due weightage to other regions of the erstwhile kingdom of Maharaja Hari Singh. A noteworthy development is that the debate over the legitimacy of Articles 370 and 35-A has finally begun.

*

NOTES

1 Shakspo, Sonam Wangchuk, Kushok Bakula Rinpoche: The Architect of Modern Ladakh, Delhi, 2017, p. 132. See also, Arpi, Claude, The land of the passes, July 5, 2002. https://www.rediff.com/news/2002/jul/05spec1.htm.

2 Om, Hari, Ladakh demands UT status: J&K division only solution, December 15, 2009. http://www.vijayvaani.com/ArticleDisplay.aspx?aid=987.

3 Shakspo, Sonam Wangchuk, Kushok Bakula Rinpoche, op. cit., p. 43.

4 NAI, Ministry of States (Kashmir), Secret, 19(16)-K52, "Buddhists in Ladakh; Representations from Head Lama of Ladakh; General position re: Ladakh", cited in Shakspo, Sonam Wangchuk, Kushok Bakula Rinpoche, op. cit., p. 80.

5 Shakspo, Sonam Wangchuk, Kushok Bakula Rinpoche, op. cit., pp. 80-1.

6 Ibid., pp. 370-74.

7 For details, see, Shakspo, Sonam Wangchuk, Kushok Bakula Rinpoche

8 Ibid., pp. 132-34.

9 Shakspo, Sonam Wangchuk, op. cit., pp. 4-5.

10 Arpi, op. cit.

11 Shakspo, Sonam Wangchuk, Kushok Bakula Rinpoche, op. cit., p. 37.

12 As discussed in the Rinpoche budget speech, mentioned above.

13 Richen became the youngest recipient of the Mahavir Chakra for his role in the defence of Nubra Valley, and retired as a highly decorated Colonel in 1984. He served in the 1962 India-China war and 1971 India-Pakistan war.

14 Tanks at 11,500 feet – The Battle for Zojila. http://www.soldier2ndlife.com/card/tanks-the-battle-for-zojila.
15 Shakspo, Sonam Wangchuk, Kushok Bakula Rinpoche, op. cit., pp. 180-83.
16 Ibid., pp. 57-60.
17 Ibid., pp. 100-101.
18 Ibid., p. 102. However, as Nehru had already ignored Sardar Patel's warning (November 7, 1950), issued one month after the People's Liberation Army entered Tibet, this appeal also fell on deaf ears.
19 Shakspo, Sonam Wangchuk, Kushok Bakula Rinpoche, op. cit., p. 379.
20 Ibid., pp. 146-151.
21 Ibid., pp. 127-29.
22 Ibid., pp. 142-44.
23 Ladakh is getting its first ever university, approval passed by J&K government, Dec. 17, 2018. https://www.indiatoday.in/education-today/news/story/ladakh-is-getting-its-first-ever-university-html-1411229-2018-12-17.
24 SAC approves University for Ladakh, *Daily Excelsior*, Dec. 16, 2018. http://www.dailyexcelsior.com/sac-approves-university-for-ladakh/.
25 Arpi, Claude, Why Ladakh needs special status, Dec. 12, 2018. http://claudearpi.blogspot.com/2018/12/why-ladakh-needs-special-status.html.
26 Stobdan, P., A case for Ladakh University, April 28, 2015. http://www.reachladakh.com/news-details.php?pID=2810.
27 PM inaugurates work for Asia's longest Zojila tunnel, May 19, 2018. https://www.telegraphindia.com/india/pm-inaugurates-work-for-asia-39-s-longest-zojila-tunnel-nbsp-nbsp/cid/1345578.
28 Ladakh demands opening of new Kailash Mansarovar Yatra route, August 12, 2014. https://www.dailypioneer.com/2014/top-stories/ladakh-demands-opening-of-new-kailash-mansarovar-yatra-route.html.
29 Arpi, Claude, New silk road, April 6, 2015. http://claudearpi.blogspot.com/2015/04/new-silk-road.html.
30 Shakspo, Sonam Wangchuk, Kushok Bakula Rinpoche, op. cit., pp. 144-45.
31 The agreement was signed by P.P. Srivastava, Additional Secretary in the Ministry of Home Affairs, on behalf of the central government; Ashok Jaitley, Additional Chief Secretary, on behalf of the J&K government; and Thupstan Chhewang, President of the LBA, in the presence of Union Home Minister Buta Singh, J&K ministers Mangat Ram Sharma and Mohammad Shafi, and Bakula Rinpoche, P. Namgyal and other dignitaries.
32 Shakspo, Sonam Wangchuk, Kushok Bakula Rinpoche, op. cit., pp. 185-92.
33 Ibid., pp. 180-83.
34 Shakspo, Nawang Tsering, Ladakh Deserves Divisional Status, July 5, 2012. https://www.greaterkashmir.com/print/ladakh-deserves-divisional-status/124465.html.
35 Arpi, Why Ladakh needs special status, op. cit..
36 "All Pleas Fell on Deaf Ears": After Resigning, BJP MP from Ladakh Writes to Modi, Nov. 20, 2018. https://thewire.in/politics/bjp-ladakh-narendra-modi-thuostan-chhewang-resignation.
37 Chosphel, Stanzin, Union territory for Ladakh: Issues and challenges, May 17, 2017. http://www.reachladakh.com/news-details.php?pID=3780.

CHAPTER EIGHT

Articles 370 and 35-A: Genesis and Consequences

Abha Khanna

The constitutional validity of the controversial Articles 370 and 35-A of the Constitution of India, both of which pertain exclusively to the State of Jammu and Kashmir and are perceived as discriminatory towards other Indian citizens and state subjects, respectively, have been challenged in the Supreme Court of India. The interlinked statutes will most likely be decided by a Constitutional Bench. Article 370 is well recognised as a "temporary" provision that some persons are now trying to enshrine as a "basic feature" of the Constitution even as others strive for its abolition. The dispute regarding Article 35-A centres round the startling fact that Parliament was bypassed when President Rajendra Prasad, on the advice (read insistence) of Jawaharlal Nehru, incorporated the said Constitution (Application to Jammu and Kashmir) Order of 1954 in the Constitution. The Order was a consequence of a personal understanding between Prime Minister Nehru and Sheikh Abdullah (the then Prime Minister of Jammu and Kashmir) in 1952. The "understanding" came to be known as the Delhi Agreement and extended Indian citizenship to the 'state subjects' of Jammu and Kashmir.

President Rajendra Prasad modified the Constitution of India under Article 370(1)(d) which empowers the President to make any exceptions or modifications with the concurrence of the Government of the State (of Jammu and Kashmir). This was astonishing because under Article 368(i) only Parliament can amend the Constitution. Barring this episode, the Indian

Constitution has never been amended other than by prescribed parliamentary procedure. In *Puranlal Lakhanpal vs. The President of India* (AIR 1961 SC 1519), a five-judge Bench of the Supreme Court discussed the President's powers under Article 370 to 'modify' the Constitution. The Court upheld the right of the President to modify an existing provision in the Constitution under Article 370, but maintained silence on whether the President can, without Parliament's knowledge, introduce an entirely new Article into the statute book. This question remains open.

A group known as 'We the Citizens' has challenged the validity of both Article 370 and Article 35-A on grounds that Jammu and Kashmir had four representatives in the Constituent Assembly of India; that the State had no special status in the Constitution; and that Article 370 was a 'temporary provision' which was never intended to serve as an instrument to usher in permanent amendments on the lines of Article 35-A. The group attacked Article 35-A as contrary to the "very spirit of oneness of India" as it creates a "class within a class of Indian citizens". It violates fundamental rights under Articles 14, 19 and 21 of the Constitution of India by prohibiting citizens from other States from getting employment or buying property in Jammu and Kashmir. Another petition filed by a state citizen, Charu Wali Khanna, states that the impugned Article 35-A impinges on women's basic right to property in the event of marriage to a non-native man and affects the inheritance rights of children.

Jammu and Kashmir has long been a victim of political mishandling by successive leaders.[1] Observations over the past seven decades increasingly converge on Article 370 as a major impediment to the progress of the State and the people. A look at the historical sequence of events in the pre- and post-independence period, especially the insertion of Article 370 followed by Article 35-A in the Constitution, and the consequences for the nation and the people of Jammu and Kashmir would be instructive.

Pre-Independence Status

The British Raj used two different administrative arrangements to rule the country. British India included provinces that were administered directly by the British Parliament through its nominated representative, the Viceroy, and comprised 60 per cent of the land area of the sub-continent. The Princely States that comprised the remaining area were ruled by the traditional rulers (maharajas, nawabs, rajas), who owed allegiance to the British Crown but retained control over their internal affairs such as law and order, civil liberties, health, education and economic development. The kingdom of Jammu and Kashmir was one such State.

On February 20, 1947 the British Government announced in the House of Commons that it proposed to grant independence to British India, which would simultaneously be divided into two dominions, India and Pakistan, the latter extracted from Muslim-majority areas on the subcontinent's eastern and western flanks.[2] With regard to the Princely States, under the policy announced by the Cabinet Mission on May 12, 1946, British paramountcy would end and all political arrangements between the British Crown and the Princely States would terminate. A Department of States was established in India and Pakistan to link the Princely States to one of the Dominions.[3] The situation for India was more challenging as the number of States involved was greater than in the case of Pakistan. Sardar Vallabhbhai Patel played a sterling role as head of the Department of States to bring the Princely States into the Indian fold. On October 26, 1947, Maharaja Hari Singh signed the Instrument of Accession[4] and Jammu and Kashmir became an integral part of India.

Constituent Assembly

After the accession of the Princely States to India, it was decided that the representatives/Princes of all States would participate in the Constituent Assembly to frame the Constitution of the Union. Sheikh Muhammad Abdullah, Motiram Baigra, Mirza Mohammad Afzal Beg and Maulana Mohammad Sayeed Masoodi participated in the Constituent Assembly debates as representatives of Jammu and Kashmir.[5] The Constitution of India was promulgated and came into effect on January 26, 1950.

Article 370 has been placed in Part XXI of the Constitution of India. Its title, "Temporary provisions with respect to the State of Jammu and Kashmir," clearly indicates that it was intended to be temporary and was to be repealed as soon as the process of the constitutional integration of Jammu and Kashmir with India was over,[6] as was the case with other parts of India. The question arises why Article 370 was listed as a 'temporary' provision when no other Article in the Constitution of India was similarly labelled even though a number of Articles were repealed later. Yet, Article 370 still exists on the statute. A scrutiny of the Constituent Assembly debates may throw some light on the matter.

The original Article 370 was discussed as Draft Article 306(A) in the Constituent Assembly and debated on October 17, 1949. N. Gopalaswami Ayyangar informed the members, "The States have been integrated with the federal Republic in such a manner that they do not have to accede or execute a document of Accession for the purpose of becoming units of the Republic, but they are mentioned in the Constitution itself; and, in the case of practically all States other than the State of Jammu and Kashmir, their constitutions also have been embodied in the Constitution for the whole of India...". This deserves a brief explanation. At independence, the Princely States joining the Dominion of India were given the liberty to draft their own state constitutions,[7] which would be subsidiary to the Indian Constitution. This arrangement was made in view of the federal structure and the Instrument of Accession signed by the rulers; Maharaja Hari Singh signed the same document. Thereafter, some Princely States began preparing constitutions for their respective States, but eventually gave up the exercise and accepted the Indian Constitution fully.

Ayyangar further asserted that the State of Jammu and Kashmir was now a part of India: "The effect of this article is that the Jammu & Kashmir State which is now a part of India will continue to be a part of India, will be a unit of the future Federal Republic of India and the Union Legislature will get jurisdiction to enact laws on matters specified either in the Instrument of Accession or by later addition with the concurrence of the Government of State." Thereafter, he categorically stated, "Now, if you remember the viewpoints that I have mentioned, it is an inevitable conclusion that, at the present moment, we could establish only an interim system. Article 306 (A) is an attempt to establish such a system." The stated intention behind the insertion of Article 370 was that it would exist for a limited period and until the state endorsed the Constitution of India. Though the Constitution of India was applied to Jammu and Kashmir by the Regent, Karan Singh, by issuing the necessary ordinance, Jammu and Kashmir prepared its own Constitution. This Constitution was limited to the State and subsidiary to the Indian Constitution. Article 370 should have ceased to exist the moment the Constitution of Jammu and Kashmir was adopted on January 26, 1957.[8]

Temporary and Transitional

The Constitution makers made their intentions clear by putting Article 370 in Chapter XXI of the Constitution, titled "Temporary and Transitional." It is emphatically not a "special" provision. The perverse argument that the State enjoys special status is based on the title as it stands today, "Temporary, Transitional and Special Provisions." What is pertinent is that the word "special" was added through the 13th Constitutional Amendment when Articles 371 (A to I) were added to Chapter XXI. The Statement of Objects and Reasons of the Amendment gives the reason for insertion of this provision: "The word 'special' is limited to Articles 371 A to I and cannot apply to a posterior provision Article 370". If "special" was to extend to Article 370 as well, the 13th Constitutional Amendment would have changed the marginal note of 370 as well. This stands as it originally was, "Temporary provisions with respect to the State of Jammu and Kashmir".[9]

Article 370 contains three sub-articles. Article 370(1)(a) says that Article 238 of the Constitution does not apply to the State of Jammu and Kashmir. Article 238 had categorized the States of India into two parts: 'Part A' States (Governed by the British) and 'Part B' states (Governed by Princes). Article 238 was deleted from the Constitution at the time of the States Reorganisation Act, 1956. Article 370(1)(a) is therefore a redundant provision. Other provisions are also redundant, as shall be discussed.

Article 370(1)(b) stipulates the mechanism for applying legislations made by the Union Parliament relating to entries in the Union List and Concurrent List of the Constitution. It nowhere states that the Parliament of India cannot make laws with respect to the State of Jammu and Kashmir. There are two limitations on this application. First, on issues which have been declared to correspond to subjects in the Instrument of Accession, namely, defence, foreign affairs and telecommunications, the Central Government can apply the Union legislation after "consultations" with the State Government. The ordinary meaning of "consultation" means a discussion, which would not be binding on the Central Government. Second, for those subjects that fall beyond these three, the Central Government will have to take the "concurrence" of the State Government to apply the laws passed by Parliament. "Concurrence" is an active and binding nature of the opinion of the State Government. This is simply an additional legislative mechanism to apply the laws passed by Parliament to the State of Jammu and Kashmir.[10]

Article 370(1)(c) is the very soul of Article 370 and eviscerates any argument of incomplete integration or special status of Jammu and Kashmir. It declares that the provisions of Article 1 would apply to the State of Jammu and Kashmir. Article 1(1) of the Constitution says, "India, that is Bharat, shall be a Union of States." Article 1(2) states that the States and their territories are mentioned in the First Schedule. The First Schedule mentions the State of Jammu and Kashmir at Item 15 and defines 'territory' to mean "the territory which immediately before the commencement of this Constitution was comprised in the Indian State of Jammu and Kashmir." It is pertinent that as per the Constitution, the territory of Jammu and Kashmir, illegally occupied by Pakistan and called "Pak Occupied Kashmir" is legally a part of India. This provision puts the State of Jammu and Kashmir at par with all other states and does not grant it any higher or special status. It is insidious to claim that integration of the State with India is incomplete.

Article 370(1)(d) is an exposition on the Constitutional relationship between the Centre and State. Discretion in the manner of application of the Indian Constitution is given to the President of India. The situation is similar to Union legislation in (1)(b). For issues relating to defence, foreign affairs and telecommunication, the President is required to "consult" the State Government, whereas on other issues "concurrence" of State Government is required. Most provisions of the Indian Constitution are applied to the State of Jammu and Kashmir and the supremacy of the Indian Constitution has been acknowledged by the Constitution of Jammu and Kashmir.[11]

There is mischief in the application of the Constitution of India to protect restrictions on non-residents of the State of Jammu and Kashmir from purchasing property because of the necessity of "Permanent Resident Certificate (PRC)." This requirement was imposed through Article 35-A of the Constitution of India,[12] applicable only in the State of Jammu and Kashmir. The President can apply the Constitution of India with such "exceptions and modifications" to the State of Jammu and Kashmir.[13]

Article 370(2) is another important provision that exposes the temporary nature of Article 370. According to this clause, the provisions of the Constitution which were applied to Jammu and Kashmir prior to the formation of the Constituent Assembly of the State shall be placed before it for appropriate decision. As per the Constitution makers, the life of Article 370 was until the Constituent Assembly of the State was formed and it completed its function of endorsing the Constitution of India. Those who argue that following the dissolution of the Constituent Assembly of the State no further provisions of the Indian Constitution can be applied to J&K forget that the State Constitution itself adopts and applies the Indian Constitution.[14]

Article 370(3) is the exit route for Article 370. It authorizes the President of India to declare that Article 370 is modified or exceptions are created to this Article or declare the Article to be inoperative. This is to be based on the recommendation of the Constituent Assembly of the State, which no longer exists. It is incorrect to claim that the powers of the Constituent Assembly stand transferred to the State legislature or State Government because neither of these bodies can perform "constituent power" functions, which only a Constituent Assembly can perform. Also, there can be no reconvening of a Constituent Assembly once it is dissolved. Hence, Article 370(3) has become redundant, as has Article 370(1)(a). The only effective and operative part of Article 370 existing at the moment is the first portion which gives the discretion of removal of Article 370 to the President of India, which he may do anytime by issuing a notification.

This is not the only way to remove Article 370. It can be removed through a Constitutional Amendment under Article 368 of the Constitution, which requires a majority of the total membership and no less than two-thirds present and voting. Parliament has unlimited powers to amend the Constitution and remove Article 370.[15]

Maulana Hasrat Mohani resisted the idea of Article 370 for Jammu and Kashmir and questioned the basis of this discrimination.[16] Gopalaswami Ayyangar replied, "There has been a war going on within the limits of Jammu and Kashmir State. There was a ceasefire agreed to at the beginning of this year and that ceasefire is still on. Part of the State is still in the hands of rebels and enemy. We are entangled in the United Nations. The legislature which is known as Praja Sabha in the State is dead, neither that legislature nor a constituent assembly can be convoked or can function until complete peace comes to prevail. Till a constituent assembly comes into being, only an interim arrangement is possible and not an arrangement which could at once be brought into line with the arrangements that exist in the case of the other States...." Ayyangar's explanation does not stand the test of time or reason; but the one thing that emerges clearly is that Article 370 was merely a procedural mechanism for completing the process of integration. Gopalaswami Ayyangar also mentioned that, "We have said that Article 238 will not apply to the Jammu and Kashmir State. But that cannot be a permanent feature of the Constitution of the State." This means that once the State Constituent Assembly was convened and had performed its requisite tasks, Article 370 would be abrogated/repealed (as in the case of Article 238). This did not require a constitutional amendment by Parliament and could be done through a simple Presidential order. It defies reason that it has not been done so far and that any attempt to raise the issue creates a nationwide furore. A White Paper on Indian States, published by the Ministry of States in 1950, declared that Article 370 is not a permanent feature of the Constitution.[17] Legally and constitutionally, therefore, the position of Jammu and Kashmir is/was the same as that of the other acceding states.

The agony of Jammu and Kashmir began with her becoming a victim of the personal ambitions of Sheikh Mohammad Abdullah, mishandling of the affairs by national leaders and international conspiracies to separate Jammu and Kashmir from India. American intelligence followed Kashmir affairs closely and prepared a profile of Sheikh Abdullah, which was declassified in December 1999; it is safe to assume that they would have established links with the major political figures of Jammu and Kashmir.[18] While New Delhi indulged the Sheikh for long, turning a blind eye to his actions and forcing Maharaja Hari Singh into exile, Abdullah tried to retard the process of offering more subjects for inclusion in the Union List from the State List even after coming to an understanding with Prime Minister Nehru in 1952; the so-called Delhi Pact was just an 'understanding' between the two leaders, yet it was given weightage by the Government of India.[19] This understanding was actually a statement of intent by Pandit Nehru and Sheikh Abdullah that was announced in the Indian Parliament and State of Jammu and Kashmir.

At the grassroots level, nationalists did not back this accord and favoured Union, State and Concurrent Lists at par with other Indian States. A grassroots movement erupted in the State against the local government and received some support from other parts of the country. Even in Parliament, the attitude of Sheikh Abdullah and the manner in which the Centre was handling J&K affairs was opposed by senior parliamentarians and constitutional experts like Dr. Syama Prasad Mookerjee and N.C. Chatterjee. Mookerjee died in mysterious circumstances in Kashmir while trying to foil the designs of Sheikh Abdullah in 1953.[20]

Shades of the Nehru-Sheikh understanding in 1952 found reflection in the Constitution (Application to Jammu and Kashmir) Order 1954 of May 14, 1954. This Order, issued by the President of India, was an unconstitutional order issued under the cover of Article 370 of the Constitution of India; it amended the Constitution of India whereas no such authority could be drawn by the President from Article 370. Worse, it enabled the Government of Jammu and Kashmir to tread on the rights of Indians living outside the State of Jammu and Kashmir.

Implications of Article 370

The retention of Article 370 even after the expiry of its raison d'être created many problems for the citizens, as it became a mechanism to obstruct welfare measures and the percolation of democratic rights to the grassroots. The State Government enjoys the right of giving its "concurrence" to the application of Union laws and application of Constitutional provisions. But the political abuse of Article 370 has resulted in a situation wherein more than 130 constitutional provisions are not applicable in Jammu and Kashmir, to the detriment of the people.[21]

The six-year term of the State Assembly is a grim reminder of the authoritarian period of the Emergency (1975-77) during which Prime Minister Indira Gandhi imposed the infamous 42nd Amendment (1976) of the Constitution to defer elections to Parliament and the State legislatures to extend her tenure by another year. The Amendment was promptly reversed when the Janata Party came to power in 1977. However, Sheikh Abdullah, who had fortuitously been restored to office in 1975, quickly adopted the 42nd Amendment extending the term of the Assembly to 6 years and turned a blind eye to the subsequent 44th Amendment that restored the original tenure of five years. As a result, the J&K Assembly term continues to be six years.

Difficulties to bring Development to the Grassroots

As Prime Minister, Rajiv Gandhi tried to take development to the grassroots by empowering the panchayats, but despite being part of the government of Jammu and Kashmir in coalition with either the National Conference or People's Democratic Party for two terms, the Congress was unable to get the 73rd and 74th amendments to the Constitution of India incorporated into the J&K Panchayati Raj Act 1989. Panchayat elections were held in 2001 and the term of the panchayats ended in 2006, but during this tenure, elections to the next level of block and district were not held. This story was repeated in the 2011 panchayat elections. As a result, panchayati raj institutions in the State are in a very poor state. States with strong panchayati raj institutions, such as Kerala and Karnataka, transfer 45-50 per cent of funds to the local bodies. In Jammu and Kashmir, barely one per cent is transferred to the local institutions.

The Union Ministry of Panchayati Raj allocates substantial funds for the smooth functioning of panchayats, but under the 73rd Amendment funds cannot be allocated to States which fail to set up PRIs. Jammu and Kashmir is probably the only State that has forfeited funds meant for panchayats due to its failure to constitute panchayats year after year. Even in 2011, panchayat elections were held perhaps only to ensure resumption of funds to the State coffers. This mockery of developmental initiatives under the cover of Article 370 does not stop here; the State Government allotted only Rs. 1 lakh each to panchayats across the State.

Accountability and Transparency

The Right to Information Act is an important tool to keep a check on government activities. However, Jammu and Kashmir has its own version of the Right to Information Act, which limits the rights of citizens to gain information. Even the report of the Central Government's interlocutors (2012) admitted that there is no local self-governance and there is "nepotism," "corruption," and "unemployment." The report, however, failed to identify the true culprit, namely, Article 370.

Two-thirds of the State budget is borne by the Central Government and the State has a deficit of 10 per cent of State income. State debt is two-thirds of the gross domestic product (GDP) and the State is unable to generate revenue sufficient to run its own affairs. Article 35-A, protected by virtue of Article 370, obstructs the setting up of industries in the State, which in turn has spawned massive unemployment, lack of development and low standard of living.

State Constitution above Indian Constitution

High Court judges, members of Legislative Assembly and Legislative Council and ministers in the State of Jammu and Kashmir take oath of office through a text that is different from that applicable to the rest of the country.[22] All these dignitaries are answerable to the State Constitution of Jammu and Kashmir instead of the Union Constitution.

Right to Education

The Constitution (Eighty-sixth Amendment) Act, 2002 inserted Article 21-A in the Constitution of India to provide free and compulsory education to all children in the age group of six to 14 years as a Fundamental Right in such manner as the State may, by law, determine. The Right of Children to Free and Compulsory Education (RTE) Act 2009, which represents the consequential legislation envisaged under Article 21-A, means that every child has a right to full-time elementary education of satisfactory and equitable quality in a formal school that satisfies certain essential norms and standards. But the same is not implemented in Jammu and Kashmir. The question arises: how does providing free elementary education conflict with the so-called special status of the State?

Financial Accountability Missing

The Prevention of Corruption Act, 1989 is not implemented in the State; nor is the Lokpal. The Comptroller and Auditor General has reported that there is no financial accountability in the State. CAG reports have at times pointed to systematic institutional mis-governance, all of which discourage institutional investment in the State. The constitutional amendment regarding "fundamental duties" is not applicable in J&K.

ARTICLE 35-A

A Fraud on the Constitution of India

On May 14, 1954, the President of India issued an order called the Constitution (Application to Jammu and Kashmir) Order 1954. Though issued by President Dr. Rajendra Prasad, he raised several doubts about the move in a lengthy epistle to Prime Minister Nehru on September 6, 1952. The Order came into effect immediately and superseded the Constitution (Application to Jammu and Kashmir) Order 1950. Besides carrying out many modifications and changes, this presidential order 'added' a new "Article 35-A" after Article 35 to the Constitution of India. The addition or deletion of an Article amounts to an amendment to the Constitution. And the Constitution can be amended only by Parliament as per procedure clearly laid out in Article 368. However, Article 35-A was never presented before the Parliament of India. In other words, the President (read Government headed by Jawaharlal Nehru) bypassed the constitutional procedure and added the new Article 35-A. In the process, Article 368 of the Constitution, in its application to Jammu and Kashmir, was also amended. The President of India did not have the legislative power to do this, but in this case he clearly performed the function of Parliament itself.

The 1954 order states it is being issued "in exercise of powers conferred by clause (1) of Article 370 of the Constitution, the President, with the concurrence of the Government of Jammu and Kashmir, is pleased to make the following order..." Yet it is pertinent that Article 370 nowhere confers on the President executive powers so vast that he can amend the Constitution and insert new provisions therein. It also does not state that the President can bypass Parliament and invoke executive powers so vast and devastating that neither the Lok Sabha nor the Rajya Sabha can do anything about the amendment being carried out. It is true that the President of India only acts on the advice of the Council of Ministers headed by the Prime Minister. But again, the Constitution *does not* authorize the Council of Ministers, i.e., the Union Cabinet, to aid and advise the President to add any provision to the Constitution that is contrary to constitutional permissibility, not even in relation and application to the State of Jammu and Kashmir. The Union Cabinet can only promulgate an ordinance, which automatically expires after six months unless passed by Parliament. The constituent power to amend the Constitution of India–by way of addition, variation or repeal of any provisions – belongs *only* to Parliament under the umbrella of Article 368. This power is an essential constituent function that cannot be effaced or abdicated or handed down to any other agency of the Government, not even the President of India.

Curiously, this 'amendment' to the Constitution was concealed from the general public by not mentioning it in the text of editions of the main Constitution. Most constitutional experts were until very recently completely unaware of Article 35-A and its implications. To explain, when a new article, Right to Education, was inserted in the Constitution as a fundamental right some years ago, it was inserted right after Article 21 and designated as Article 21A. It was followed by Article 22. Accordingly, new copies of the Constitution display the same in sequence, viz., Article 21, Article 21A and Article 22. In similar vein, Article 35-A should be inserted between Article 35 and Article 36. However, Article 35-A is missing from this sequence because it was never presented to Parliament, never enacted by Parliament and hence could not occupy its logical place in the statute. Moreover, Article 35-A does not figure in the list of amendments to the Constitution, which lists all amendments made to the Constitution of India, from the first one in 1951 till the latest. On careful scrutiny, one finds Article 35-A stealthily inserted in Appendix I to the Constitution.

Purpose of Article 35-A

Article 35-A empowers the State Assembly to define 'permanent residents' and give them special rights and privileges, while restricting the rights and privileges of citizens of India who do not fit the criteria of 'permanent resident'. It has denied basic rights to lakhs of citizens living in Jammu and Kashmir for the past seven decades. It has taken away the right of Indians living outside Jammu and Kashmir to settle in a state which is an integral part of India. None except those defined as 'permanent residents' are entitled to property rights; employment in the state government; participation in panchayat, municipal and legislative assembly elections; admission to government-run technical education institutions; scholarships and other social benefits.

Residents who fulfil the conditions required for being a Permanent Resident are entitled to issuance of a Permanent Resident Certificate (PRC). In Jammu & Kashmir, PRC is a very important document and is needed at many places, in different walks of life. Whenever the State government issues an advertisement for jobs, only persons with a PRC can apply, or one has to produce an "under process" certificate and produce the PRC on a later date. In State-run professional colleges such as medical or engineering colleges only persons with valid PRCs can apply. One needs a PRC to buy and sell immovable property. The rights of Permanent Residents are defined clearly and they have some rights which Non-Permanent Residents do not have.

The Presidential Order says: "after Article 35, the following new article shall be added, namely: Article 35-A:Saving of laws with respect to permanent residents and their rights.

(a) Defining the classes of persons who are, or shall be, permanent residents of the State of Jammu and Kashmir;
(b) Conferring on such permanent residents any special rights and privileges, or imposing upon other persons any restrictions, as respects:
  (i) Employment under the State Government;
  (ii) Acquisition of immovable property in the State;
  (iii) Settlement in the State; or
  (iv) Right to scholarships and such other forms of aid as the State Government may provide, shall be void on the ground that it is inconsistent with or takes away or abridges any rights conferred on the other citizens of India by any provisions of this Part.

The Constitution of Jammu and Kashmir defined permanent resident status through sections 6 to 10 of Part III of the State Constitution in a manner that denied Permanent Resident Certificates to refugees from West Pakistan.

(1) Every person who is, or is deemed to be, a citizen of India under the provisions of the Constitution of India shall be a permanent resident of the State, if on the fourteenth day of May, 1954:

(a) He was a State Subject of Class I or of Class II; or

(b) Having lawfully acquired immovable property in the State, he has been ordinarily resident in the State for not less than ten years prior to that date.

(2) Any person who, before the fourteenth day of May, 1954, was a State Subject of Class I or of Class II and who having migrated after the first day of March, 1947, to the territory now included in Pakistan, returns to the State under a permit for resettlement in the State or for permanent return issued by or under the authority of any law made by the State Legislature shall on such return be a permanent resident of the State.

Impact of 35-A

On West Pakistan Refugees: Partition was accompanied by serious communal clashes in several areas. Hindus and Sikhs were uprooted from areas that became Pakistan and moved towards Indian territories. Sialkot and other contiguous areas of West Punjab had substantial Hindu and Sikh populations which moved towards Jammu and other areas of J&K which had a Hindu majority, and settled there. Refugees who moved to other parts of India (Delhi, Mumbai, Surat, etc.) were rehabilitated with a number of welfare measures such as allotment of houses, jobs, etc., and integrated into the mainstream seamlessly, enjoying all rights and privileges at par with all citizens. But even after more than seven decades of freedom, the 5,764 families consisting of 47,215 persons who moved to Jammu Division have been denied their due rehabilitation. They are citizens of India but not of the State of Jammu and Kashmir, due to Article 35-A. The West Pakistan refugees are not entitled to vote in Assembly and local body elections, but can vote in Parliamentary elections. They cannot apply for jobs in the State government, and their children cannot get higher education in State institutions.[23] Nor can the West Pakistan refugees own their homes. They were allowed to retain the land on which they settled initially, but title to the land was not conferred upon them on grounds of non-permanent resident status. Thus, while they can stay on this land, they cannot sell it or buy any other property.

West Pakistan Refugees (WPR) hailed mostly from deprived sections of society and more than 80 per cent were Scheduled Castes. The J&K law ensures that they can be tillers, labourers and tenants but not landowners and landlords. Today, their population has grown manifold and is estimated at around three lakh. The land permitted to them after 1947 is no longer sufficient. Denial of 'permanent resident status' denies them access to State Government employment and the benefit of various social welfare schemes of the State Government. No other benefits of any kind have been granted to them. Their children are not entitled to scholarships and freeships available to PRC holders or for admissions to any state-run professional colleges.

On Valmikis: In 1957, around 200 Valmiki (Scheduled Caste) families were invited to Jammu and Kashmir by the then government to work in the municipality as the sweepers of Jammu had gone on strike for over a month. They were promised that the 'permanent resident' clause would be relaxed in their favour. However, due to Article 35-A, despite living and working in the state for more than 60 years, the Valmikis have not been given any rights. They are not allowed to take up any government job other than that of sweeper in the Jammu municipality. Their children have become graduates but are not eligible to apply for government jobs. The disabilities attached to West Pakistan refugees apply equally to them and even the colony allotted to *safai karamcharis* (Valmiki Colony, Gandhi Nagar, Jammu) has not been regularized till date. The denial of rights extends to inhibiting Valmikis from joining Central services like the Armed Forces due to non-issuance of domicile certificate. Recently however, the domicile certificate has begun to be issued at the intervention of the Centre.

On Gorkha Community: Gorkhas settled in Jammu-Kashmir in the 18th century and a majority of them were soldiers who fought in the army of Maharaja Ranjit Singh of Punjab, whose commander-in-chief was Gulab Singh, a landlord of Jammu. Their population numbers around one lakh and is spread across the State, including Kashmir Valley. They have resided in Jammu and Kashmir for more than a century and have made supreme sacrifices for the integrity of India and the safety of Jammu and Kashmir. Despite this, Gorkhas face huge hurdles in getting the Permanent Residence Certificate (PRC), without which educated young Gorkha boys and girls cannot get a government job or admission into educational institutes. Hence, they remain economically, socially and educationally backward.

On Women: Article 370 has indirectly provided a means, via Article 35-A, to violate the social, legal and property rights of women with permanent resident status. It discriminates against women, irrespective of religion. If they marry outside the State, they can lose the right to own and acquire property in the State and are not entitled for employment in government service. Various welfare legislations for the empowerment of women are not applied in the State.

Prior to 2002, a woman was liable to lose her Permanent Resident status if she married a non-Permanent Resident. This discriminatory practice was struck down in *Dr. Susheela Sawhney Vs State of Jammu and Kashmir* (2002), wherein the Court ruled, "daughter of a permanent resident of the State of Jammu and Kashmir will not lose status as a permanent resident of the State of Jammu and Kashmir on her marriage with a person who is not a permanent resident of the State of Jammu and Kashmir".[24] The State Government challenged the verdict in the Supreme Court but later withdrew. However, it made another attempt by bringing "The Jammu and Kashmir Permanent Resident (Disqualification) Bill 2004" which was passed in the Legislative Assembly but fell in the Legislative Council.[25] Nevertheless, there are many cases of Jammu and Kashmir women who marry in other parts of the country and their children are deprived of permanent resident rights in their maternal land.[26] Even the wife of a Union Minister, (late) Sunanda Pushkar, faced difficulties in purchasing land in the State as her husband did not have PRC status.

Though the women of Jammu and Kashmir won the right to maintain their Permanent Resident status in 2002, the discrimination continues as their children are still not eligible for PRC, which means they cannot get admissions to professional colleges and cannot apply for state government jobs. They cannot inherit their mother's property or buy property themselves. This creates a traumatic situation for women who marry 'outsiders' and later get widowed or divorced. Their children have no future in Jammu and Kashmir. This situation afflicts Hindu and Muslim women equally, though numerically, more Hindu women are affected as more of them have married outside the State. The PRC provisions impact Jammu region more than Kashmir region, mainly because many parts of Jammu are contiguous to Punjab and Himachal Pradesh and cultural and familial bonds lead to inter-state marriages.

On Development of the State: The Permanent Resident Certificate bars people from other States from buying property in Jammu and Kashmir. It is understandable if such a provision is made to protect agricultural lands, but there is no rationale to disallow free purchase of non-agricultural lands. A serious concern is the absence of industry in the State, but no industrialist would invest if he cannot own the land on which his factory will stand. If small scale, non-polluting industries are allowed to purchase land and set up units, it would provide local employment and improve the standard of living.

On Scheduled Tribes: Tribals comprise nearly 15 per cent of the State's population, but political reservations for Scheduled Tribes are non-existent. Again, Article 35-A is invoked to deny social justice and equitable distribution of opportunities to deprived/weaker sections such as scheduled tribes, scheduled castes, other backward classes, women, refugees et al as the process of offering more subjects from the J&K specific State List to the Union List has been stalled by not using the provisions of Article 370 and the State not making better welfare laws.

On Education Sector: As per the provisions of Article 35-A, no person from outside Jammu and Kashmir is allowed to take up any government job. This has caused a serious dearth of qualified experts in professional medical and engineering and such other educational institutions. This has been detrimental to the quality of professional education and students are suffering as a consequence.

On Health Sector: Due to 35-A, qualified doctors, specialists and researchers from other states do not work in Jammu & Kashmir. There is an acute shortage of doctors in super specialty hospitals and professors in the medical colleges.

The cumulative impact of Article 370 and Article 35-A on Jammu and Kashmir is suffocating. While Jammu and Ladakh resent the political weightage given to the Kashmir Valley and its domination of the entire state, the flip side is that it has choked the development and efflorescence of the State by denying non-permanent residents the right to settle, work, and invest in the region. India's high growth cities (Mumbai, Surat, Bengaluru, Hyderabad, Pune, Gurugram, etc.) embrace Indian and international talent and investment. Jammu and Ladakh yearn to embrace the Indian nation directly; Kashmir alone spurns the national embrace. Yet the state cannot thrive without revisiting this peculiarly calibrated isolationism. Jammu and Kashmir depends for two-thirds of its budget on the Central Government. Escape from the clutches of Article 370 could open the door to an era of prosperity.

*

NOTES

1 Kumar, P., Ed., *Article 370: Evolving Clarity beyond the Conundrum*, Mewar University Press: 2015, p. 1.

2 All about the Indian Independence Act that partitioned the country. https://

www.indiatoday.in/education-today/gk-current-affairs/story/indian-independence-act-329774-2016-07-18

3 *White Paper on Indian States*, Ministry of States, Govt. of India, Government of India Press: 1950, p. 32.

4 Instrument of Accession 1947, Home Department, F. No.P-1/20/47, p. 2.

5 *Constituent Assembly Debates Official Report* (CAD), Book no. 3, volume 8, p. 915. Reprint by Lok Sabha Secretariat, New Delhi: 2009.

6 Lok Sabha Debates, September 11, 1964, p. 1282.

7 See Vellodi Committee Report; this committee was set up under the chairmanship of M. K. Vellodi.

8 *Constituent Assembly Debates Official Report* (CAD), book 3, volume 8, p. 915. Reprint by Lok Sabha Secretariat, New Delhi: 2009.

9 See Original Constitution of India as enforced from January 26, 1950.

10 Kumar, P., Ed., *Article 370: Evolving Clarity beyond the Conundrum*, Mewar University Press: 2015, p. 1.

11 See Section 5 of the Constitution of Jammu and Kashmir, Law Department Codification Cell: Ranbir Government Press, Jammu.

12 The Constitution (Application to Jammu & Kashmir) Order, 1954, C.O 48.

13 Article 370 Cl.(1)(d).

14 Original Constitution of India as enforced from January 26, 1950.

15 For details, see landmark judgment of *Kesavananda Bharti Vs. State of Kerala* (1973) 4 SCC.

16 Constituent Assembly Debates Official Report, October 17, 1949; Reprint by Lok Sabha Secretariat, New Delhi: 2009.

17 White Paper on Indian States, Government of India, Ministry of States, Govt. of India Press: 1950.

18 See https://www.cia.gov/library/readingroom/document/cia-rdp79-00927a0044000 90003-4. Also see, Sheikh Abdullah: A CIA Profile, December 5, 2016. https://kashmirlife.net/sheikh-abdullah-a-cia-profile-125468/

19 Kaul, Jawaharlal and Daya Sagar, eds., *Article 35-A: Face the Facts*, Jammu Kashmir Study Centre: 2017, p. 10.

20 Roy, Tathagata, *The Life and Times of Dr. Syama Prasad Mookerjee: A Complete Biography*, Prabhat Prakashan: 2012, p. 356.

21 See Slathia, B.S., 'Constitution of India (as applicable to the State of Jammu Kashmir),' *Jay Kay Law Reporter*: 2016.

22 See Constitution of Jammu Kashmir, Fifth Schedule, Form D.

23 Report no. 183 by Department-related Parliamentary Standing Committee on Home Affairs, presented to Rajya Sabha on December 22, 2014, p. 16.

24 State of Jammu Kashmir Vs. Dr. Susheela Sawhney and others, AIR 2003 JK.

25 Ashai, Sehla, The Jammu and Kashmir State Subjects Controversy of 2004, *Drexel Law Review*, vol. 2:537, pp. 549-50. http://thejammuheight.in/wp-content/uploads/2016/06/Ashai53755.pdf

26 Sharma, Sant Kumar, *Article 370: Deceit and Fraudulent Communication*, Makhanlal Chaturvedi National University of Journalism and Communication: 2016, chapter 3.

CHAPTER NINE

J&K Accession: Some Historical and Legal Facts

Pankaj Gupta

Jammu & Kashmir (J&K) is famed for its mesmerising beauty that has drawn people through the ages, though its peace has been marred by terrorist violence in the past few decades. Some visit the state for its scenic wonders and great ancient monuments, others for its celebrated pilgrimages. Though the entire state legally belongs to India, a major portion is under the illegal occupation of Pakistan and China due to the nefarious designs of Pakistan in 1947 and later by both the countries. The original kingdom of Jammu and Kashmir shared borders with Afghanistan, Pakistan, Tajikistan (part of former USSR), China and Tibet. Before August 15, 1947, the entire state of Jammu and Kashmir was administratively divided into four distinct regions, viz., Jammu, Kashmir, Ladakh and Gilgit Provinces.[1]

Historically, Gurez Valley was part of Gilgit. But after the invasion by tribals backed by the Pakistan Army in October 1947, a major portion of Gilgit came to be illegally occupied by Pakistan. Thereafter, Gurez Valley was included in the Kashmir region for administrative convenience. This valley is spread over roughly 2,000 km^2. whereas the entire Kashmir province is spread over an estimated 16,000 km^2. The population of Gurez Valley is cent per cent converted to Islam but no terrorist or separatist activities have been reported from this region in the last seventy years. The people are ethnic Dard/ Shin and speak 'Shina'; many words are similar to Sanskrit. For instance, 'forehead' is *mastak*, 'river' is Sindhu, 'sword' is *khadag* and 'Sunday' is

Adityawar, which clearly establishes a link between ancient 'Shina' and the languages that developed in the Indian mainland. Gilgit-Baltistan is the gateway to Central Asia and Europe, the route historically taken by monks, saints and traders en route to Central Asia and Europe. Buddhism travelled to Central Asia from where news of the faith reached China and triggered the pilgrimages of countless Chinese monks to India.

Kashmir is one of the smallest segments of the state and encompasses three valleys, viz., Kashmir or Srinagar valley, Gurez valley and Lolab valley. Of these, the latter two are largely peaceful and no incident of separatism and terrorism has been reported from there; only some districts of the Kashmir valley are problematic. However, terrorism must be seen in the context of Pakistani aggression and its consequent effects on the life of the people of Jammu and Kashmir who began to be manipulated during the movement for the creation of Pakistan, though it could not then convert the majority of the people in favour of Pakistan. Jammu and Kashmir's history has mainly centred round the personalities and roles played by Sheikh Abdullah, Lord Louis Mountbatten and Jawaharlal Nehru. The Indian Independence Act, the critical role of Maharaja Hari Singh and the Instrument of Accession have not received due recognition. Even in institutions of higher education, the curriculum does not include a serious study of the Indian Independence Act and accession of the Princely States, before and after Independence. As the entire narrative regarding the problem in Jammu and Kashmir was cornered by some personalities to suit a political agenda, access to authentic information has been a challenge. For long, the account put forward by Pandit Nehru or Sheikh Abdullah was taken as the whole truth. As Sheikh Abdullah was succeeded by his son, Dr. Farooq Abdullah, and then his son, Omar Abdullah, who also became chief minister of Jammu and Kashmir, there was a strong vested interest in perpetuating myths.

Kuldip Chand Agnihotri[2] portrays Maharaja Hari Singh as a progressive ruler who took many developmental initiatives for the welfare of his subjects such as prohibition of child marriage, widow remarriage, ban on female foeticide and practice of *sati*, prohibition of prostitution and trafficking of women, promotion of education and vocational skills, independent judiciary, prohibition on smoking in public places, legislation on state subjects, minimum wages, industrialisation, extension of health services, parliamentary system of governance, local self-governance and many others.

As Partition and Independence loomed, Maharaja Hari Singh, under the influence of his prime minister, Ramchandra Kak, proposed a Standstill Agreement with India and Pakistan. Hari Singh was an avid supporter of Indian independence at the Round Table Conference in London in 1930, but later become apprehensive due to the rise of Jawaharlal Nehru and his close proximity to Sheikh Abdullah (who had launched the 'Quit Kashmir' movement against the monarch in 1946). Hari Singh was not against the accession of J&K to India. In fact, he wanted to accede to India immediately after the lapse of British paramountcy over Princely States, but Nehru's unreasoned support to Abdullah and insistence that power be transferred to the latter as a prelude to accepting the accession was the main reason why the Instrument of Accession was signed after Abdullah was released from jail and made interim prime minister of the State.[3] Mohammad Ali Jinnah accepted the Standstill Agreement but India wanted further discussions with the Maharaja. This irked Pakistan and it broke off the Standstill Agreement on August 31, 1947.

The Indian Independence Act gave legal form to the two-nation theory and created a new British dominion, namely, Pakistan. Among its various provisions, sections 2, 5 and 7 are critical to the understanding of Jammu and Kashmir's accession to India. Section 2 of the said Act divided British India into two dominions, leaving aside more than 550 small and large princely states that were governed by the British through political agents placed in the courts of the respective rulers. The fate of the princely states was to be decided by their respective rulers and they had to choose to join either of the two dominions – India or Pakistan. Section 5 concerns the provision of a Governor-General for the two dominions. Section 7 states that on the appointed day, August 15, 1947, British rule will come to an end in British India and the princely states. More importantly, Section 7 empowered the rulers of the princely states to take decisions in certain matters, wherein the legislative provisions were to be abrogated. This section mentioned that from the appointed day (August 15), the Government of the United Kingdom would have no responsibility vis-à-vis the government of any of the territories hitherto included in British India; the suzerainty of the British monarch over the Indian states lapsed along with all treaties and agreements, functions and obligations, powers, rights, authority or jurisdiction *et al.* This provision applied equally to treaties or agreements in the tribal areas, though provisions which relate to customs, transit and communications, posts and telegraphs, and such matters, shall continue until the provisions in question are denounced by the Ruler of the Indian state or a person having authority in the tribal areas on the one hand, or by the Dominion or Province concerned on the other hand, or are superseded by subsequent agreements. This section was thus explicit that the appropriate authority in the matter of princely states was the ruler and the assent of the rulers was of paramount importance in abrogation or addition of any provision relating to the said princely states. Besides, Section 6(1) of the Government of India Act (1935) through the India (Provisional Constitution) Order, 1947 clearly mentioned, "an Indian State shall be deemed to have acceded to the Dominion if the Governor General has signified his acceptance of an Instrument of Accession executed by the ruler thereof",[4] which amply clarified that the final authority in the matter of accession of the princely states were the respective rulers alone.

The Indian Independence Act was passed by the British Parliament on June 17, 1947, and received royal assent on July 18, 1947; but the fate of the princely states was largely decided on May 12, 1946, when the Memorandum on State Treaties and Paramountcy was presented to the Nawab of Bhopal and Chancellor of the Chamber of Princes in India by the Cabinet Mission.[5] There was no pre-condition for accession except the decision of the rulers, though Mountbatten did emphasise the importance of geographical contiguity to the rulers. The Mountbatten Plan of July 25, 1947, discussed the partition of India and advised the rulers of the princely states to join either of the two dominions in their own interest.[6] On July 25, 1947, Mountbatten addressed a special meeting of the Chamber of Princes and reiterated the need to use the Instrument of Accession to accede to either of the two dominions. Maharaja Hari Singh joined India through this instrument like the other princely states. This instrument was full and final, not subject to challenge and irrevocable. Sadly, these facts were not presented before the nation in this unequivocal manner and Mountbatten's mischievous interjections – unchallenged by the new government – allowed false propaganda to prevail. As a result, most of the public discourse has focused on a few personalities who added fuel to the fire.

The kingdom of Jammu and Kashmir acceded to India on October 26, 1947, when Maharaja Hari Singh signed the Instrument of Accession (IoA)[7] to the Government of India and sought help to beat back an invasion by the Pakistan Army which had begun on October 22. It was accepted by Lord Mountbatten, Governor General of India, on October 27, 1947. Thereafter, India was obligated to safeguard the territory and the lives of the people who had become its citizens. It bears reiteration that this Instrument of Accession was the standard instrument through which more than 550 princely states had acceded to India or Pakistan.[8] Later, in 1954, the Jammu and Kashmir Constituent Assembly ratified the Instrument of Accession,[9] thereby conveying the wishes of the people for complete integration with India. While accepting the accession, Lord Mountbatten asserted that the Indian Government would ascertain the wishes of the people regarding the accession of Jammu and Kashmir to India. In his letter dated October 27, 1947, he said:

> "Your Highness' letter dated 26 October has been delivered to me by Mr. V. P. Menon. In the special circumstances mentioned by Your Highness, my Government have decided to accept the accession of Kashmir State to the Dominion of India. Consistent with their policy that in the case of any State where the issue of accession has been the subject of dispute, the question of accession should be decided in accordance with the wishes of the people of the State, it is my Government's wish that as soon as law and order have been restored in Kashmir and her soil cleared of the invader the question of the State's accession should be settled by a reference to the people. Meanwhile in response to your Highness' appeal for military aid action has been taken today to send troops of the Indian Army to Kashmir to help your own forces to defend your territory and to protect the lives, property and honour of your people. My Government and I note with satisfaction that your Highness has decided to invite Sheikh Abdullah to form an interim Government to work with your prime minister".[10]

It bears stating that Lord Mountbatten's letter of October 27, 1947 had no legal sanctity as there was no pre-condition in the Accession process which enjoined the ruler to ascertain the wishes of the people before acceding to either Dominion. Moreover, at the time of the accession there was no opposition or protest against the decision of Maharaja Hari Singh. In fact, people participated in the election to the Constituent Assembly so that it could prepare the constitution of the state. Maharaja Hari Singh, in his letter dated October 26, 1947, to Lord Mountbatten, explained his reasons for not acceding to either India or Pakistan and the urgency created by the Pakistani aggression and the need for Indian intervention to save the precious lives of his subjects.[11]

Hari Singh wrote,[12]

> "I have to inform your Excellency that a grave emergency has arisen in my State and request immediate assistance of your Government.
>
> "As your Excellency is aware the State of Jammu and Kashmir has not acceded to the Dominion of India or to Pakistan. Geographically my State

is contiguous to both the Dominions. It has vital economical and cultural links with both of them. Besides, my State has a common boundary with the Soviet Republic and China. In their external relations, the Dominions of India and Pakistan cannot ignore this fact.

"I accordingly approached the Dominions of India and Pakistan to enter into Standstill Agreement with my State. The Pakistan Government accepted this Agreement. The Dominion of India desired further discussions with representatives of my Government. I could not arrange this in view of the developments indicated below. In fact, the Pakistan Government are operating Post and Telegraph system inside the State.

"Though we have got a Standstill Agreement with the Pakistan Government that Government permitted steady and increasing strangulation of supplies like food, salt and petrol to my State.

"Afridis, soldiers in plain clothes, and desperadoes with modern weapons have been allowed to infiltrate into the State, at first in Poonch and then in Sialkot and finally in mass area adjoining Hazara District on the Ramkot side. The result has been that the limited number of troops at the disposal of the State had to be dispersed and thus had to face the enemy at the several points simultaneously, that it has become difficult to stop the wanton destruction of life and property and looting. The Mahora powerhouse which supplies the electric current to the whole of Srinagar has been burnt. The number of women who have been kidnapped and raped makes my heart bleed. The wild forces thus let loose on the State are marching on with the aim of capturing Srinagar, the summer capital of my Government, as first step to over-running the whole State.

"The mass infiltration of tribesmen drawn from distant areas of the North-West Frontier coming regularly in motor trucks using Mansehra-Muzaffarabad Road and fully armed with up-to-date weapons cannot possibly be done without the knowledge of the Provisional Government of the North-West Frontier Province and the Government of Pakistan. In spite of repeated requests made by my Government, no attempt has been made to check these raiders or stop them from coming into my State. The Pakistan Radio even put out a story that a Provisional Government had been set up in Kashmir. The people of my State, both the Muslims and non-Muslims, generally have taken no part at all.

"With the conditions obtaining at present in my State and the great emergency of the situation as it exists, I have no option but to ask for help from the Indian Dominion. Naturally, they cannot send the help asked for by me without my State acceding to the Dominion of India. I have accordingly decided to do so and I attach the Instrument of Accession for acceptance by your Government. The other alternative is to leave my State and my people to free-booters. On this basis, no civilized Government can exist or be maintained. This alternative I will never allow to happen as long as I am Ruler of the State and I have life to defend my country.

"I am also to inform your Excellency's Government that it is my intention at once to set up an interim Government and ask Sheikh Abdullah to carry the responsibilities in this emergency with my Prime Minister.

"If my State has to be saved, immediate assistance must be available at Srinagar. Mr. Menon is fully aware of the situation and he will explain to you, if further explanation is needed."

Hari Singh's letter is self-explanatory and reveals Pakistan's unprovoked aggression on the kingdom. The Pakistan Army was killing innocent civilians, including Muslims, and making the life of ordinary residents of the state miserable. Accession to Pakistan was unthinkable under such circumstances There is an erroneous belief that Jammu and Kashmir being a Muslim majority region should have gone to Pakistan. Under the criteria for princely states, the rulers were empowered to decide. A pertinent example is that of Amarkot (now Umarkot) in Sindh, Pakistan, where the Hindu population was 90 per cent at the time of independence. The principality was ruled by Raja Rana Chandra Singh, a Hindu, but went to Pakistan because the Raja chose to accede to Pakistan and not to India.[13] If accession was to be settled by religious demography, then this princely state should have been part of India. Moreover, it is a mischievous obfuscation of facts that all of India was divided on communal lines and that the kingdom of Jammu and Kashmir should have gone to Pakistan because Kashmir province had a Muslim majority. Undoubtedly, religious separatism was invoked to ensure the partition of India, but religious demography did not determine the decision of the princely states to accede to India or Pakistan. Moreover, Kashmir province does not represent the entire state of Jammu and Kashmir and there was no provision in the Indian Independence Act whereby a portion of a princely state could go to one Dominion and the other portion(s) to the other Dominion.

At the time of the invasion, the tallest leaders in the State, Sheikh Abdullah from Kashmir valley, Pandit Prem Nath Dogra from Jammu and Kushok Bakula Rinpoche from Ladakh, rallied to safeguard the state. According to Agnihotri,[14] Kushok Bakula Rinpoche created an army of Ladakhi youth, the 'Nubra Guard', to fight against the Pakistani invaders. The Nubra Guard successfully defended and saved the Nubra Valley in the northeast of Ladakh valley. Participating in the debate in the United Nations Security Council (UNSC) on February 5, 1948, Sheikh Abdullah challenged Pakistan's claims before the international body regarding the State of Jammu and Kashmir, but also gave indications of a repositioning on his part vis-à-vis the Republic of India. He said

> "I have heard with patience, attention and respect the statements made by the representatives of Pakistan and members of the Security Council, as well as the statements made on various occasions by the members of my own delegation....I have heard patiently to the debate in the Security Council, but I feel that I am rather confused. After all, what is the point in dispute? The point in dispute is not that the sovereignty of the Prince is in question, as the representative of Pakistan stated yesterday.... The subject of the dispute before the Security Council is not the maladministration of the Princely State of Kashmir.... the dispute revolves around the fact that Kashmir acceded legally and constitutionally to the Dominion of India...the tribesmen across the border have poured into my country. They have been helped and are being helped by the Pakistan Government, with the result that there is the possibility of a greater conflagration between India and Pakistan. But (the representative of Pakistan) completely denied that any support was being given by the Government of Pakistan to either the tribesmen or those who are in revolt within the State against the constituted authority....
>
> "Today Pakistan has become the champion of our liberty. I know very well that in 1946, when I raised the cry of 'Quit Kashmir', the leader of the Pakistan Government, who is the Governor-General now, Mr. Mohammad Ali Jinnah, opposed my movement, declaring that this movement was a movement of a few renegades and that Muslims as such had nothing to do with the movement. The Muslim Conference, which has been talked about so much, opposed my movement and declared its loyalty to the Prince. The representative of Pakistan now says that Sheikh Abdullah, once the supporter of 'Quit Kashmir', has joined hands with the Maharaja of Kashmir...But the State of Jammu and Kashmir, and its people, kept calm...Why was that so? It was because I and my organisation never believed in the formula that Muslims and Hindus form separate nations. We do not believe in the two-nation theory nor in communal hatred or communalism itself. We believed that religion had no place in politics. Therefore, when we launched our movement of 'Quit Kashmir' it was not only Muslims who suffered, but our Hindu and Sikh comrades as well...The situation was worsening day by day and the minority in our State was feeling very nervous.
>
> "Some friends from Pakistan met me in Srinagar. I had a heart-to-heart discussion with them and explained my point of view... While I was engaged in these conversations and negotiations with friends from Pakistan, I sent

one of my colleagues to Lahore, where he met the Prime Minister of Pakistan, Mr. Liaquat Ali Khan and other high dignitaries of the West Punjab Government. He placed the same point of view before them and requested that they should allow us time to consider this vital question, first helping us to achieve our liberation instead of forcing us to declare our decision one way or the other.

"Then, one fine morning, while these negotiations were proceeding, I received news that a full-fledged attack had been carried out by the raiders on Muzaffarabad, frontier town in the Kashmir Province...While the raiders came to our land, massacred thousands of people – mostly Hindus and Sikhs, but Muslims too – abducted thousands of girls, Hindu, Sikh and Muslim alike, looted our property and almost reached the gates of our summer capital, Srinagar, the result was that the civil, military and police administration failed. How Pakistan wanted to force this position of slavery upon us? Pakistan had no interest in our liberation or it would not have opposed our freedom movement....

"We realized that Pakistan would not allow us any time, that we had either to suffer the fate of our kith and kin of Muzaffarabad, Baramulla, Srinagar and other towns and villages, or to seek help from some outside authority.

"Under those circumstances, both the Maharaja and the people of Kashmir requested the Government of India to accept our accession.

"The Security Council should not confuse the issue. The question is not that we want internal freedom; the question is not how the Maharaja got his State, or whether or not he is sovereign. These points are not before the Security Council. Whether Kashmir has lawfully acceded to India – complaints on that score have been brought before the Security Council on behalf of Pakistan – is not the point at issue. If that were the point at issue then we should discuss that subject. We should prove before the Security Council that Kashmir and the people of Kashmir have lawfully and constitutionally acceded to the Dominion of India, and Pakistan has no right to question that accession...'[15]

The UN Security Council acknowledged that the entire State of Jammu and Kashmir belonged to India, but did not take any strong action to free the part held by Pakistani intruders because of covert lobbying by the Western powers in favour of Pakistan, which was needed in the context of the emerging Cold War. This was compounded by the Indian Government's neglect of Maharaja Hari Singh who was the more appropriate candidate to represent the Indian Government at the UNSC. Hari Singh conveyed his unhappiness regarding the Pakistani aggression against his erstwhile kingdom to Deputy Prime

Minister Sardar Vallabhbhai Patel through a letter dated January 31, 1948. In this letter, the Maharaja lamented,

> "The military situation as you know has been quite depressing since the arrival of Indian troops. Except the first gains in the Kashmir Valley there has been a debit balance throughout so far as achievements are concerned. The Indian troops arrived in the Valley on 27 October. At that time we were in possession of about 3/4ths of Poonch and the whole of Mirpur district. We had by then lost only small bits of Poonch and Muzaffarabad district. After the recapture of Baramulla and Uri, there has been a standstill. Two months have passed and the Indian troops are still at Uri. They attempted a venture to the town of Poonch and though they reached it, it was at great cost and the road was eventually lost. In the Poonch Jagir which was held by the State troops, inch by inch we had to withdraw and eventually lost the whole of the Jagir except the town itself where about 40,000 people are besieged along with 4 battalions (3 State and 1 Indian). The situation is by no means satisfactory.
>
> "I may mention that in the August disturbances, with two battalions of the State troops we cleared the whole of the Poonch Jagir, peace was restored, the whole of the revenue was realised and the Administration was functioning normally. It was only in the second week of October that trouble again began in Poonch and our troops resisted it till about the end of December. But as no help was given they had eventually to fall back on Poonch town. If the Indian troops had ventured forward along with the State troops in Poonch, there would have been no difficulty in clearing that area of the raiders. I feel that the Indian military advisers take an exaggerated view about the difficulty of fighting in Poonch. I know some of that area myself and as a soldier can say that it is not difficult to clear Poonch of the raiders in the course of a fortnight or so if a strong military venture (with modern weapons and equipment) is undertaken, but they would have to act mercilessly and not leniently.
>
> "In Mirpur district at the time when the Indian forces arrived we were still holding Mangla and our territory along the Jhelum Canal bank, but during the last two months we have lost Mangla, Alibeg, Gurdwara and the town of Mirpur, the town of Bhimber and the villages of Deva and Battala, the town of Rajouri and the whole of the area adjoining Chhamb and Noshera. Jhangar, a key-place both for Mirpur and Kotli, was lost after a defeat. These defeats have been a heavy blow to us and undermined the prestige of the Indian forces. Not a single town has so far been recovered by the Indian troops. The people judge an army from results and not from propaganda carried on about it. On the Kathua-Sialkot border attacks have intensified. Every day there is one raid or another. A number of villages have been

burnt, people have been looted, women abducted and there have been killings also. The result is that all the border villages have been vacated and we have about 70,000 to 80,000 refugees in the city of Jammu. Crops, houses and valuables have been lost. Most of the people are also now vacating Jammu and its suburbs and are going to East Punjab. The situation, therefore, is worsening every day.

"The name of the Indian Army is getting into the mud in spite of its brilliant record. I was a member of the War Cabinet. I travelled in war zones during the Great War. The name of the Indian Army was at its highest pitch and it pains me to see that the name of that Army has become a topic of every tongue during these days and it is daily losing prestige...Since your departure, nothing has been done and as I have said, we had more serious attacks. The effort on the part of Pakistan is gaining ground every day. Their morale owing to success is going up. They loot property, they take away cattle and women and when they go back to Pakistan they incite people and tell them how much loot and what benefits there are to raid our territory. On the other hand, our morale is rapidly going down....

"Apart from the military situation the reference to the UNO and the proceedings that are hanging fire there are causing great uncertainty and perplexity not only to me but to every Hindu and Sikh in the State as well as to those who belong to the National Conference. The feeling is strongly gaining ground that the UN Security Council will take an adverse decision and that the State will eventually have to accede to Pakistan as a result of what the Security Council will decide. The Hindus and Sikhs have therefore started going away from the State as they anticipate that their fate as a result of the UNO decision will be the same as what happened in West Punjab and therefore it is much better to clear out of the State before that eventuality arises. The National Conference leaders also feel that they may eventually be let down by accepting the decision of the Security Council and that would be disastrous for them.

"My position in this matter is also precarious. You know I definitely acceded to the Indian Union with the idea that the Union will not let us down and the State would remain acceded to the Union and my position and that of my dynasty would remain secure. It was for this reason that I accepted the advice of the Indian Union in the matter of internal administration. If we have to go to Pakistan it was wholly unnecessary to accede to India or to mould the internal administration according to the desire of the Indian Union. I feel that the internal administration or the question of accession is wholly foreign to the jurisdiction of the Security Council. The Indian Union only referred a limited question to the Security Council, but the whole issue has been enlarged and not only the matter of aggression by one

> Dominion over the other is being considered by the Security Council but internal questions of the formation of Interim Government and the matter of accession have all been taken notice of by them. It was a wrong step in going on the limited issue to the Security Council and then agreeing to the enlargement of the agenda before that Council....
>
> "I am prepared to take over command of my own forces along with the forces of the Indian Army as volunteers to help the State. I am prepared to lead my Army personally and to command, if the Indian Union agrees, also their troops. It would certainly hearten my people and the troops. I know my country much better than any of your generals will know it even during the next several months or years and I am prepared to take the venture boldly rather than merely keep on sitting here doing nothing...I am prepared to be a constitutional Ruler of the State and when a new constitution is framed I am quite willing to give responsible Government, but I am not prepared to go beyond the Mysore model because I am not satisfied that the leaders of the National Conference are for the time being very fit administrators or command the confidence of the Hindus and Sikhs and even of a large section of the Muslims. I must therefore keep certain reserved powers of which you are already aware and I must have a Dewan of my free choice as a member of the Cabinet and possibly as President...What should have been done and achieved a month before can still be achieved during the next month, but if matters are delayed and if owing to the UNO reference and the attitude of compromise the situation remains at a standstill it would become terribly grave after the expiry of a month".[16]

Hari Singh was well informed about the developments in the State and was deeply pained at the loss of Mangla Valley, Alibeg, Gurudwara, Mirpur, Bhimber, Devi and Kotli within just two months. He had deep anxiety that the UNSC would give a biased decree in favour of Pakistan, which would make it difficult for Hindus and Sikhs to live in the state. In the same letter, he observed that the National Conference did not have the confidence of Hindus, Sikhs and a large chunk of Muslim subjects. Expressing grief and frustration over the bloodbath, he wanted to be allowed to lead the battle against the enemy and urged greater efforts to vacate the regions occupied by the invaders. Areas particularly affected by the bloodbath included Bhimber, Kotli, Mirpur, Muzzaffarabad and Rajouri, where thousands of men, women and children were murdered in a single day.

Under UN pressure, on January 1, 1949, the Indian Government declared a ceasefire, leaving around 85,000 km^2 of territory with the Pakistan Army. Decades later, on February 22, 1994 the Indian Parliament passed a unanimous resolution affirming that Pakistan Occupied Jammu and Kashmir and China Occupied Jammu and Kashmir are integral parts of India, which would be taken back someday and no government could compromise on this issue.[17] Pakistan is thus in possession of Gilgit, Skardu, Diamir, Mirpur, Muzzaffarabad and part of Poonch; China occupied Aksai Chin in 1962 and approximately 5,100 km^2 of Shaksgam valley was given to China by Pakistan in 1963, though Pakistan was not competent to do so as per the Instrument of Accession, which was executed in favour of India.

India went to the UNSC to appeal against the Pakistani aggression in J&K, and the UN implicitly accepted the validity of the Accession when it ruled that Pakistan should vacate its forces from the territory of Jammu and Kashmir. The UNSC resolution of April 21, 1948 (S/726 stated, "The Government of Pakistan should undertake to use its best endeavours to secure the withdrawal from the State of Jammu and Kashmir of tribesmen and Pakistani nationals not normally resident therein who have entered the State for the purpose of fighting, and to prevent any intrusion into the State such elements and any furnishing of material aid to those fighting in the State".[18]

Sheikh Abdullah endorsed the accession of Jammu and Kashmir to India in his speech at the UNSC on February 5, 1948, and in the State Constituent Assembly on November 5, 1951. On the latter occasion, he said:

> "The most powerful argument which can be advanced in her favour is that Pakistan is a Muslim State, and a big majority of our people being Muslim the State must accede to Pakistan. This claim of being a Muslim state is of course only a camouflage. It is a screen to dupe the common man, so that he may not see clearly that Pakistan is a feudal State in which a clique is trying by these methods to maintain itself in power. In addition, the appeal to religion constitutes a sentimental and a wrong approach to the question. Sentiment has its own place in life, but often it leads to irrational action. Some argue, supposedly natural corollary to this, that on our acceding to Pakistan, our annihilation or survival depends. Facts have disproved this; right thinking men would point out that Pakistan is not an organic unity of all the Muslims in this subcontinent. It has, on the contrary, caused dispersion of the Indian Muslims for whose benefit it was claimed to have been created.
>
> "There are two Pakistans at least a thousand miles apart from each other. The total population of western Pakistan which is contiguous to our State is hardly 25 million, while the total number of Muslims resident in India is as many as 40 million. As one Muslim is as good as another, the Kashmiri

> Muslims, if they are worried by such considerations, should choose the 40 million living in India. Looking at the matter too from a more modern political angle, religious affinities alone do not and should not normally determine the political alliances of State. We do not find a Christian bloc, a Buddhist bloc or even a Muslim bloc, about which there is so much talk now-a-days in Pakistan. These days, economic interests and a community of political ideals influence the policies of state more appropriately …
>
> "Our weakness was exploited by the neighbours with whom we had a valid Standstill Agreement. The State was invaded. What is the guarantee that in future too we may not be victims of a similar aggression?"[19]

In this speech, Abdullah categorically asserted that he wanted the State of Jammu and Kashmir to accede to India and not to the Muslim majority country, i.e., Pakistan, and that he did not believe in the two-nation theory. He lamented the massacre of residents of the State and was ready to justify the accession to India. In his speech before the UNSC, he spoke of the common wish of the Maharaja and the people of the State to accede to India. He even said that the Prime Minister of India showed his gesture of gratitude when he said that 'India does not want to take advantage of the difficult situation in Kashmir' but will seek the ratification of the people of the State once it is freed from Pakistani invaders.

The issue of plebiscite has long bedevilled discussions on the topic of Jammu and Kashmir. Here again we may refer to the Indian Independence Act, 1947, that only the ruler had the authority to decide which Dominion he wanted to accede to; there was no clause for a plebiscite. Mountbatten conveyed as much to all the Princes, barring Jammu and Kashmir, where he clearly had a vested interest in compelling it to join Pakistan. This is why he raised the bogey of plebiscite in the case of Jammu and Kashmir; Nehru fell into the trap. Even then the Government of India said in the United Nations that it was ready for a plebiscite provided that the conditions stipulated by the UN were fulfilled, viz., ceasefire and withdrawal of Pakistani intruders from the soil of the state. This never happened and as the UN made no move to help vacate the territory of the State of the invaders, a stalemate developed that persists to this day.

On January 23, 1957, V.K. Krishna Menon, India's representative to the UN, emphasised before the Security Council that Jammu and Kashmir including Pakistan Occupied Jammu and Kashmir (PoJK) belonged to India alone. He said, "The Government of India request the Security Council to call upon Pakistan to put an end immediately to the giving of such assistance immediately, on 1 January 1948, and today we are nine years away from it, which is an act of aggression against India. I shall quote these words more than once before I have concluded, in order to discharge my responsibility as the representative of my Government: ...which is an act of aggression against India.... I repeat this point, to which we shall come back again and again, that it must be planted firmly in your minds that the issue is aggression. The issue is invasion; it is a violation of territory. It is not necessary for me to prove the unquestioned sovereignty of India in regard to Kashmir.... The Security Council regards this as a dispute. It is not a dispute for territory. There is only one problem before you – whether you will face it or not, and if you do not face it, I say with great respect it is a matter between yourselves and the instructed judgement of your governments – and that problem is the problem of aggression".[20]

Article 370

The Constitution of India mentions Article 370 as a temporary provision.[21] As per Schedule 1 of the Indian Constitution, Jammu and Kashmir is the fifteenth state of India and Article 370 is a temporary and most controversial Article in the Constitution. Dr. Bhimrao Ramji Ambedkar, chairman of the Drafting Committee, was vehemently opposed to this article and refused to draft it, after which the task was assigned to Gopalaswami Ayyangar, a former *diwan* (prime minister) of Jammu and Kashmir (1937-43) and member of the Drafting Committee. That Ambedkar drafted all provisions barring Article 370 shows it was imposed with ulterior motives. Article 370 provided two types of arrangements with the State of Jammu and Kashmir. The first is related to those matters that are listed in the Union List and Concurrent List and correspond to matters specified in the Instrument of Accession, where only consultation with the State government is required. The second arrangement was that no law passed by the Parliament of India could be applied to the State of Jammu and Kashmir unless the Legislative Assembly of the State passed a concurring legislation; this included the social justice provisions. As a result, the Fundamental Rights enshrined in the Constitution of India are not available to citizens residing in the State.

Pradeep K. Sharma notes that the differences between Ambedkar and Prime Minister Nehru burst into the open when the former tendered his resignation as Union Law Minister on September 28, 1951, impugning the Congress policy on Kashmir as one of the reasons for quitting.[22] The first draft of the Constitution did not have any temporary and transitional provision. Ambedkar rebuffed suggestions by Sheikh Abdullah to permit residents of the State to receive benefits at par with other citizens of India while residents of the rest of India would be denied the same benefits in Jammu and Kashmir, and said he could not betray his country in this manner. This resulted in the backdoor entry of Gopalaswami Ayyangar, a Minister without portfolio in the Cabinet, to create the controversial Article 370 at the behest of Jawaharlal Nehru and Sheikh Abdullah. Any discussion on Jammu and Kashmir must consider these historical facts. Yet, the legislative provisions of the Indian Independence Act in relation to J&K have never been adequately discussed in the public arena, which has made it virtually impossible to separate the wheat from the chaff. While India runs according to the Constitution and laws framed by Parliament and State legislatures, J&K runs according to the whims of its political class. They have suppressed much relevant material in the public discourse within the State.

Important Provisions of the Constitution of J&K

Jammu and Kashmir is an integral part of India and its separation from India is impossible, as it is embedded in the Constitution of the State. The Preamble of the Jammu and Kashmir Constitution states,

> WE, THE PEOPLE OF THE STATE OF JAMMU AND KASHMIR, having solemnly resolved, in pursuance of the accession of this State to India which took place on the twenty-sixth day of October, 1947 to further define the existing relationship of the State with the Union of India as an integral part thereof, and to secure to ourselves – JUSTICE, social, economic and political; LIBERTY of thought, expression, belief, faith and worship; EQUALITY of status and of opportunity; and to promote among us all; FRATERNITY assuring the dignity of the individual and the unity of the Nation; IN OUR CONSTITUENT ASSEMBLY This seventeenth day of November, 1956 do hereby ADOPT ENACT AND GIVE TO OURSELVES THIS CONSTITUTION.

Article 3 of the Jammu and Kashmir Constitution states "The State of Jammu and Kashmir is and shall be an integral part of the Union of India." Article 5 mentions "The executive and legislative power of the State extends to all matters except those with respect to which Parliament has power to make laws for the State under the provisions of the Constitution of India".

Article 147 "An amendment of this Constitution may be initiated only by the introduction of a Bill for the purpose in the Legislative Assembly and when the Bill is passed in each House by a majority of not less than two thirds of the total membership of that House, it shall be presented to the Governor for his assent and, upon such assent being given to the Bill, the Constitution shall stand amended in accordance with the terms of the Bill:

Provided that a Bill providing for the abolition of the Legislative Council may be introduced in the Legislative Assembly and passed by it by a majority of the total membership of Assembly and by a majority of not less than two-thirds of the members of the Assembly present and voting:

Provided further that no Bill or amendment seeking to make any change in:

(a) this section; or
(b) the provisions of sections 3 and 5; or
(c) the provisions of the Constitution of India as applicable, in relation to the State, shall be introduced or moved in either House of the Legislature".

It is thus evident that the Constitution of Jammu and Kashmir is explicit that separation of the State from India is impossible. It is therefore strange that the mainstream media has been perpetuating fallacies and has not made serious efforts to dispel the misinformation and confusion in this regard among ordinary citizens of the country, including residents of Jammu and Kashmir. The Accession of Jammu and Kashmir was a milestone in the history of independent India and Indians should be proud of it. Unfortunately, the discourse is held captive to disturbances in five districts of Kashmir Valley, namely, Srinagar, Baramullah, Anantnag, Shopian and Pulwama, where incidents of violence and stone-pelting against security forces have taken place, even as Jammu and Ladakh have remained largely peaceful. Moreover, the Gujjars, Shias, Pahadis, nationalist Muslims, Kashmiri Sikhs, Pandits, Ladakhis, Dogras and Buddhists have never joined any demand for separation of Jammu and Kashmir from India. It is therefore logical to conclude that the majority population of Jammu and Kashmir desires to remain with India and that Maharaja Hari Singh reflected the wishes and best interests of his subjects when he signed the Instrument of Accession to India. This was ratified by the State Constituent Assembly in 1954. There is no rationale for reopening a settled chapter of history.

NOTES

1 For details, see verdict on Gilgit and Baltistan (Northern Areas), High Court of Judicature Azad Jammu and Kashmir, March 08, 1993, p. 4.

2 Agnihotri, Kuldip Chand, *Jammu Kashmir ke Jannayak: Maharaja Hari Singh*, Delhi: Prabhat Prakashan: 2016.

3 The Chief Minister of State of Jammu and Kashmir was called Prime Minister. For details, refer Hakeem, Abdul, *Paradise on Fire: Syed Ali Geelani and the Struggle for Freedom in Kashmir*, United Kingdom: Revival Publications: 2014.

4 For details, refer Jain, M. P., *Indian Constitutional Law, 2003*, (Fifth Ed), vol. 2, Maharashtra: Wadhwa, Nagpur.

5 For details, refer, 'Legal Documents on Jammu and Kashmir,' Jammu & Kashmir Study Centre, Delhi: 2016.

6 For details, refer Dutt, R.P., 'The Mountbatten Plan for India.' *Labour Monthly*, July 1947, pp. 210-219. https://www.marxists.org/history/international/comintern/sections/britain/periodicals/labour_monthly/1947/07/1947-07-india.htm (accessed Jan 15, 2019)

7 Instrument of Accession (1947a). Jammu & Kashmir State: Instrument of accession and standstill agreement signed by Shriman Inder Mahander Rajrajeswar Maharajadhiraj Shri Hari Singh, ruler of Jammu and Kashmir, Naresh Tatha Tibbetadi Deshadhipathi, Ruler of Jammu and Kashmir. F. No. B-II/1/47, Home Department, Government of India.

8 For details, refer 'White Paper on Indian States' (1950), Ministry of States, Government of India. New Delhi: Govt. of India Press.

9 For details, refer Athar, G.M., 'The instrument of accession: Issue of authenticity, legitimacy and validity,' 2016, (accessed Jan 15, 2019), http://brighterkashmir.com/the-instrument-of-accessionissue-of-authenticitylegitimacy-and-validity/

10 For details, see text of Lord Mountbatten's letter dated October 27, 1947 (accessed Jan 15, 2019). https://www.mtholyoke.edu/acad/intrel/kasmount.htm

11 For details, see Sagar, Daya, *Jammu & Kashmir: A Victim of Personal Ambitions of some and Mishandling by the core Indian Leadership*, Delhi: Ocean Paperbacks: 2015, p. 63.

12 For details refer Government of India Publication, October 26, 1947. http://www.jammu-kashmir.com/documents/harisingh47.html (accessed Jan 15, 2019)

13 For details, see *The Myth of Kashmir Problem*, Jammu & Kashmir Study Centre, Delhi, 2016.

14 For details, see Agnihotri, Kuldip Chand, op. cit.

15 See Excerpts of Sheikh Abdullah's February 5, 1948 speech in the UN Security Council, (accessed Jan 15, 2019). http://www.satp.org/satporgtp/countries/india/states/jandk/documents/papers/excerpts_of_sheikh_abdullah%27s_february_5_1948_speech.htm

16 Letter from Maharaja Hari Singh to Sardar Patel, January 31, 1948. http://www.claudearpi.net/wp-content/uploads/2016/12/1948-01-31-Maharaja-to-Patel.pdf (accessed Jan 15, 2019)

17 For details, see Teng, M. K., Bhatt, R.K.K. & Kaul, Santosh, *Kashmir Constitutional History and Documents*, Delhi: Light & Life Publishers: 1977.

18 United Nation Security Council 47 (1948) of 21 April 1948 (S/726), (accessed Jan 15, 2019). http://www.un.org/en/ga/search/view_doc.asp?symbol=S/RES/47(1948)

19 For details, see Jammu and Kashmir Constituent Assembly Debate, Part I, First Volume, (1951-1955), (accessed Jan 15, 2019). http://jklegislativeassembly.nic.in/debates/debate%20Part%20I.pdf

20 For details, see United Nations Security Council (1957). 762nd, 763rd and 764th meeting: 23 -24 January, 1957 held in New York. S/PV.762, 763 and 764, http://ask.un.org/faq/37127 (accessed Jan. 15, 2019).

21 Constitution of India, Article 370.

22 See Sharma, P. K. (2016). 'Article 370: Why can't we at least debate its pros and cons?' *International Journal for Social Studies*, 2(5), pp. 1-6.

CHAPTER TEN

Hari Singh: Exiled King of Jammu and Kashmir

Yashraj Singh Bundela

Maharaja Hari Singh was a heroic and tragic personality whose role and contributions to nation building have been deliberately eclipsed and erased by the leadership of newly-independent India and the academic establishment that vigorously defended that political edifice for several decades thereafter. Historians of the post-independence era have generally portrayed him as a weak, confused, selfish and incompetent ruler, who could not administer his state efficiently and whose subjects were mostly unhappy with his rule. Some went to the extent of painting him as a communal ruler who did not care for the well-being of his Muslim subjects; some tried to tar him as a pawn of British paramountcy. However, a very different picture emerges when we examine facts culled from long-ignored chronicles. Some important pages from the history of Jammu and Kashmir were intentionally expunged or distorted to put the burden of responsibility for what went awry in the land of the Tawi, the Chinar and the Lama, on the shoulders of the person who was least responsible and was in fact its greatest victim.

Hari Singh was caught in a pincer between the communal leadership of Sheikh Mohammad Abdullah, an alumna of Aligarh Muslim University who wore the guise of a social reformist and had earned popularity as a powerful orator, and the imperial power represented by Lord Louis Mountbatten, last Viceroy of India, who played a key role in the unfolding events, guiding Jawaharlal Nehru, who trusted him more than he trusted his own cabinet colleagues. Trapped between these crafty personalities, and having been compelled to surrender his powers for the good of his besieged people, the lonely king was swiftly consigned to oblivion. And history was written by the victors. Yet, under Hari Singh's leadership, the State of J&K was miles ahead of regions run by the British Crown. Other princely states like Baroda, Mysore, Travancore, etc., were also far ahead of the Raj. Maharaja Hari Singh understood his State in terms of its geography, social structure and people's psychology; that was the reason why he wished to participate in the Indian Army's strategies and even volunteered to lead the troops in the battlefield to save his people from the atrocities unleashed by the regular troops of the Pakistani Army along with the tribal raiders in the 1947 War. Sadly, the rise of powers inimical to him, in Delhi and in the Valley, ruled this out. Sardar Vallabhbhai Patel was of the view that after the accession, the Maharaja's influence should be utilised to streamline the administrative framework in the State on the lines of other princely states, but his advice was ignored.[1] With hindsight, it would seem that the greatest mistake committed by the Congress leadership's handling of the J&K issue was that Nehru put all his eggs in the basket of Sheikh Abdullah to the detriment of the Maharaja, who could have galvanised a powerful response to the Pakistani aggression at that critical time.

Family Background

The ancestors of Maharaja Hari Singh hailed from the village of Ramgarh, situated 20 kilometres west of Jammu on the India-Pakistan border. His great grandfather, Gulab Singh, who lived in Ramgarh with his brothers Dhyan Singh and Sachet Singh, came into the limelight when, in 1808, under the command of Bhai Hukum Singh, the army of Maharaja Ranjit Singh marched towards Jammu, then ruled by Maharaja Jeet Singh. The latter decided to fight against the invading army to safeguard Jammu. Gulab Singh was just 17 years old at the time. Though the army of Jeet Singh was routed, Gulab Singh impressed all including Hukum Singh with his exemplary valour on the battlefield. After the battle, Gulab Singh and his brothers, Dhyan Singh and Sachet Singh, moved towards the Punjab and joined the Army of Maharaja Ranjit Singh in 1809.[2]

In 1816, Maharaja Ranjit Singh merged the *jagir* of Jammu in his territory. In 1819, he further expanded his territories by expelling the Afghans from Kashmir region; in this expedition, he was accompanied by Gulab Singh who displayed extraordinary ability. In 1820, Ranjit Singh appointed Raja Kishore

Singh as Governor of Jammu, but after the latter's demise in 1822, he rewarded Gulab Singh and appointed him as Governor of Jammu with the title of Raja. Gulab Singh's brothers were gifted the *jagir* of Ramnagar. Subsequently, Raja Gulab Singh was also recognised by Jeet Singh, the deposed Maharaja of Jammu. Thereafter, the ambitious armies of Gulab Singh under the command of General Zorawar Singh conquered Ladakh, Gilgit, Baltistan, Zanskar and Skardu. Kashmir was already under Ranjit Singh, who had appointed a Governor there. However, after the death of Ranjit Singh in 1839, infighting in the Lahore Darbar led to the murder of Gulab Singh's brothers and their sons, though Gulab Singh managed to escape from Lahore and reach Jammu safely.

After the Anglo-Sikh War, Gulab Singh negotiated the peace between the Lahore Darbar and the British East India Company. The Treaty of Amritsar, 1846, gave control of Jammu and Kashmir region to Maharaja Gulab Singh in return for a war indemnity of Rs. 75,00,000 (Rs seventy five lakh) which the Lahore Darbar was unable to pay.[3] Under the treaty, Kashmir officially belonged to the East India Company, but actual control was with the Subedar of Lahore Darbar, Sheikh Imam-ud-din, who refused to vacate his control even after the treaty. Subsequently, Maharaja Gulab Singh's army defeated Sheikh Imam-ud-din with the help of the Lahore Darbar, and thus the whole State of Jammu and Kashmir came under the control of Maharaja Gulab Singh. On February 8, 1856, due to ill health, Gulab Singh stepped down from the throne in favour of his son, Ranbir Singh; he passed away on August 2, 1857.[4]

Maharaja Gulab Singh's control over Jammu and Kashmir has great significance with regard to its integration with India in 1947. If the State had become part of British India in 1846 or annexed with the Punjab in 1849, the percentage of Muslims in Punjab (including J&K) would have totalled 55 per cent and all of Punjab (including J&K) would have gone to Pakistan, as it would have been a Muslim-majority area in terms of the policy mooted by the British for the partition of India.

After Ranbir Singh, his son Pratap Singh became the Maharaja. Pratap Singh did not have any son and his brother, Amar Singh, passed away during his lifetime (1909). Therefore, Amar Singh's son, Hari Singh, was declared successor to the throne; he became Maharaja in 1925. Hari Singh was born on September 23, 1895. His early school education was at Mayo College, Ajmer, after which he was sent to Imperial Cadet Corps, Dehradun, for military training. In 1918, he was designated as Commander-in-Chief of the State Armed Forces and in the same year, he was given the title of Raja, confirming him as successor to the throne. The British Government conferred upon him the designation of Captain as per the then existing norms. In 1922, he was made senior member in the State Council. After the demise of Pratap Singh in 1925, he became the Maharaja of Jammu and Kashmir and soon thereafter, in 1926, the British Government conferred upon him the honorary rank of Colonel.[5]

Hari Singh and the Raj

Being a border state sharing boundaries with the erstwhile USSR, Afghanistan, China and Tibet, the British kept a close eye on J&K and tried to take administrative control over the State, but were impeded by the Amritsar and Lahore Treaties. The British Government in fact conspired to take control of the state from Maharaja Pratap Singh but did not fully succeed, though they managed to ensconce a Resident who constantly interfered in the internal affairs of the state. When the British realized that Hari Singh was going to be the heir to the throne, they tried to dispute his succession on the ground that he was not a direct descendant of Maharaja Pratap Singh, but the plot failed due to the provisions of the Treaty of Amritsar.

Hari Singh's character can be gauged from the report written by J.B. Wood, British Resident in Srinagar, to the Secretary of the Political and Foreign Department on January 22, 1926:

> "In the recent past it has happened for the first time that the State of Jammu and Kashmir is seen as a well organized State, and the ruler who is ruling the State has got all the power.... The Administration of the State is in much better condition than that of many other Princely States. There is no doubt about the fact that Maharaja is intelligent and he has got ability to do work. He is influential amongst the people and he has got the ability to determine the course of this important border State."[6]

In another letter to the Secretary of the Political and Foreign Department, Wood wrote:

> "Though it will not be appropriate to reach to any final conclusion about Maharaja Hari Singh, but there is no doubt about the fact that before the death of Maharaja Pratap Singh, Maharaja Hari Singh has served as the senior member of the State Council for foreign affairs and there he left permanent impression of his administrative abilities".[7]

Hari Singh resented British control and strove to disempower the British agents in his realm. The kingdom had a practice of taking the winter capital to Jammu. On one occasion when the Darbar moved from Srinagar to Jammu, Hari Singh protested when the Resident also moved and conveyed to him that if he could not handle the cold weather of Srinagar, he might like to move to Sialkot in neighbouring Punjab instead. On various occasions, Hari Singh refused the Resident permission to use the hunting lodge for his guests and refused permission to provide cars from his transport department.[8] He believed the relationship of the princely states was directly with the British Crown and therefore the interference of any British official (who was subordinate in status to the Maharaja) in the internal administration of the State was unwarranted and detrimental to the position of the princely states; hence he maintained a firm hold on the kingdom's internal administration.[9]

Hari Singh was uncomfortable with the agents appointed by the political department of the British Government; he urged them to remove their agents from Gilgit Agency.[10] Russia's growing presence in Central Asia forced London to keep close watch on developments in the region. The Agent for the northern areas, Col. John Biddulph, established Gilgit Agency in 1877 and was appointed officer on special duty. Gilgit Agency included Chilas, Gilgit, Yasin, Ghizr, Iskoman, Humza and Nagar Valley; the region remained part of J&K State. London attempted to get Gilgit Agency made part of British India (under the Crown), but failed. On July 20, 1881, the post of officer on special duty in Gilgit Agency was abolished and Col. Biddulph recalled, but the struggle for control of Gilgit region continued and became intense after the demise of Maharaja Ranbir Singh and the office of Resident Commissioner in Srinagar was established without even informing Maharaja Pratap Singh. The aim was to somehow take control of the State, for which many plots were hatched. On one occasion, Pratap Singh was falsely accused of establishing ties with the Russians, but the ruse was exposed by the newspaper, *Amrit Bazar Patrika*, with a report under the title '*Condemned Unheard*'. The story reverberated in the British Parliament and Maharaja Pratap Singh could not be removed for conspiring with Russia In 1885, the British sent William Lockhart to Gilgit to conduct scientific geo-strategic mapping of the region and on his recommendation sent Col. Algernon Durand to strengthen British control over Gilgit Agency. London ultimately managed to get Gilgit Agency on lease for 60 years in 1935, though the Maharaja remained sovereign; it was returned on August 1, 1947, prior to independence.

FIRST ROUND TABLE CONFERENCE

Maharaja Hari Singh's role at the first Round Table Conference in London in 1930 shows that far from being weak and incompetent, he was a bold, intelligent and strong leader with an overwhelming patriotic sentiment. The Round Table Conference was organised by the British to discuss Indian independence with various stakeholders and overcome the inadequacy of the Simon Commission Report. The Congress did not participate as Gandhi had launched a Civil Disobedience Movement and many leaders were in jail, but representatives of the Muslim League, Hindu Mahasabha and Princely States were present. Hari Singh was invited as representative of the Chamber of Princes. London's strategy was to deny any claims regarding independence and unification of the whole of India into one federation without taking the blame for it by asserting that the British Government had a duty to take care of the interests of the princely states and conveying that the latter were against the idea of independence as detrimental to their (princely) interests. This task was to be performed by Sir Samuel Hoare, Secretary of State for India. Hari Singh foiled the plan to make the princely states the scapegoat when he delivered two bold and fiery speeches and shook the foundations of the Raj. He created a flutter when he said that the princely states would join an "All India Federation". Moreover, while replying to the inaugural address by the King Emperor, George V, he pleaded for equality of status for Indians in the British Commonwealth. Hari Singh said:

> ...This is the first occasion on which the Princes of India meet in person at a conference table along with the representatives of British India and his Majesty's Government to discuss the political future of India........
>
> ...As Indians and loyal to the land where we derive our birth and infant nurture, we stand as solidly as the rest of our countrymen for our land's enjoyment of a position of honour and equality in the British Common Wealth of Nations...
>
> Neither England nor India can afford to see this conference in failure. The task confronting this Conference is a gigantic one. Two years ago, speaking at a conference of Chamber of Princes, I said, with regard to certain activities in British India, that in my view, federation was a higher ideal than isolation. I feel deeply gratified at the progress which has been made with the scheme of an All-India Federation as worked out in this conference, some surprise has been expressed in various quarters in India and in England at the willingness of the princes to join an All-India Federation. It is said that the princes have forced the pace and that in any case they should have opposed

> a federation with British India.... I have never disguised from my friends, my warm support of the idea of an All-India Federation....
>
> To British India, Federation ensures unity of our country and prevents the hopeless splitting up of our Motherland into two distinct political entities working in watertight compartments... To the people and governments of our States, federation must make a very particular appeal, as it ensures to us that voice in matters of common concern which we have been working for, for a long time, and in absence of which the fiscal and economic interest and development of our States and of our people would have been seriously jeopardized...
>
> ......Lastly, it would not be unreasonable attitude to adopt that until the question, which are at present forming the basis of our negotiations with His Excellency the Viceroy and his Majesty's Government, are put on a mutually satisfactory basis, namely, those relating to Paramountcy and personal dynastic issues, it would be difficult to express agreement to enter an All India Federation. But, with all these details and considerations present in my mind, I say, with deep sense of responsibility, that I am prepared cordially to bless this Scheme of Sankey Committee and that, so far as my own State is concerned, I will, in the interest of the Greater India, be ready to join federation....."[11]

The Maharaja's speech spoiled the game plan of the British and was celebrated all over the country.[12] When he returned from England, Congress leader Sarojini Naidu went to receive him and congratulated him for his bold and nationalistic stand at the conference. Laxman Das Chadak referred to this speech of Hari Singh in Parliament on September 27, 1954. Karan Singh also mentioned this speech in his autobiography.[13] In response to the British proposal of formulating a Council of British India and of Princely States, Hari Singh said, "Our motherland is unfortunately divided into two different political arrangements. Both the units work without any coordination. The proposed federation will ensure the unity of the country."[14] (January 15, 1931) Hari Singh's speeches enraged the British and the Raj began plotting against him to gain greater control over the kingdom.

Communal Turbulence: A British Conspiracy

To achieve their twin objectives of curbing Hari Singh's bold nationalist approach and thwarting Russian influence in the region as a part of the Great Game,[15] the British sought control over Gilgit and other parts of Jammu and Kashmir, administratively and militarily. They began fomenting conspiracies and communal charges against the Maharaja and the Hindu community with a view to aggravate the law and order problem to such an extent that the Maharaja became weak and could be forced to cede more space to the British officials in the kingdom. The Home and Finance Ministers, B.J. Glancy and Sir Elvin Banerjee (an Anglo Indian) played a significant role in designing these conspiracies.[16] Even before Hari Singh could return to India after the Round Table Conference of 1930-31, the British began spreading rumours and instigating unrest in the kingdom. In one incident, a head constable named Labhram reportedly tried to make a subordinate (a Muslim) get up from a *charpai* (cot); when the latter refused, Labhram insisted. At this, the subordinate started shouting and claimed that Labhram had insulted the Koran by throwing it on the ground; he raised slogans like "Dogra Raj Murdabad."[17] News of the incident spread like wildfire and large-scale rioting began. Many such incidents were created all over the realm. The incident gave an opportunity to a young group of scholars from Aligarh Muslim University, popularly known as the Reading Room Party, led by Sheikh Mohammad Abdullah and clandestinely supported by the British Government, to establish themselves in the politics of the region; they actively participated in the rioting on grounds of religion and propagated falsehoods about the Maharaja's rule.[18] Maulvis started using masjids to spread rumours and raised slogans of 'Islam in danger,' 'Dogra Raj Murdabad'. On June 21, 1931, similar speeches and slogans were made at Masjid Khangah-e-Maula. The Maharaja called a delegation to consider the demands of those shouting slogans against him. When the delegation arrived, a person suddenly stood up and started shouting and instigating people to initiate *jihad* against the *kafirs* (Hindus) in Kashmir; he was later identified as Abdul Kadir, but his real identity is still unknown.[19] Abdul Kadir created a chaotic situation that resulted in the death of many Hindus in the Kashmir valley. The police arrested Kadir and registered a criminal case against him; the trial started in Central Jail, Srinagar.

On July 13, 1931, as the hearing of Abdul Kadir's case was under way, people started gathering in large numbers; some, in a meticulously planned manner, began to break the doors of the jail to set Abdul Kadir free.[20] As the situation began to go out of control, police opened fire in which some persons died. This gave an opportunity to the *agent provocateurs* to begin large-scale rioting in Kashmir in which a large number of Hindus were killed, their properties destroyed, shops burned down. This was the first time after the end of Afghan rule in Kashmir that Hindus were killed in the name of religion on such a large scale.[21] An interesting aspect of the incident is that Sheikh Abdullah and his associates from Aligarh Muslim University, who played a leading part in the rioting on religious grounds, received clandestine support from the Ahmadiyas of Kadiyan Nagar of Punjab province, who were considered to be the closest supporters of British rule in India.

It later came to light that incidents such as June 21, 1931, and July 31, 1931, were part of a well-planned conspiracy of the Political Department of British India to destabilise the Maharaja and gain control of Gilgit Agency. Major Gibyn Kingsley Butt of the Yorkshire Regiment, posted in Peshawar, had come to Kashmir for his summer vacations, bringing Abdul Kadir Pathan along with him as his cook;[22] Sheikh Abdullah and his Aligarh team, the Ahmadiyas and others, merely played the role of British pawns. This was substantiated by the Barjor Dalal Committee Report (September 24, 1931). The Barjor Dalal Committee was constituted under the leadership of the Chief Justice of Jammu and Kashmir High Court, Sir Barjor Dalal, to investigate the causes behind the rioting of June and July 1931; its other members were Mr. B.R. Sahni and Mr. Abdul Kayyum. The report established with documentary, oral and circumstantial evidence that Mr. G.E.C. Wakefield, prime minister and in-charge of the kingdom's defence ministry, played a prominent role in plotting the mischief through false propaganda such as the allegedly disrespectful treatment of the Koran (July 4, 1931). The investigation showed that most incidents had never taken place.[23]

The years of rioting and violence ended in 1935 when the British secured Gilgit Agency (Wazarat) from the Maharaja on a 60-year lease. And after March 29, 1935, the All-India Kashmir Committee which was constituted in Lahore and Simla and responsible for spreading the violence all around the Valley simply disappeared. Though London gained administrative control of Gilgit Wazarat, it remained part of J&K and all mining rights in the region still vested with the kingdom; only the Maharaja was entitled to execute all the necessary religious ceremonies in the region; at the official building of the Agency it was mandatory to hoist the State's flag along with the Union Jack, and restrictions on cow slaughter continued. The British relinquished control back to the Maharaja just weeks before independence.

Within weeks of independence, however, Gilgit, Baltistan and other areas were handed over to Pakistan by Maj. William A. Brown of the Gilgit Scouts, aided by Capt. Matherson and Sub.-Maj. Babar Khan (a close relation of the Mir of Hunza). When the British returned Gilgit Agency to the Maharaja in July, he appointed Brig. Ghansara Singh as the new Governor on August 1, 1947. This was welcomed by the Raja of Punial and chieftains of Koh Gizar,

Yashin and Askoman, but resented by the Mirs of Hunza and Nagar. Their hostility proved disastrous as 75 per cent of the troops of Gilgit Scouts belonged to these two principalities. Hari Singh had wanted to appoint a trusted lieutenant as head of Gilgit Scouts, but the British Government insisted on the appointment of Major Brown who was serving in Chitral Scouts. Lt. Col. Roger Bacon, then political agent in Gilgit, before departing from Gilgit, indicated the role Brown was expected to play there. Major Brown clandestinely galvanised the locals and the Muslim officers and soldiers of Gilgit Scouts and of the Maharaja's army. On the intervening night of Oct. 31-Nov. 01, 1947, around one hundred men of the Gilgit Scouts under Major Brown, Lt. Hyder Khan and Sub.-Maj. Babar Khan surrounded the Governor's house. Ghansara Singh was captured and most of his Hindu and Sikh soldiers killed in cold blood. On November 3, 1947, a provisional Government was formed and Major Brown hoisted the Pakistani flag in the Scout lines. Brown was awarded the MBE (Member of the Most Excellent Order of the British Empire) in 1948, which suggests London's complicity in his actions. In Skardu, Maj. Sher Jung Thapa displayed exemplary courage and endurance during a six month-long siege, but ultimately failed.[24]

Social and Administrative Reforms

Amidst this political turbulence Hari Singh took several measures for the welfare of his people. These have been erased from the historical narrative in order to justify the British-backed Muslim agitations aimed at tarnishing the Maharaja's image.

Ban on female infanticide: Soon after ascending the throne, Hari Singh constituted a committee to consider prohibition of the practice of female infanticide in the realm, especially amongst the Rajput community. The committee submitted its report on December 15, 1925. On May 18, 1929, another committee was constituted to examine how the recommendations could be implemented. Hari Singh proposed a unique formula. To encourage people to let the female child live, it was decided that the government would gift one acre of land to the family giving birth to a female child, and another sum would be given at the time of the marriage of the daughter for which purpose Hari Singh constituted the "Dhan Devi Memorial Kanya Fund". At the same time, he instituted a strict law prohibiting female infanticide, punishable with a fine.

Law against Sati: The law prohibiting Sati, introduced in the Bengal Presidency in 1829, was legally challenged and ultimately went up to the Privy Council which upheld the law, as a result of which it could be implemented in 1932. Soon after this law was implemented in the Bengal Presidency, Hari Singh decided to enforce a law prohibiting sati in his kingdom even though it was not much prevalent there.

Law prohibiting the sale of women: A practice that considered women as property that could be sold was prevalent in some parts of the country, including J&K. Hari Singh, under the influence of the Arya Samaj, considered this an affront to the honour and dignity of women and decided to put an end to it. He increased the punishment for persons indulging in the practice from three years to seven years.

Hari Singh was sensitive to the plight of women and treated them with utmost respect and expected the same conduct from those around him. On one occasion, whilst returning to Udhampur from a hunting trip with his ADCs, Kawal Singh and Captain Prithi Singh, they saw some women taking water from a *baoli* (stepwell). Prithi Singh made a comment which infuriated Hari Singh who made him get out of the car and walk the rest of the way back, some eight or nine kilometres. He later told Prithi Singh that every girl in the kingdom, irrespective of religion or caste, was his daughter and 'you dared to pass a comment on my daughter'.[25] A senior People's Democratic Party leader in 2011 informed the State Assembly about an incident in which the Maharaja of Patiala asked a Kashmiri girl in his court to dance; Hari Singh always considered every girl from Kashmir as his daughter and walked out of the darbar. Thereafter, he never invited the Patiala ruler to his kingdom.[26]

Prohibition of child marriage: Hari Singh called a meeting of people from different sections of society in May 1927 to eradicate the evil of child marriage. Most of those who attended the meeting denounced the custom and encouraged by their support the Maharaja promulgated a law prohibiting child marriage in the kingdom on June 18, 1928. The law fixed the minimum age of the bride at 14 years and bridegroom at 18 years. The Child Marriage Prohibition Act 1985 (Vikram Samvat) provided that a person who is a major and marries a minor child of less than 14 years will be punished with imprisonment of one year, and a person who acts as an accomplice in a child marriage will undergo the same sentence. The Act provided stricter punishment for marriage between unequals; if a 50-year-old adult marries a minor girl or acts as accomplice in such a marriage the punishment would be imprisonment for three years. This remarkable legislation preceded the SARDA Act, 1929. Even the British Resident, Col. O. Gilin, appreciated the Maharaja's efforts in eradicating social evils.[27] In 1940, Hari Singh prohibited the practice of marriage of a female child or adult in exchange for money. In 1941, he penalised the practice of polygamy in Ladakh region.[28]

Widow Remarriage: Considering the deplorable condition of women due to child marriage, especially those widowed young, Hari Singh introduced legal changes to allow widow remarriage.

Education: Efforts had been made from the time of Maharaja Pratap Singh to improve education in the kingdom. The Director of Education in British India, Mr. Henry Sharp, was invited to examine the issue and give recommendations. Sharp submitted his report in 1916 and accordingly measures were taken to implement it. However, substantial improvements were made by Hari Singh who, having toured Europe prior to becoming king, understood the importance of modern education to equip his subjects for future challenges. Hari Singh introduced free and compulsory primary education in 1930, under which the state also provided free books and stationery to children coming to school, including the girl child.[29] A separate Women Education Department was established in 1928. To encourage girls to study, provision was made for scholarships for them. State scholarship was provided to students to study in prominent universities outside the state such as Aligarh Muslim University, Banaras Hindu University, Punjab University, etc. By 1941, in Jammu division, there was a primary school for a population of 3602 and a high school in almost every district.[30] Hari Singh emphasized the importance of skill development for the youth, along with formal education.[31] Various institutions were set up for teacher education. Between 1931 and 1941, the percentage of educated persons increased by 12 per cent, an impressive growth rate.[32]

Judicial Reforms: On becoming king in 1925, Hari Singh's first declaration was *'justice is my religion'* and throughout his life he remained true to his words.[33] Jammu and Kashmir was the first princely state to establish a High Court (1928) to render independent and impartial justice to all persons living in the state. In 1930, the powers of the Residency Courts were also transferred to the High Court, which helped in reducing British influence in the administrative activities of the state. The kingdom's penal code had a provision that protected Brahmins and Rajputs from being given the death penalty, but in 1936, the Maharaja amended the penal code and removed this privilege.[34]

In 1943, the High Court got the power of Letter Patent. During Hari Singh's reign, the judiciary became fully independent of the executive.[35]

One incident captures Hari Singh's attitude towards justice. Land was once being acquired in Karan Nagar for a public purpose and most people vacated their land, but one Sambhu Nath Shastri refused to surrender his land and wanted to register a case against the Maharaja for the land acquisition, for which the prior permission of the Maharaja was required. Accordingly, Sambhu Nath made an application before the Maharaja, which was granted; the Maharaja himself pleaded his case in court and ultimately lost to Sambhu Nath.[36]

State Subject Law: The British found the cool climes of J&K very congenial and similar to that of England. Many British officers regularly visited popular tourist spots such as Gulmarg, Patni Top, etc. As the connectivity of the State improved with other parts of the country, many influential Britishers were keen to acquire properties in the State; this posed a danger because it would have increased their interference in the State administration, which the Maharaja did not welcome. At the same time, the improved education facilities in the state had created a significant population of educated persons available for employment and hence it was necessary to prevent English people or their favourites from taking away jobs that could be taken by these citizens. Hence, the Maharaja promulgated the State Subject law[37] which defined four categories of State Subjects, Class I, II, III and IV, whereby only state subjects could be employed in the state and acquire immovable property. However, the notification of June 27, 1932, permitted a person to acquire the status of a State Subject after acquiring immovable property on the basis of *ijazatnama* and on obtaining *rayatnama* after ten years of continuous residence in the State (L/1989). During this time, the house boats on Dal Lake became popular among the British as they did not fall in the definition of land and could be purchased for residential purposes.

Constitutional and Democratic Reforms: Hari Singh took the unprecedented decision of appointing the B.J. Glancy Commission to suggest constitutional reforms to usher in a more democratic set-up in the State and improve the quality of administration (November 12, 1931). On May 31, 1932, he accepted its recommendations and declared the constitution of a legislative assembly, designated as Praja Sabha. In 1934, he introduced the Jammu and Kashmir Regulation, 1991 (Sambat) which constitutionally recognized the existence of the Praja Sabha. The first session of the Praja Sabha was held on October 17,

1934. As per the 1934 Regulation, the legislature was bicameral, with a legislative council and a legislative assembly. In the Council, all members were nominated by the Maharaja and included the prime minister and other ministers. The Legislative Assembly (Praja Sabha) comprised 75 members, of which 33 were elected and the rest were either ministers or nominated by the Maharaja. Elected members were to be elected in appropriate proportion of their population so all communities could get some representation. The 1934 Regulation was amended in 1939 to make it compatible with the Government of India Act 1935. Hari Singh was so unbiased that he appointed Mirza Afzal Beg of the National Conference as revenue minister, though the latter was among the elected members who were agitating against the monarchy.

Other Important Reforms

In 1929, Hari Singh introduced a regulation prohibiting children under the age of 18 years from smoking or consuming tobacco products in public places; violations were punishable with a fine of up to Rs. 100. The remarkable feature of the regulation was that for effective implementation not only the police, but a doctor, lawyer, engineer, lambardar, jaildar, teacher or magistrate was allowed to take any tobacco product away from a child using it and destroy it. Hari Singh also banned the practice of *begaari* under which a subject was bound to carry government supplies from one place to another without any remuneration.

To promote industrial development, Hari Singh promulgated a regulation in 1935 to provide loans for industries, guarantee for those taking loans, subsidy on the purchase of machinery, easy access to land, water, wood, making machinery available on hire-purchase basis, providing easy access to raw materials, creation of a large number of industrial credit cooperative societies and set up the Jammu and Kashmir Bank in 1938. Many new industries were opened, viz., Biroja Factory in 1940, Srinagar Emporium in 1941, sugar mill in Ranbir Singh Pura, construction of bridges, construction of first electricity house in 1935, and so on. Three hospitals were opened in Jammu, Srinagar and Kotli to provide good medical facilities to the subjects. Another hospital was set up in Mirpur.

In 1935, the Gram Panchayat Regulation was introduced to democratise the system up to village level and a Panchayat and Village Development Department was set up in 1937. In 1940, Hari Singh introduced the Town Area Development Act and established the Town Planning Department. To bring transparency in the selection of employees in the State services, a Public Service Commission was established. Deeply influenced by the philosophy of the Arya Samaj, Hari Singh made various attempts to eradicate untouchability from his realm. In 1936, he ordered the opening of all schools and public wells for all people, including those from the scheduled castes. He opened the doors of government employment for them as well as places of worship so that they could offer prayers in the temples. Initially, the Brahmins opposed these changes but the Maharaja was undeterred. When the priest of the Raghunath temple, Rajguru Pandit Devraj, expressed unhappiness with this policy, the Maharaja removed him and appointed his brother Pandit Balkishan on condition that he would not prevent any 'untouchable' from entering the temple.[38] In 1939, he introduced a provision in the Penal Code to penalize persons who prevented persons of the subordinate classes from taking water from public water resources or from entering temples.

Hari Singh was aware that though Rajputs owned large tracts of agricultural land, they never engaged in cultivation. They either joined the Army or preferred to remain unemployed. To break this practice, the Maharaja took up the plough and started cultivating to encourage all his subjects to participate in agricultural activities. Further, to protect farmers from extortion by moneylenders, he promulgated the Kastgar Protection Regulation in 1928 and in 1936, introduced the Land Improvement and Kastgar Relief Regulation. Under the Land Alienation Act, no land belonging to a kastgar (farmer) could be transferred to a non-kastgar. If a merchant exerted force on a kastgar, the latter could approach the court for a solution and the court was given wide powers to reduce the rate of interest being charged by the merchant.

Hari Singh introduced the Press and Publication Act 1932 to replace the extant law of 1914 to strengthen independent media. When he ascended the throne, there was only one newspaper in circulation, but by 1949 there were 67 newspapers in the State.

Having a nationalist view, Hari Singh always promoted the use of Hindi along with Urdu and Arabic, especially for educational purposes, to connect J&K with the rest of the country. In 1936, he constituted a committee for the promotion of Hindi. Previously, Government Notification No. 99, October 05, 1934, gave a new nomenclature to several official posts, namely, Executive Council – Amatya Mandal; Prime Minister – Pradhan Amatya; Minister – Amatya.[39]

Bold Personality

In 1921, Jammu was seriously afflicted with the plague. As Commander-in-Chief of the Army, Hari Singh directed the Army to ensure that no one entered the city. One day, Hari Singh entered the city in ordinary dress and was accosted by a soldier on duty; as Hari Singh tried to bribe him, the angry soldier took him to the Company officer. The officer recognised Hari Singh and saluted him, to the shock and dismay of the soldier. But the Maharaja appreciated his commitment and promoted him to the rank of hawaldar.[40]

Hari Singh maintained a clear distinction between personal and state property. Soon after he ascended the throne, the Bhaderwah jagir given to him by his uncle as a personal jagir was merged with state property. He used to draw a salary of Rs. 2 lakh from the rajkosh (treasury) for his personal expenses and discouraged the use of state machinery for personal reasons. Once, Captain Deewan Singh used a government vehicle for his dogs, for which the Maharaja reprimanded him; Captain Deewan Singh himself narrated this incident.[41]

Hari Singh was an excellent sportsman; he loved shooting, playing polo and horse riding. He was a connoisseur of the arts and patronised the famous singer, Malika Pukhraj.[42] He was appalled when she decided to move to Pakistan though there had been no communal tension or violence in Jammu and Kashmir.

Accession and Integration

The shadow of partition loomed as the dawn of independence approached. Britain was determined to create a new nation called Pakistan, as demanded by the Muslim League. With this arose the question of the fate of the over 550 princely states that had to be merged with India to give the newly-independent country territorial and cultural coherence and integrity. Most princely states joined the nation building process before August 15, 1947, but there were a few exceptions. States that signed the Instrument of Accession after August 15, 1947, included Jammu and Kashmir, Patna, Manipur, Sikkim, Pondicherry, Hyderabad, Travancore, and Goa. It is truly unfortunate that J&K is always cited with the states of Travancore, Junagadh and Hyderabad, whose rulers either wanted independence or wanted to join Pakistan. It has often been alleged that Hari Singh favoured independence and some have suggested that he was in touch with Pakistan. Another allegation frequently levelled against the hapless king is that when Pakistan marched swiftly into the border districts of the state, the Maharaja moved from Srinagar to Jammu for his personal safety; these are baseless canards.

Under the Indian Independence Act, 1947, and Government of India Act, 1935, as amended in 1947, the rulers of the princely states had full authority to decide as to which Dominion, India or Pakistan, they wished to join.[43] In order to accomplish the task of accession and integration, the Government of India set up a States Department. Sardar Vallabhbhai Patel took charge of the department on July 5, 1947 and invited the princely states to accede to the Dominion on three subjects of Defence, Foreign Affairs and Communication.[44] In his address to the Chamber of Princes on July 25, Mountbatten advised the rulers that it would not be in the interests of the princely states to remain independent and they should surrender matters of common concern to the Dominion they may have to join. Further, they would have to respect the geographical contiguity of their state while acceding to any Dominion.[45]

The hill state of J&K shared borders with Afghanistan, Tajikistan, China and Tibet,[46] and was ideal for keeping an eye on Russia. Hence, the USA and the UK wanted it to go with Pakistan or somehow remain independent, or be partitioned as a last resort. In pursuit of this objective, Mountbatten visited the state from June 19 to 23, 1947, where, according to Allen Campbell Johnson, media in-charge in the Viceroy's office, he repeatedly told Hari Singh not to sign the Instrument of Accession in favour of any of the Dominions before ascertaining the wishes of the people.[47] According to some authors, Mountbatten even suggested that Hari Singh should defer a decision till a Constituent Assembly of Pakistan was convened.[48] Hari Singh narrated his consecutive meetings with Mountbatten in Srinagar, "Lord Mountbatten chose to visit the State in June 1947 and we had several talks. Lord Mountbatten then urged me and my Prime Minister, Kak, not to make any declaration of independence but to find out in one way or another, the will of the people of Kashmir as soon as possible and to announce our intention by the 14th August to send representative accordingly to one Constituent Assembly or the other. Lord Mountbatten further told us that the newly created States Department was prepared to give an assurance that if Kashmir went to Pakistan, it would not be regarded as an unfriendly act by the Government of India. Lord Mountbatten stressed the dangerous situation in which Kashmir would find itself if it lacked the support of one of the two dominions by the date of the transfer of power. The impression which I gathered from my talks with Lord

Mountbatten who explained the situation with plans and maps was that, in his opinion, it was advisable for me to accede to Pakistan."[49]

In his reply to Mountbatten, Hari Singh strongly repudiated any inclination towards joining Pakistan. In fact, on the last day of his visit to Srinagar, when Mountbatten again sought to meet the Maharaja, the latter feigned sickness to avoid the Viceroy who was repeatedly urging him to join Pakistan.[50] According to Mehr Chand Mahajan, who visited Mountbatten on September 29, 1947, in Delhi, before taking charge as prime minister of Jammu and Kashmir, "*during talks I realized that Lord Mountbatten even now believed that Jammu and Kashmir should go with Pakistan even in terms of its geography*".[51]

While Mountbatten was exerting pressure on Hari Singh to accede to Pakistan and persuading him to otherwise delay accession to either dominion, Prime Minister Nehru was working on a different tangent. He wanted power to be transferred first to Sheikh Abdullah and under his command an elected constituent assembly of the State would pass the resolution for the accession of the State to India; thus the accession would take place after ascertaining the wishes of the people.[52] Nehru emphasised the need to release Abdullah, who was undergoing a three-year prison sentence for his agitation against the monarchy in 1946. In fact, when the State police arrested Abdullah during this agitation, Nehru personally attempted to enter the State to get him released despite repeated warnings from the Maharaja. Nehru was detained and deported after making an illegal entry, a fact he held against Hari Singh forever, to the detriment of the state. It deserves mention that when Hari Singh sent prime minister Ram Chandra Kak to Delhi to discuss the accession, in July 1947, the latter was told that the subject would be discussed only after Abdullah was released from jail, power transferred to him and the wishes of the people ascertained.[53] There is an enduring controversy about the role of Ram Chandra Kak, who had a Scottish wife.[54] During his Delhi visit, Kak met Mountbatten, who especially arranged for him to meet Mohammad Ali Jinnah,[55] with whom he is alleged to have remained in touch.[56] Rumours that the Maharaja was willing to remain independent have long been attributed to him. Even Mehr Chand Mahajan who later became prime minister of the state wrote in his autobiography that Pandit Kak was openly working for accession to Pakistan.[57] Kak misguided Hari Singh on the issue of accession and made attempts to prevent accession to India, a fact told to Mahajan by the Maharaja himself.[58]

At the instance of Sardar Patel, Mahatma Gandhi visited Srinagar from July 31 to August 2, 1947, and met Hari Singh at Gulab Bhawan. Though there is no written record of the discussion, it frightened the Muslim Conference, which opposed the visit with mass agitations in Baramulla. Immediately after Gandhi's visit to Srinagar, Kak was sacked on grounds of suspicious activities and detained by state forces while trying to flee,[59] and the aged Major-General Janak Singh appointed as acting prime minister. The posts of Inspector-General and Chief of General Staff of Army were eliminated as it was observed that they were working in British interests. A new bridge was constructed on the Ravi river, telegraph lines were spread between Jammu and Srinagar, state roads repaired and in all these activities the Government of India played an active role. The influence of Mahatma Gandhi on Hari Singh was reported in *The Times*, London, on October 25, 1947. Hari Singh sent Standstill Agreements to both India and Pakistan on August 12 in the hope of continuing to receive necessary supplies from Pakistan as the British had built most connecting roads via Pakistan, while giving the Government of India leeway to interfere in case of Pakistani mischief, as it was the responsibility of the Successor State to give protection to the princely states in terms of the Indian Independence Act, 1947, and Government of India Act, 1935. While Pakistan formally accepted the agreement, India did not give an immediate response.[60]

Narendra Singh Sarila, ADC to Mountbatten, observed that by the end of August, Hari Singh had decided to join the Indian constitutional and administrative arrangement but the accession was being delayed only because Nehru was adamant that power be transferred to Sheikh Abdullah and a government led by him.[61] With Sardar Patel's efforts, Mehr Chand Mahajan was appointed prime minister of J&K; before taking charge, Mahajan called on Nehru on August 29, 1947, and conveyed that the Maharaja was ready for accession and administrative reforms would follow the accession, but Nehru insisted on the release of Abdullah and transfer of power to him.[62] Eventually, to further the accession process, Hari Singh agreed to release Abdullah in return for an apology letter from jail on September 29, 1947, and again sent his representative to propose accession. The offer was again rebuffed[63] and the concerned officers instructed by Nehru that so long as power was not handed over to Abdullah, no talks should be initiated on accession.[64] It is evident that Hari Singh was not responsible for the delay in accession. As Sarila observed, it was only Hari Singh who blocked the accession of Jammu and Kashmir to Pakistan under the British Plan.[65]

Mehr Chand Mahajan took charge on October 15, 1947, and immediately thereafter, Jinnah's representative, Major A.S.B. Shah, offered him a blank Instrument of Accession to insert any conditions in return for accession to Pakistan. He also warned that if the Maharaja did not sign the Instrument of Accession with Pakistan he should be ready for dire consequences. When Mahajan told Hari Singh what had transpired in the meeting with Major Shah, the latter responded, "even if I have to construct a road via Bhadrawah-Kistwar in order to connect with Chamba-Dalhousie, I will do that but I will not accede to Pakistan".[66]

Realising that precious time was being lost, Sardar Patel arranged for a meeting between Hari Singh and M.S. Golwalkar (Guruji), Sarsanghachalak of the Rashtriya Swayamsevak Sangh (RSS). During this visit to Srinagar on October 17,1947, Delhi prant pracharak Vasant Rao Oak, Punjab prant pracharak Madhav Rao Mulye, Srinagar pracharak Harish Bhanot and Srinagar karyawah Balraj Madhok accompanied Golwalkar. The meeting between Hari Singh and Guruji was private; Guruji reportedly advised the Maharaja that given the difficult situation, he should take a decision without regard to personal honour.[67]

From October 19 to 22, Hari Singh visited troubled areas along the Jammu border, but when he reached Srinagar on October 23, he received news of the attack on Muzaffarabad. He immediately sent his deputy prime minister, Ram Lal Batra, to Delhi along with the signed copy of the Instrument of Accession and a letter requesting the Indian Government for defence assistance.[68] When this letter was placed before the Defence Committee on October 25, 1947, Mountbatten placed the condition that no defence-related assistance could be given to the state until the Instrument of Accession was signed by both sides. Nehru was adamant that Abdullah should head the government and he wanted a written assurance for that from the Maharaja himself. Ultimately, on October 26, V.P. Menon, Secretary of the States Department, was sent to Srinagar with a copy of the Instrument of Accession and instructed to bring Mehr Chand Mahajan to Delhi to ascertain if the Maharaja would transfer power to Sheikh Abdullah. Menon obtained Hari Singh's signature on the Instrument of Accession and returned to Delhi the same day with Mahajan. Before leaving Srinagar, Menon and Mahajan advised the Maharaja to move to Jammu as his security was under serious threat in Srinagar, which was the immediate target of the raiders.

Mahajan apprised Nehru of the sufferings of the state, but Nehru remained unmoved until assured that power would be handed over to Abdullah. Mahajan returned to Srinagar with Menon as Nehru wanted some insertions in the letter the Maharaja had written on October 26, 1947. This read as, "I want to bring it to the knowledge of the Hon'ble Governor General that I wish to form an Interim Government in the State with immediate effect and I invite Sheikh Abdullah to share the responsibility of administering the Interim Government along with my Prime Minister".[69] Thereafter, Mountbatten accepted the Instrument of Accession while cunningly adding a condition that the wishes of the people would be ascertained at an appropriate time. This proviso had no legal sanctity in terms of the Indian Independence Act, 1947, and Government of India Act, 1935.

The Maharaja also wrote a lengthy epistle to Mountbatten narrating the sequence of events and his reasons for acceding to India: "*...Consistently with their policy that in the case of any State where the issue of accession has been the subject of dispute, the question of accession should be decided in accordance with the wishes of the people of the State, it is my Government's wish that as soon as law and order have been restored in Kashmir and her soil cleared of the invader, the question of the State's accession should be settled by a reference to the people...*". This was a diplomatic surrender to the obduracy of Mountbatten and Nehru, who tolerated the invasion of the kingdom and untold brutalities on the population for four critical days during which the Pakistan Army reached within striking distance of Srinagar, in order to secure a political arrangement of their wishes. Hari Singh swallowed 'poison' to uphold the cultural and geographical integrity of India.

Sheikh Abdullah and the National Conference later maliciously alleged that the Maharaja abandoned Srinagar at a time when it was under attack. The truth is that immediately after the visit of Golwalkar on October 19, 1947, Hari Singh disregarded his own security and visited the border areas of Jammu at a time when an attack from Pakistan appeared imminent, and he was the most valuable target for the enemy. In some places, arson had already begun, but Hari Singh visited Kathua, Bhimber, Mirpur and Kotli. At Gujrat in Jammu region (now under Pakistan occupation), a dak bungalow was attacked at a time when the Maharaja was scheduled to visit the place but he had fortuitously visited this place one day previously.[70] Hari Singh moved to Jammu because Menon and Mahajan insisted that any threat to his person in the existing circumstances was a threat to the accession and integration of the State with India. Moreover, the Darbar normally moved to the winter capital of Jammu in October and most officers of the state administration had already moved there. The move to Jammu was thus both routine and imperative in the circumstances of the war.

Once Rawalpindi was convinced that Hari Singh was not going to accede to Pakistan under any circumstances, it attacked J&K with full force with Pathans and Afridis aided by serving members of the Pakistan Army, equipped with sophisticated military weapons and other machinery. On October 22, the raiders reached and captured Muzaffarabad, killing all soldiers of the Maharaja's army, including Col. Narain Singh who was in charge of the post.[71] When Hari Singh got news of the attack, he called his recently-appointed Chief of the State army, Brig. Rajendra Singh Jamwal, who replaced Major-General H.L. Scott. The Maharaja was keen to visit the troubled area but Brig. Rajendra Singh warned that the Maharaja's security was of utmost importance for the future of the state. At the end of the meeting, Hari Singh instructed Brig. Rajendra Singh to fight till the last man and the last bullet.[72] After visiting affected areas in Jammu and giving charge of the military operation to Brig. Rajendra Singh, Hari Singh reached Srinagar on October 23, 1947. He now took the extraordinarily bold step of celebrating Dussehra (October 24) with the usual festivity to keep up the morale of his subjects in that time of calamity.

With the war in full swing, the Maharaja found himself unable to give succour to his subjects who were suffering terrible atrocities. As the interim government was in the hands of Sheikh Abdullah and military operations of Indian forces still under the command of Gen. Sir Macgregor Macdonald, he could not play any significant role for his own state. Aggrieved at the manner in which military operations were being conducted, Hari Singh expressed his anguish in a letter to Sardar Patel (January 31, 1948).[73] The letter also expressed unhappiness at the manner in which Jammu and Kashmir was being handled in the United Nations.

Exile of the Maharaja

Patel and Nehru had fundamental differences over Hari Singh; Patel wanted to use the Maharaja's influence in the state's integration and Nehru wanted all credit to go to Sheikh Abdullah. Patel also had reservations about the manner in which Gopalaswami Ayyangar was handling the situation at Nehru's instance, surpassing the role of the States Department headed by Patel. When Patel tried to manage the critical situation in the state, Nehru sidelined him. The letter Nehru wrote to Patel on December 23, 1947, was so offensive and disrespectful that Patel even wrote his resignation as Minister of States Department, but relented after Gandhi intervened.

Patel advised Hari Singh to go amongst his subjects and express his views regarding the future of the state. As the Maharaja was highly regarded, Abdullah grew alarmed and planned to oust the Maharaja from the State, as he had previously ousted Mehr Chand Mahajan, using an obliging Nehru. Hari Singh was invited to Delhi in April along with his family and on April 29, Sardar Patel was made to convey the news that the Government of India wanted him to stay out of the state for some time. He was politely asked to delegate his remaining powers as Maharaja under the State Constitution of 1939, which was still in force, in favour of his son Karan Singh by appointing the latter as Regent of the state.[74] Nehru followed this up by convincing Karan Singh to accept the position of Regent for the future of the state and the nation as the Maharaja could not understand the new order and the changes the nation was passing through.

Sheikh Abdullah was now in a position of authority in the state. To consolidate his position, he demanded the establishment of a Constituent Assembly to prepare a separate constitution for the State. This required Hari Singh's assent. Hari Singh was sent a format of the proclamation he was to make for constitution of a Constituent Assembly. The Maharaja understood the Sheikh's designs and instructed his son not to sign any such proclamation without obtaining his permission. He also wrote a letter to Sardar Patel on December 10, 1950, wherein he agreed with the fundamental objective sought to be achieved by formation of the Constituent Assembly, but wanted a clear demarcation of powers and responsibilities of the Constituent Assembly; the issues kept out of its authority; and that it should report to the ruler and on necessary issues the ruler will obtain the advice of Parliament.[75] Clearly, the Maharaja was trying to establish a link with Parliament which would have got a supervisory role in the affairs of the Constituent Assembly of Jammu and Kashmir; this would have created a necessary check on Sheikh Abdullah. However, five days after the Maharaja's missive, Sardar Patel passed away on December 15, 1950. Thereafter, Hari Singh tried to apprise Gopalaswami Ayyangar[76] of his concerns, but Ayyangar in a letter to the Maharaja dated April 5, 1951, did not give substantive assurances. Ultimately on April 21, 1951, Karan Singh signed the proclamation for formulation of a Constituent Assembly in the state.

In the elections to the Constituent Assembly, all 75 candidates of the

National Conference were virtually elected unopposed as the nominations of 41 out of 59 candidates of the Praja Parishad were rejected on trivial grounds while ignoring deficiencies in the nominations of National Conference candidates. In anger, the Praja Parishad boycotted the election. Sheikh Abdullah now began to unveil his ambitions. On March 24, 1952 his revenue minister, Mirza Afzal Beg, declared in the Assembly that in the Union of States, Jammu and Kashmir will be a sovereign republic that will have its own prime minister, national assembly and judiciary.[77] On March 30,1952, Abdullah announced in the Assembly that no other Parliament would have any role to play in the State Constituent Assembly.[78] But his most venomous speech was on April 10, 1952, at Ranbir Singh Pura, where he openly declared that the Constitution of India would have no application in J&K.[79] All the concerns that the Maharaja had raised with Patel and Ayyangar were coming true, but still no lessons were learnt.

Abdullah now wanted the total removal of the monarchy, to which Nehru was agreeable; again Karan Singh was convinced to get nominated in place of his father.[80] Nehru defended his actions in Parliament on June 26, 1952, even going to the extent of saying that the provisions of the Constitution cannot have application in states against the wishes of the people.[81] After this speech, Hari Singh wrote to Dr. Kailash Nath Katju[82] on June 29, 1952, pointing out how constitutional provisions were being ignored one after another by the Constituent Assembly of the State under the command of Sheikh Abdullah by making all attempts to remove him from the position of the Ruler, "*completely ignoring the fact that all my decisions were taken in national interest so that State could be integrated with India like other States and India's position could be strengthened in the United Nations*".[83] Instead of Dr. Katju, Nehru himself, vide letter dated July 5, 1952, volunteered to answer the issues raised by Hari Singh and tried to demonstrate that whatever might be his (Maharaja's) legal authority, practically he had no powers left. Nehru questioned Hari Singh's wisdom in being unable to adjust to the new constitutional order, but evaded the substantive issues raised by the Maharaja regarding non-compliance of constitutional provisions by the Constituent Assembly of the state.

In the interim period, Nehru and Abdullah after long deliberations in July formulated the terms of the Nehru-Sheikh Accord, also called the Delhi Accord, 1952. By this time, Abdullah had begun to dominate Nehru, who surrendered on various significant aspects of the constitutional position of Jammu and Kashmir State qua Union of India, especially regarding the appointment of the constitutional head of the state and his nomenclature.[84] After hearing Nehru's speech of August 7, 1952, in Parliament regarding his decisions in the state of Jammu and Kashmir, Hari Singh again wrote to Dr. Katju questioning the idealistic talk of Nehru in Parliament and its non-application on the ground.

When Nehru sought an amendment in the provision of Article 370 through a Presidential Order to smoothen the path to remove the Maharaja from the position of Ruler, Hari Singh made a detailed representation to the President of India. He questioned the things done in the name of the public which had no role to play in the matter and was in fact kept in the dark in almost all decisions taken by the so-called popular leaders.[85] Even the President of India, Dr. Rajendra Prasad, vide his letter dated September 6, 1952, to the Government of India questioned the repeated exercise of the power conferred upon the President under Article 370 to make changes in the provision of the Constitution by exercising its executive power. But even Dr. Rajendra Prasad had to surrender before the adamant Nehru; he issued the executive order to amend the provisions of Article 370 and the word *Sadar-e-Riyasat* (Regent) was added in place of Ruler. Accordingly, on November 15, 1952, Karan Singh was appointed Sadar-i-Riyasat in place of Maharaja Hari Singh to prevent public outrage at the way in which the Maharaja was humiliated. Less than a year later, in an act of poetic justice, Nehru himself had to pass the order for sacking Sheikh Abdullah from the post of prime minister of J&K and have him arrested on August 8, 1953, for consistent separatist and anti-national activities, after Indian intelligence warned that he was conniving with Western powers to declare an independent nation.[86]

Maharaja Hari Singh spent the last years of his life privately in Mumbai. Mindful always of India's interests in the United Nations, he never made any public speech, nor wrote any book or diary. But today, as separatism, fundamentalism and terrorism wreak havoc in Jammu and Kashmir, there is a clamour to restore the Maharaja's honour in history; abrogate Article 370 and its tail, Article 35-A, and fully integrate the State with the Union of India, as the Maharaja had originally intended. The Africans have a saying, 'Until the lions have their own historians, the history of the hunt will always glorify the hunter'. For seven decades, the hunters dominated the pages of history. Now it's the turn of the lions.

*

NOTES

1 For details, see Sagar, Daya, *Jammu Kashmir: A Victim of Personal Ambitions of Some and Mishandling by the Core Indian Leadership*, Prabhat Prakashan, Delhi: 2015.

2 Wakhlu, Somnath, *Hari Singh: The Maharaja, the Man and the Times: Biography of Maharaja of Jammu and Kashmir, 1895-1961*, National Publishing House: 2006, p. 31.

3 For the Treaty of Lahore dated March 9 & 11, 1846, and Treaty of Amritsar dated March 16, 1846 see, *Legal Documents on Jammu and Kashmir*, Jammu Kashmir Study Centre, 2016.

4 Kripa Ram, Diwan, *Gulabnama: A History of Maharaja Gulab Singh of Jammu & Kashmir*, Gulshan Books: 2005; Panikkar, K.M., *Gulab Singh*, Martin Hopkinson Ltd.: 1930; Singh, Jagjit K., "*Gulab Singh (1792-1857): Encyclopedia of Sikhism*" Punjabi University Patiala: 2017.

5 Wakhlu, Somnath, *Hari Singh: The Maharaja, the Man and the Times*, op. cit., pp. 31-33.

6 Jamwal, Shailendra Singh, *Jammu and Kashmir: Autocracy to Democracy*, Saksham Books International: 2011, p. 37.

7 Jamwal, Shailendra Singh, *Jammu and Kashmir*, op. cit., p. 38.

8 Jamwal, Shailendra Singh, Barjor Dalal's report of the Srinagar Riot Enquiry Committee, 1931, Saksham Books International: 2013, p. 7.

9 Saxena, Hori Lal, *Sheikh Mohammad Abdullah and Kashmir*, in *Encyclopedia of Kashmir*, vol. 7, ed. S.R. Sharma & S.R. Bakshi, Anmol Publications: 1995, pp. 7-8.

10 For more details, see Bansal, Alok, *Gilgit-Baltistan: Gilgit-Baltistan and Its Saga of Unending Human Rights Violations*, Pentagon Press: 2018; Chouhan, Amar Singh, *The Gilgit Agency, 1877-1935*, Atlantic Publishers: 1997; Dewan, Parvez, *A History of Ladakh, Gilgit, Baltistan*, Manas Publication: 2007; *Military Report and Gazetteer of the Gilgit Agency and the Independent Territories of Tangir and Darel*, General Staff, India, 1927, Government of India Press, Shimla: 1928; F. M. Hussnain, *Gilgit: The Northern Gate of India,* Sterling, 1978; *Pakistan Occupied Kashmir: Changing the Discourse*, PoK Project Report, Institute for Defence Studies and Analyses, New Delhi: 2011.

11 Saxena, Hori Lal, 'Sheikh Mohammad Abdullah and Kashmir', in *Encyclopedia of Kashmir*, vol. 3, op. cit., pp. 284-285; Agnihotri, Kuldip, *Jammu Kashmir ke Jannayak: Maharaja Hari Singh*, Prabhat Prakashan: 2016, p. 279.

12 Interestingly, Sir Akbar Hyderi, Hyderabad's delegate to the conference, saved the British Government during the Round Table Conference by recommending a federation with a weak centre, which diluted the idea of forming a Greater Federation of India as demanded by the nationalists. Hyderi's approach was guided by London and supported by Mohammad Ali Jinnah.See http://www.dailyexcelsior.com/remember-maharaja-hari-singh/ (accessed Jan. 15, 2019).

13 Singh, Karan, *Autobiography*, Oxford University Press: 2003, pp. 32-33.

14 Agnihotri, Kuldip, op. cit., p. 279.

15 The 'Great Game' refers to the shadow boxing between the British and Russian empires over Afghanistan and the Khanates of Central and Southern Asia, from 1830 onwards. While Russia dreaded British commercial and military inroads into Central Asia, Britain feared Russian designs on India. The term 'Great Game' gained currency after Rudyard

Kipling made it famous in his novel, *Kim* (1901). As J&K shared borders with Afghanistan, Tibet and Russia, Gilgit region became of critical importance in the contest. For more, see: Sarila, Narendra Singh, *The Shadow of the Great Game: The Untold Story of India's Partition*, Harper Collins: 2009; Weller, Charles R., review of*The Great Game, 1856-1907: Russo-British Relations in Central and East Asia*, (Review No. 1611); Ewans, Martin, *The Great Game: Britain and Russia in Central Asia*, volume 1, Routledge, Curzon, Oxon UK: 2004; Hopkirk, Peter, *The Great Game: The Struggle for Empire in Central Asia,* Kodansha Globe: 1994; Huttenback, Robert A., The 'Great Game' in the Pamirs and the Hindu-Kush: The British Conquest of Hunza and Nagar, *Modern Asian Studies*, vol. 9, no. 1, 1975, pp. 1-29.

16 Saraf, Mulk Raj, *Fifty years as a Journalist: Unknown Binding*, Raj Mahal, Publishers: 1967, pp. 48-49, also narrated in Jamwal, Shailendra Singh, Barjor Dalal's report of the Srinagar Riot Enquiry Committee, op. cit. p. 9; Bamzai, P.N.K., *A History of Kashmir*, Gulshan Books, Kashmir: 2009, p. 707; Thomas, Christopher, *Faultline Kashmir*, op. cit., pp. 99-100.

17 Agnihotri, Kuldip, *Jammu Kashmir ke Jannayak*, op. cit., p. 71; Alastair Lamb, *Kashmir: A Disputed Legacy*, Oxford Books: 1991, p. 89.

18 Jamwal, Shailendra Singh, Barjor Dalal's report, op. cit.

19 The man's real identity could never be ascertained. See, Akbar, M. J., *Kashmir Behind the Veil*, Roli Books: 2017, p. 70.

20 This incident, rooted in false propaganda, has resulted in July 13 being observed as Martyrs Day in J&K.

21 Akbar, M.J., *Kashmir Behind the Veil*, Roli Books: 2017; Jamwal, Shailendra Singh, Barjor Dalal's report, op. cit.

22 Hussain, Taffazull, *Sheikh Abdullah: A Biography: The Crucial Period 1905-1939*, Wordclay, annotated edition, 2016.

23 Choudhary, Shabir, *Kashmir Dispute, Pakistan and the UN Resolution*, Author House: 2017 Chapter 6; Tikoo, Tej K., *Kashmir: Its Aborigines and Their Exodus*, Lancer Interconsult: 2012, p. 133.

24 See Brown, William, *Gilgit Rebellion: The Major Who Mutinied Over Partition of India*, Pen & Sword Military: 2014; Tikoo, Tej K., *1947-48 Indo-Pak War: Fall of Gilgit and Siege and Fall of Skardu*, Vivekananda International Foundation: 2013, https://www.vifindia.org/sites/default/files/1947-48-indo-pak-war-fall-of-gilgit-and-siege-and-fall-of-skardu.pdf; Khanna, K.K., *Art of Generalship*, Vij Books India: 2015; Bamzai, Sandeep, 'How Gilgit was Lost Forever,' *The Asian Age*, Sept. 23, 2018 http://www.asianage.com/columnists/how-gilgit-was-lost-forever-574.

25 Thomas, Christopher, *Faultline Kashmir*, op. cit., p. 67.

26 Excelsior, Jammu, March 10, 2011.

27 Sooden, Surjeet Singh, *Jammu under the Reign of Maharaja Hari Singh: A Study on Socio Economic Conditions*, Vinod Publishers & Distributors: 1999, p. 135.

28 Agnihotri, Kuldip, *Jammu Kashmir ke Jannayak*, op. cit., p. 209.

29 Jammu and Kashmir, Free and Compulsory Primary Education Regulation, 1930.

30 Sooden, Surjeet Singh, *Jammu under the Reign of Maharaja Hari Singh*, op. cit., p. 160.

31 Ibid., p. 98.

32 *Dainik Ranbir*, 7 June, 1943, Itihas Darpan, p. 375, vol. 18(2); Article of Jawahar Abbas, cited in *'Jammu Kashmir ke Jannayak'* by Agnihotri, Kuldip, op. cit., p. 218.
33 Singh, Harbans, *Maharaja Hari Singh: The Troubled Years*, Brahaspati Publication: 2011, pp. xix; Also, Singh, Karan, *Autobiography*
34 Wakhlu, Somnath, *Hari Singh: The Maharaja, the Man and the Times*, op. cit., p. 92.
35 S.R. Sharma & S.R. Bakshi, *Encyclopedia of Kashmir*, vol. 3, Anmol Publications: 1995, p. 270.
36 *Excelsior*, 23.09.2013, Singh, J. P.
37 Notification No. I-L/84 dated 20.4.1927, issued by His Highness the Maharaja Bahadur, Published in Gov. Gazette.
38 Singh, Harbans, *Maharaja Hari Singh: The Troubled Years*, Brahaspati Publications: 2011.
39 Jerath, Ashok, *Dogra Legends of Arts and Culture*, Indus Publishing: 1998.
40 Wakhlu, Somnath, *Hari Singh*, op. cit., pp. 174- 175.
41 Thomas, Christopher, *Faultline Kashmir*, op. cit., p. 196.
42 Jayrath, Ashok, *Jammu Kashmir me Hindi Sahitya ka Itihas*, p. 61.
44 White Paper on Indian States, Govt. of India Press, New Delhi, July 1948, p. 34 and Appendix IV.
45 Press Communique dated 25 July, 1947, released from Viceroy's House after the Meeting of Lord Mountbatten with the Chamber of Princes, cited in *Legal Documents on Jammu and Kashmir*, op. cit., p. 29.
46 Bhatnagar, Ashutosh, *Jammu Kashmir: An Analysis of Facts*, Jammu and Kashmir Study Center: 2013, p. 10.
47 Johnson, Allen Campbell, *Mission with Mountbatten*, Atheneum Books: 1985.
48 Hudson, H.V., *The Great Divide: Britain-India-Pakistan,* Atheneum Books: 1969, p. 442.
49 Menon, V. P., *The Story of the Integration of the Indian States*, Orient BlackSwan Publication: 2014, pp. 95-96.
50 Agnihotri, Kuldip, *Jammu Kashmir ke Jan Nayak*, op. cit., p. 109.
51 Mahajan, Mehr Chand, *Looking Back*, Har Anand Publications Pvt. Ltd.: rpt. 2018 [1963], p. 268.
52 Singh, Karan, *Jammu and Kashmir: 1949-64*, ed. Jawaid Alam, Penguin India: 2006, pp. 145-46.
53 Thomas, Christopher, *Faultline Kashmir* op. cit., p. 144.
54 Agnihotri, Kuldip, in *Jammu Kashmir ke Jannayak* states that Ram Chandra Kak's wife took keen interest in the politics of Jammu and Kashmir and its future.
55 Menon, V.P., *The Story of Integration of Indian States*, op. cit., pp. 95-96.
56 Agnihotri, Kuldip, *Jammu Kashmir ke Jan Nayak,* op. cit., p. 112.
57 Mahajan, Mehr Chand, *Looking Back*, op. cit., p. 131.
58 Mahajan, Mehr Chand, *Looking Back*, op. cit., p. 142.
59 Agnihotri, Kuldip, *Jammu Kashmir ke Jan Nayak*, op. cit., p. 113.
60 Singh, Karan, *Jammu and Kashmir: 1949-64*, op. cit., p. 313.
61 Sarila, Narendra Singh, *The Shadow of the Great Game*, op. cit., p. 349.
62 Mahajan, Mehr Chand, *Looking Back*, op. cit., p. 126.
63 Thomas, Christopher, *Faultline Kashmir*, op. cit., p. 144.

64 S. Gopal, *Jawahar Lal Nehru, A Biography*, Oxford University Press, India: 2003, p. 189.

65 Sarila, Narendra Singh, *The Shadow of the Great Game*, op. cit., p. 348.

66 Mahajan, Mehr Chand, *Looking Back*, op. cit., p. 142.

67 See also Sehgal, Narendra, *Vyathit Jammu & Kashmir*, Prabhat Prakashan: 2013, pp. 144-145; Kapoor, M.L., *Maharaja Hari Singh: 1895-1961*, Har Anand Publications: 1995, p. 135.

68 Mahajan, Mehr Chand, *Looking Back*, op. cit., p.150.

69 Letter from Maharaja Hari Singh to Lord Mountbatten along with Instrument of Accession, 26 October, 1947, in Sagar, Daya, *Jammu Kashmir: A Victim*, op. cit., p. 258.

70 Mahajan, Mehr Chand, *Looking Back*, op. cit., p. 144.

71 Hari Singh anticipated an attack from the Kishan Ganga Bridge and ordered its demolition, but there was no dynamite to execute the order. Someone was sent to Delhi to bring dynamite, but by that time the raiders had already crossed the bridge. The situation was aggravated by some troops deserting on communal lines. See Menon, V.P., *Integration of the Indian States*; Prasad, S.N. and Dharam Pal, *Operations in Jammu & Kashmir (1947-48)*, Natraj Publishers, UK: 2011; Bajwa, Kuldip Singh, *Jammu and Kashmir War, 1947-1948: Political and Military Perspective*, Har-Anand Publications: 2003; Singh, Harbans, *Maharaja Hari Singh: The Troubled Years*, op. cit.

72 Brig. Rajendra Singh's sacrifice is unforgettable as he saved three crucial days while engaging his small number of troops with minimum resources against a larger and better equipped force. True to his promise, he fought till the last bullet and made the supreme sacrifice. See Singh, Karan, *Autobiography*, pp. 87-88. Other heroes include Maqbool Sherwani (civilian), Major Somnath Sharma, Lt. Col. Ranjit Kumar, and Major Sher Jung Thapa.

73 Chopra, P.N., *Sardar Patel: Kashmir aur Hyderabad*, Prabhat Prakashan: 2015, p. 79. In November 1948, Cariappa planned to reoccupy Mirpur and Muzaffarabad, but General Roy Bucher with the help of the Defence Committee prevented the supply of additional troops needed for the operation. Thereafter, the UN under the influence of the UK and USA compelled India to declare a ceasefire which was declared on January 1, 1949. At this time, all strategic areas which London and Washington considered important to counter Russian influence were under the control of Pakistan. See also Devadas, David, *In Search of a Future: The Story of Kashmir*, Penguin Viking: 2007.

74 See Singh, Karan, *Autobiography*. Hari Singh also narrated this incident in a letter to Dr. Rajendra Prasad, published in Singh, Karan, *Jammu and Kashmir: 1949-64*, ed. Jawaid Alam, Penguin India: 2006.

75 Singh, Karan, *Autobiography*, Oxford University Press: 2003, pp. 156-157.

76 After the death of Patel, Nehru handed over the States Department to Gopalaswami Ayyangar.

77 Nehru Abdullah Pact: An unholy agreement and a fraud, A pamphlet published by Praja Parishad, p. 1.

78 Singh, Karan, *Autobiography*, op. cit., p. 155

79 Akbar, M. J., *Kashmir Behind the Veil*, Roli Books: 2017, p. 148; Agnihotri, Kuldip Chandra, op. cit., p. 131.

80 Singh, Karan, *Jammu and Kashmir: 1949-64*, op. cit., p. 323.

81 *Selected Works of Jawahar Lal Nehru*, vol. 19, pp. 295-296.

82 Dr. Kailash Nath Katju was appointed as minister of States Department in place of Gopalaswami Ayyangar.

83 Singh, Karan, *Jammu and Kashmir: 1949-64*, op. cit., pp. 342-345.

84 Agnihotri, Kuldip Chand, op. cit. p. 131. The Governor was appointed by the President in all states, but in J&K he was to be elected by the legislative assembly, with the consent of the President. This was changed later.

85 Singh, Karan, *Jammu and Kashmir: 1949-64*, op. cit. p. 350.

86 For details, see Mullick, B.N., *My Years with Nehru: Kashmir*, Allied Publishers: 1971.

CHAPTER ELEVEN

Delimitation and Unequal Representation

Shakti Munshi and Divya Roy

The word "delimitation" literally means the act or process of fixing limits or boundaries of territorial constituencies in a country or a province having a legislative body. In India, the responsibility of delimitation is assigned to the Delimitation Commission of India, constituted by the Central Government under a law enacted by Parliament. The Delimitation Commission is an autonomous statutory body. The key aspects of delimitation in India began with the need to demarcate the boundaries of Parliamentary and Assembly constituencies, largely on the basis of population. Successive Delimitation Commissions later accommodated reservation of seats for the Scheduled Castes and Scheduled Tribes, and other factors, such as physical features and existing boundaries of administrative units, facilities of communication, and public conveniences.

The allocation of seats for Scheduled Castes and Scheduled Tribes in the Lok Sabha was on the basis of the proportion of Scheduled Castes and Scheduled Tribes in the State concerned to that of the total population, vide provisions contained in Article 330 of the Constitution of India read with Section 3 of the Representation of the Peoples Act, 1950 (RP Act). All Delimitation Commission orders have the force of law and cannot be challenged in any court of law. However, the mandate for all Delimitation Commissions was that delimitation should be executed in such manner as to ensure equal distribution of legislative power and prevent imbalance of the population across the constituencies. The constitutional scheme of India itself provides for boundary fixation for the purposes of seat determination in Lok Sabha and State Assemblies.

Delimitation Commissions till date

The first Delimitation Commission was established in 1952 under the Delimitation Act 1952 that came into force on January 7, 1953. Headed by Justice N. Chandrasekhara Aiyar, it not only dealt with the readjustment of parliamentary and state assembly constituencies but also took into account the formation of the States on linguistic basis by the States Reorganisation Act of 1956. Consequently, the delimitation orders were finalized only in 1956. The apportionment of seats for the 1957 general elections was based on population figures from the 1951 Census.

Under the second Delimitation Commission, set up in 1963 under Delimitation Act 1962, the associate members were increased to nine; four of whom were to be members of the House of the People representing that State and five from members of the Legislative Assembly of that State. All constituencies, as far as practicable, had to be geographically compact areas, and in delimiting them, physical features, existing boundaries of administrative units, facilities of communication and public convenience were to be taken into consideration. The third Delimitation Commission, established in 1973 under Delimitation Act 1972, was based on the 1971 Census and completed its work in 1975. The associate members were increased to 10: five from the House of the People representing that State and five from the Legislative Assembly of that State.

The fourth Delimitation Commission, established in 2002 under Delimitation Act 2002, was undertaken after three decades and was based on Census 2001. The population of India had increased by almost 87 per cent and the nature of constituencies had become disproportional. But by the Constitution 87th Amendment Act, 2003, Parliament froze the total number of seats in the Lok Sabha and State Assemblies. The Delimitation Commission's operations were suspended over a dispute whether Census 1991 or Census 2001 figures were to be used for calculating the number of reserved constituencies. This was resolved by passing the Constitutional Amendment Act of 2003, which settled the issue in favour of Census 2001. As a result of the delay, delimitation could not be carried out in time for the 2004 parliamentary elections and continued till 2007. In response to a petition, the

Supreme Court in December 2007 issued notice to the Government of India for non-implementation. On January 4, 2008, the Cabinet Committee on Political Affairs (CCPA) decided to implement the recommendations of the Delimitation Commission, which were approved by President Pratibha Patil on February 19, 2008. Thus, the constituencies carved out on the basis of Census 2001 shall continue undisturbed till the first Census after 2026.

Articles dealing with delimitation of Constituencies

- Article 81: Deals with the composition of members of the House of the People (Lok Sabha)
- Article 82: Deals with the readjustment of constituencies after each Census. Parliament is obligated to enact a Delimitation Commission after every Census. The motive behind this Act was to ensure that there is not much disparity in the population of different constituencies, whether in the Lok Sabha or in the Vidhan Sabha.
- Article 170: Deals with the composition of Legislative Assemblies and provides at length the ratio of seats based on population and also mandates that upon the completion of each Census, the representation of the territorial constituencies in the Legislative Assembly of each State shall be readjusted by such authority, in such manner and with effect from such date as Parliament may by law determine.

Explanation: The provisions of Article 81 and clauses of Article 170 positively demonstrate that in the case of the Lok Sabha and State Assembly, the publication of figures of Census was to trigger reconstitution of a constituency or revisional change of the number of constituencies in a State because of change in the population of a particular State, as reflected in the publication of the figures of Census.

Parliament alone is vested with the constitutional mandate to provide the law for determining the number of constituencies in the Lok Sabha and number of constituencies in any State Assembly. Articles 55 and 56 of the Constitution of India, which deal with the election to the office of President, also define population as ascertained at the last preceding Census of which the relevant figures have been published.

- Article 329: Under Article 329, the validity of any law relating to the delimitation of constituencies or allotment of seats to such constituencies, made or purporting to be made under Article 327 or Article 328, shall not be called in question in any court, and further, no election to either House of Parliament or to either House of the Legislature of a State shall be called in question except by an election petition under 329(b) presented to such authority and in such manner as may be provided for by or under any law made by the appropriate Legislature. Identical provisions have been made in Section 142 of the Constitution of Jammu and Kashmir Section 142(a).

- Article 330: Deals with the reservation of seats for Scheduled Castes and Scheduled Tribes in the House of the People (Lok Sabha).
- Article 332: Deals with the reservation of seats for Scheduled Castes and Scheduled Tribes in the Legislative Assemblies of the States.
- Article 331: Gives the President the right to nominate two Anglo-Indians in the Lok Sabha
- Article 333: Gives the State Governors the right to nominate one Anglo-Indian in the Vidhan Sabha; under Article 334, this reservation has been extended to 2020.

Over the years, all these Articles were amended by the following amendment acts

1) The Constitution (Forty-second Amendment) Act, 1976, froze fresh delimitation after Census 2001. Passed during the Emergency at the behest of Sanjay Gandhi, it was argued that changing the number of seats according to population punished states that had managed to restrict their population growth. It thus protected the number of seats of southern states like Tamil Nadu, Kerala and Karnataka in the Lok Sabha, the only areas where Congress did well in the 1977 elections.[1]
2) The Constitution (Eighty-fourth Amendment) Act, 2001, further postponed the delimitation exercise from 2000 to 2026 and prevented reallocation of seats to the various States to reflect their growing population until the Census after 2026, i.e. after Census 2031, and substituted Census 1971 with Census 1991. However, the 84th amendment allowed boundaries of constituencies within the states to be redrawn so that large differences within the States could be redressed.[2]
3) The Constitutional (Eighty-seventh Amendment) Act 2003 substituted Census 1991 with Census 2001.

The cumulative effect of these three amendments to the Constitution is as follows:

- The total number of existing seats as allocated to various states in the Lok Sabha on the basis of Census 1971 shall remain unaltered till the first Census to be taken after the year 2026.
- The total number of existing seats in the Legislative Assemblies of all states as fixed on the basis of Census 1971 shall also remain unaltered till the first Census to be taken after the year 2026.
- The number of seats to be reserved for the Scheduled Castes and Scheduled Tribes in the Lok Sabha and State Legislative Assemblies shall be re-worked on the basis of Census 2001.
- Each state shall be re-delimited into territorial parliamentary and assembly constituencies on the basis of Census 2001 and the extent of such constituencies as delimited now shall remain frozen till the first Census to be taken after the year 2026.
- The constituencies shall be so re-delimited that population (on the basis of Census 2001) of each parliamentary and assembly constituency in a state shall, so far as practicable, be the same throughout the state.

Tempering of the process of delimitation

All Delimitation Commission orders come into force on a date specified by the President of India and are laid before the Lok Sabha and the State Legislative Assembly concerned. But they are not allowed to modify the same.

In spite of all measures taken to judicialise the process of delimitation, many believe it was tempered with slowly. The Delimitation Commission Act 1952 provided for a three-member Delimitation Commission made up of two Judges (or ex-Judges) and Chairman of the Election Commission (ex-officio), two to seven Associate members for each State (MLAs who were to be appointed by the Speaker of the State Legislative Assembly). The number of Associate members were gradually increased from two to seven and then to 10 in the Delimitation Commission Act 1972. The explanation given was that inputs from local politicians would help in executing the delimitation process.

Despite the Associate members having no voting rights, the number of such appointments and their privileged position at the heart of the process was bound to undermine the appearance of impartiality. The presence of

Associate members from the Lok Sabha and Vidhan Sabhas on the Delimitation Commissions was construed as political interference by Jaya Prakash Narayan even in the 1950s; he complained that "the task [of delimitation] has been practically left in the hands of single party, Congress".[3]

Thus, the history of delimitation till the last Delimitation Commission of 2002 reflects the continuing conflict between the desire to present the process as open and fair, and the temptation for politicians to control the process. As R.P. Bhalla notes, "It was regarded as a familiar device of giving an unbiased colouring to the biased proposals of the government".[4]

In 1976, the Indira Gandhi government suspended delimitation by enacting the Constitution (Forty-second Amendment) Act, 1976, which inserted Provisos to Articles 82 and 170(3) of the Constitution providing that no fresh readjustment of constituencies can be undertaken until the figures of the first Census taken after the year 2000 are published. These provisos were inserted to boost family planning norms and ensure that south India did not suffer a decline in political representation in the Lok Sabha. This tempering led to wide discrepancies in the size of constituencies, with the largest having over three million electors, and the smallest less than 50,000.

Delimitation process and position in J&K

Following the 84th and 87th amendments, the State of Jammu and Kashmir in 2002 also made amendments to the Jammu and Kashmir Representation of the People Act, 1957, and the Constitution of Jammu and Kashmir, freezing delimitation exercise in the state till the publication of the report of Census 2026. The corresponding amendments to Section 3 of the Jammu and Kashmir Representation of the People Act, 1957, and as amended from time to time, read as follows:

> **3. Constitution of Delimitation Commission**
>
> (1) As soon as may be after the completion of each Census, the Government shall constitute a Commission to be called the Delimitation Commission which shall consist of three members as follows:
>
> (a) Two members, each of whom shall be a person (who is or has) been a judge of the Supreme Court or of a High Court in India; and
>
> (b) A Deputy Election Commissioner nominated by the Chief Election Commissioner: Provided that until the relevant figures for the first Census taken after the year 2026 have been published, it shall not be necessary to

> constitute a Commission to determine the delimitation of Assembly Constituencies in the State under this sub-section.
>
> (2) The Governor shall nominate one of the members appointed under Clause (a) of Sub-section (1) to be the Chairman of the Delimitation Commission.
>
> (3) The Delimitation Commission shall determine the delimitation of Assembly Constituencies in the State within such period as may be specified by the Governor.

In line with the above-mentioned amendment, no Delimitation Commission was set up for the State of Jammu and Kashmir after the delimitation of 1995 based on Census 1971. The Census due in 1991 could not be conducted due to terrorism and ethnic cleansing of Kashmiri Hindus from the valley. The figures of Census 2001 used across the country did not reflect in Jammu and Kashmir due to the freeze imposed by the 87th amendment in 2002; it was during this period that the demography of the state changed drastically.

The State of Jammu and Kashmir, while showing promptness in making amendments in its state Constitution and Representation of People Act, did not even acknowledge the arbitrariness of these amendments, as for the rest of India, already several Delimitation Commissions had been set up and they had done their job of demarcation of constituencies in line with the mandate of the Constitution of India.

The amendments in Sub-section 3 of Section 47 of the Constitution of Jammu and Kashmir, 1957 (hereinafter referred to as Constitution of J&K) provide that

> Upon the completion of each Census, the number, extent and boundaries of the territorial constituencies shall be readjusted by such authority and in such manner as the Legislature may by law determine; Provided that such readjustment shall not effect representation in the Legislative Assembly until the dissolution of the then existing Assembly; Provided that until the relevant figures for the first Census taken after the year 2026 have been published, it shall not be necessary to readjust the total number of seats in the Legislative Assembly of the State and the division of the State into territorial constituencies under this Sub-section.

The State of Jammu and Kashmir without applying any Census publication of previous years, as was done in the other States of India, straightaway made an amendment saying that delimitation would be postponed till after the

Census of 2026, meaning thereby that any delimitation would not reflect before the Census of 2031. Under Article 370 of the Constitution of India, the President, while making modification and restriction and thereafter applying Article 81 of the Constitution of India, applied Article 81 in such a manner that Parliament is empowered to determine the number of seats of the State of J&K in Parliament. However, Parliament did not apply the Delimitation Act in relation to J&K, thereby frustrating the Constitutional provision to determine the number of seats of Lok Sabha periodically, with a view to provide adequate representation to the people of the state. Thus, a constitutional provision was defeated by a legislative provision. (*Explanation*: While Article 81 was applied in relation to J&K, at the same time the power to constitute the Delimitation Commission was left to the state legislature, thereby making the application of the constitutional provisional in the case of J&K meaningless.)

The failure on the part of the State Assembly of J&K to set up a Delimitation Commission to re-determine the number of constituencies for the State has become so fundamentally erroneous that the legitimacy of the constitution of the State Assembly after every election has become questionable. Since the Census exercise to be initiated in respect of J&K is relevant for the purposes of re-determination of constituencies for Lok Sabha and State Assembly as well, any reluctance on the part of the Central Government to initiate a process to reconstitute the parliamentary seats in Jammu and Kashmir has assumed serious dimensions.

Arguments for Delimitation in J&K

The last delimitation of J&K was in 1995 based on Census 1971 figures. It would be 60 years (till Census 2031) of injustice for the people of Jammu region. Delimitation is discouraged by the Valley-centric political parties who have controlled the State polity since 1947. None of them would like to give equitable share of membership in the Legislative Assembly to Jammu region, nor can the Kashmiri leadership digest political reservations for the Scheduled Tribes, namely, Gujjars, Bakerwals and Gaddies.

Even the Kashmiri Pandits of the valley were not spared in this manipulation. There is an entrenched feeling among Kashmiri Pandits that the three constituencies of Habba Kadal, Baramulla and Anantnag where they were numerically significant and could influence the electoral results, were subjected to gerrymandering by conducting delimitation in such a manner that merged parts of these constituencies with areas where demography could affect electoral outcomes. This ensured that all constituencies in the valley had a Muslim majority population and left Kashmiri Pandits without any representation in State politics. Sham Lal Saraf was elected from Habba Kadal and Sardar Harbans Singh Azad from Baramulla in the Constituent Assembly of 1951; D.P. Dhar won from Habba Kadal, a bastion of the Kashmiri Pandit community, in 1957 and 1962. But by 2009, Jammu and Kashmir Legislative Assembly did not have a single representative from the Kashmiri Hindu community.

The seven reserved seats for the Schedule Castes in Jammu Pradesh have not been rotated since 1996. It is pertinent to note that delimitation also means rotation of the reserved seats for Scheduled Castes and Scheduled Tribes and other weaker sections of society as enshrined in the Constitution. But there is no hope that in J&K these seven reserved Scheduled Caste seats will be rotated till 2031, thereby denying the SC population in other constituencies of any representation in the Assembly.

The Delimitation of Assembly seats has become imperative with the creation of eight new Districts in 2006, as some areas of one constituency fall under the administrative jurisdictions of two Districts. For example, Chatroo and Thakrai of Inderwal constituency fall in Kishtwar District whereas Gandoh and Thatri Tehsils of the same constituency remain with Doda District. Gool Tehsil of Gool-Arnas constituency falls under the jurisdiction of the newly created Ramban District, but Arnas Niabat falls under Reasi District. Ramgarh and Vijaypur Niabat of Vijaypur constituency fall under Samba District, whereas Bari Brahmana Niabat and Ratnu Chak continue to be with Jammu District. In Samba constituency, areas like Sidhra, Bain-Bajalta and the entire Purmandal block continue to fall under Jammu District. Parts of Hiranagar segment in Kathua District, namely, Ghagwal Niabat/Block have now been attached with Samba District. In Kashmir Valley also, a similar situation prevails in several Assembly segments. For instance, Devsar Assembly segment has been divided in Anantnag and Kulgam Districts. This sort of situation exists in many Assembly segments across the state and is bound to hamper developmental and other social welfare activities.

The electoral distribution in the state is interesting as the percentage share of the electorate at the regional level keeps on changing in each election. Sometimes Jammu region registers more electorate (voters) than Kashmir region, and at other times Kashmir region outnumbers Jammu region. This shift in numbers is for different reasons such as population growth, filing of electoral forms during each general and assembly election, migration, Kashmiri refugees from the valley settling in Jammu and so on. As per the 2002 electoral statistics of J&K State, Jammu region had two lakh more registered voters than Kashmir region.

Similarly, as per the Election Commission of India, Kashmir region registered nearly 2.50 lakh more electors in 2014 assembly elections than Jammu region. In terms of assembly seat share percentage, as per 2014 assembly election figures, Gurez and Batmaloo assembly seats represent the two extreme electoral distributions from Kashmir region, the former having merely 17,624 registered voters while the latter had 1,20,344 registered electors. Similarly, Bani and Gandhi Nagar in Jammu region represent the two extremes of electoral distribution, Bani recording a low 41,533 registered voters and Gandhi Nagar a high of 1,69,672 registered electors. Of the 15 assembly constituencies in Jammu and Kashmir that have more than one lakh registered electors each, 10 fall in Jammu region while 5 fall in Kashmir region. Similarly, of the 15 assembly constituencies with less than 60,000 voters, five are in Kashmir region, three in Ladakh and seven in Jammu region. This disproportionate spread of electors warrants delimiting to resize the electorate against each constituency. The proper and proportionate distribution of electors against each constituency is desirable to give fair representation to the electorate in both the state legislature and parliament.

The Jammu and Kashmir assembly currently comprises 111 members, including 24 seats kept vacant for the territorial constituencies under Pakistani occupation. More than 10 to 12 lakh persons of Pakistan-occupied Jammu and Kashmir (POJK) are living in refugee camps in Jammu. Their demand is that a proportionate number of these 24 seats reserved under section 47 of the state constitution for the permanent residents of POJK should be allocated to them as they have migrated to the Indian side and hold the status of permanent residents of Jammu and Kashmir State, but remain unrecognised by the political leadership.

In 2002, a common minimum programme was agreed between Congress president Sonia Gandhi, Dr Manmohan Singh, People's Democratic Party leader Mufti Mohd. Sayeed, Bhim Singh of Panther's Party and CPM leader Yousuf Tarigami to hold delimitation in J&K. Later, the PDP and Congress joined hands with the National Conference to defeat this move. Aggrieved, the Panther's Party withdrew support from the coalition government headed by Ghulam Nabi Azad in 2007.[5]

Though increase in the total number of assembly constituencies has been barred in J&K as in other States of India, legal experts believe that while the total number of Assembly constituencies is fixed, under President's rule in J&K, the Governor has the power to set up a Delimitation Commission to re-adjust the boundaries of Assembly constituencies to balance electorates and rotate the seven reserved seats for Schedule Castes: Chhamb, Domana and RS Pura in Jammu district; Samba, Hiranagar in Kathua district; Chenani in Udhampur district and Ramban, which have not been rotated since 1996.

Conclusion

Jammu has always felt aggrieved at the manner in which Jawaharlal Nehru ensured that all power was handed over to Sheikh Abdullah in 1947 before he would accept the Maharaja's accession and send military aid to the beleaguered state. Abdullah used this power to arbitrarily assign 43 seats for Kashmir region, 30 for Jammu, and 2 for Ladakh, leaving the rest for occupied regions. Though somewhat mitigated over the years, weightage to Kashmir has persisted to the present day. In the course of a conversation with this author (December 21, 2018), Bhim Singh recalled that in 2002, Jammu Pradesh had two lakh more voters than Kashmir Valley. More importantly, the Scheduled Tribes (Gujjars, Bakerwals and Gaddies) who comprise 11 per cent of the population have not been granted any political reservation in the Legislative Assembly of J&K.

The delimitation of Districts and Blocks in 2005-6 caused many Assembly constituencies to fall across two or three districts, in violation of the Representation of People Act, 1981. There is a gross violation of electoral laws on the "vote value" as some constituencies, for instance, Gurez in Kashmir Valley has less than 18,000 voters whereas Jammu West has nearly 200,000 voters. None of the Assembly constituencies in Kashmir Valley has more than 70,000 voters, whereas most Assembly constituencies in Jammu Pradesh comprise more than 80,000 to 200,000 voters. This militates against the electoral system of India that is based on a single-member constituency having roughly the same size of an electorate so that the vote of one person does not have greater weight than another's.

Till date, there is no representation for the refugees of POJK, whereas the Constitution of J&K in Section 47 reserved 24 seats for the permanent residents of POJK and nearly one-third of the population of POJK who are permanent residents of J&K and have been residing in Jammu Pradesh as refugees. These seats should be allocated to these refugees without further delay.

The Schedule Caste seats are meant to be rotated in different parts of the State. The 84th amendment allows rotation of reserved seats, but the seven assembly constituencies reserved for Scheduled Castes in the J&K State have remained in Jammu region for more than 25 years, leading to electoral manipulation similar to gerrymandering favouring valley politicians. There is thus a strong case for a fresh and rational delimitation of Lok Sabha and Assemblies constituencies in J&K State to rationalise the electorate numbers and remove the regional imbalance between Kashmir and Jammu. The Centre should also consider reservation of some seats in the Kashmir valley for the Kashmiri Pandits, to give them a political voice in the region, which they lost post the first delimitation exercise, and need to recover if the return of the families forced out in 1989-90 is seriously envisaged.

*

NOTES

1 See Sivaramakrishnan, K.C., A fear of change, Seminar, 2008. http://www.india-seminar.com/2008/586/586_k_c_sivaramakrishnan.htm.

2 See Handley, Lisa (ed.) and Bernard Grofman (ed.), *Redistricting in Comparative Perspective*, Oxford, UK: Oxford University Press, 1997.

3 See Kumar, Sanjay, The Fourth Delimitation: An Evaluation, *Economic and Political Weekly*, 44 (3), 2009, pp. 41-46. See also, McMillan, Alistair, Changing the Boundaries of Indian Democracy. https://www.nuff.ox.ac.uk/users/Mcmillan/Delimitation McMillan.pdf.

4 Bhalla, R.P., Elections in India (1950–1972), New Delhi: S Chand and Co., 1973, p. 61. See also, McMillan, op. cit.

5 Panthers Party withdraws support in J&K. June 17, 2007. https://www.hindustantimes.com/india/panthers-party-withdraws-support-in-j-k/story-ob9cOt21ZCyLjUo5Pu9ZAI.html.

CHAPTER TWELVE

Genesis of the *Praja Parishad*

Kuldip Chand Agnihotri

The last dynasty of the Kashmir region was founded in 1846, when the empire created by Maharaja Ranjit Singh was defeated in the first Anglo-Sikh War and the region was ceded to the British. The East India Company thereafter elevated the Dogra ruler of Jammu, Gulab Singh, formerly a noble in Ranjit Singh's darbar, as the Maharaja of Jammu and Kashmir. He had already expanded the northern frontiers of the kingdom to include the strategically important territories of Ladakh, Gilgit and Baltistan; his dynasty ruled until 1947 when the last ruler was deposed after falling foul of the new leaders of independent India.

Hari Singh, the great grandson of Gulab Singh, ascended the throne in 1925, by which time the British Government had become keen to bring Gilgit under its direct administration, apprehending Russian designs on India. London felt it would be useful to undermine the authority of Hari Singh, to which end it began to encourage a Muslim reading room group in Srinagar, a gathering of ex-students of Aligarh Muslim University.[1] Hari Singh did not endear himself to the British when, participating in the Round Table Conference in London in 1930, as representative of the Princely States, he asserted, "As Indians and loyal to the land, whence we derive our birth and infant nurture, we stand as solidly as the rest of our countrymen for our land's enjoyment of a position of honour and equality in the British commonwealth of nations".[2]

Backed by British patronage, Sheikh Mohammad Abdullah, an alumnus of Aligarh Muslim University and a school teacher from village Soura in

Srinagar, rose to prominence on the strength of his powerful oratory. He was linked to the Muslim reading room group by Maulvi Sayyid Masoodi, a teacher in a Government School at Muzaffarabad, who also introduced him to Mian Bashir-ud-din Mehmood at Hazara, who urged Abdullah to serve his community. After an incident of rioting in 1931, the Muslim Conference was born with Sheikh Abdullah as president. Its battle cry was, "Dogras Quit Kashmir". The party split after some time, and Sheikh became the leader of the breakaway National Conference.

By 1946, it was clear that London wanted to create a buffer state between Afghanistan and India, ostensibly to check the expansion of Communist Russia; this became the justification for Pakistan. The British wanted Jammu and Kashmir to merge with the proposed new country as its borders stretched up to Tibet, China, Russia and Afghanistan. The obstacle was the Treaty of Amritsar (1846) that created the Kingdom of Jammu and Kashmir and made Kashmir Valley part of this State. As if on cue, Sheikh Abdullah and the National Conference launched a campaign for abrogation of the Treaty of Amritsar. Maharaja Hari Singh understood the British game and arrested Sheikh Abdullah. To his astonishment, Jawaharlal Nehru rushed to Kashmir to help Abdullah. But Hari Singh stood firm and crushed the agitation.

The Viceroy, Lord Louis Mountbatten, and Jammu and Kashmir prime minister Ramchandra Kak favoured accession to Pakistan. The situation was complicated by Congress president Jawaharlal Nehru insisting that Hari Singh hand over administrative power to his friend, Sheikh Abdullah. Mountbatten visited Srinagar two months before partition (June 19-23, 1947) and reputedly nudged Hari Singh to accede to Pakistan. His press attaché, Allan Campbell Johnson, recorded in his diary (October 28, 1947) details shared by Mountbatten regarding his Srinagar visit, "(Mountbatten) said that while urging the Maharaja to make up his mind about the transfer of power, he had all along, from his visit in June onwards, exerted his whole influence to prevent him from acceding to one Dominion or the other without first taking steps to ascertain the will of his people by referendum, plebiscite, election, or even, if these methods were impracticable, by representative public meetings".[3] Mountbatten's effort to ensure that Hari Singh did not accede to either India or Pakistan before August 15 was corroborated by H.V. Hodson, "The viceroy had recounted that the advice he had given to the Maharaja was that Kashmir should not decide about joining any Constituent Assembly until the Pakistan Assembly had been set up".[4] This was also the impression gleaned by Mehr

Chand Mahajan, who visited Mountbatten on September 29, 1947, before assuming charge as prime minister of Jammu and Kashmir, "From an hour's talk I had with him, I inferred that he felt that there was no option for the Maharaja but to accede to Pakistan, in view of the geographical position of the State".[5]

Even as Mountbatten pressured Hari Singh to accede to Pakistan and suggested gauging public opinion to achieve his objective, Nehru refused to discuss accession with Hari Singh and was adamant to discuss the matter only with Sheikh Abdullah. He devoted his energies to getting Abdullah released from prison (for demanding abrogation of the Treaty of Amritsar) and put in a position of authority.[6] Nehru made this a condition for accepting the accession of Jammu and Kashmir: "In July, a month before partition, the Maharaja sent Pandit Kak, his prime minister, to Delhi to explore the terms under which Kashmir might accede to India. Kak was told there could be no accession without first ascertaining the wishes of the people – the people being Sheikh Abdullah".[7]

From the time of Mountbatten's failed trip to Srinagar, rumours were spread that the Maharaja favoured independence. Campbell Johnson observed, "Both Nehru and Gandhi have been very anxious that the Maharaja of Kashmir should make no Declaration of Independence".[8] Realising that accusing the Maharaja of wanting to keep the state could be injudicious at such a sensitive moment, Sardar Patel suggested that Mahatma Gandhi rather than Nehru should visit Srinagar. Gandhi visited the State for four days from July 31 to August 2, 1947; this agitated the Muslim Conference that demonstrated against Gandhi in Baramulla. Gandhi met Hari Singh on August 1; there are no records of the conversation. However, Karan Singh recalled that Gandhi "was urging my father to ascertain the wishes of his people, to take his people into confidence, and to align himself with rather than against them in the political turmoil that was engulfing the country".[9]

Mountbatten and Nehru were advising Hari Singh to hold a plebiscite, and so was Mahatma Gandhi. However, there was a difference in the meaning of the words uttered by the three of them, and who understood this better than the Maharaja? After the meeting with Gandhi, Hari Singh dismissed Ramchandra Kak from office on August 11 and replaced him with Major General Janak Singh of Himachal Pradesh. Kak, who supported Pakistan, attempted to escape, but was put under house arrest. The Inspector General of Police and Chief of the General Staff of the State Forces were also dismissed.

Construction began for a new bridge across the river Tawi and telegraph lines were laid in Jammu and Kashmir, while roads were repaired in Jammu and Kathua, all of which pointed to Hari Singh's intention to join India.

Standstill Agreement and Invasion

Trapped between Mountbatten and the Muslim League pressure to accede to Pakistan and New Delhi's failure to negotiate with him, Hari Singh proposed a Standstill Agreement with both Dominions on August 12. Karachi immediately sent a telegram accepting the proposal, but Nehru stonewalled, despite the fact that the conditions for the Standstill Agreement sent to Delhi favoured the new federal system of the country. Under international law, the Indian Dominion that remained after partition was the successor state of British India and inherited the obligations inherent in the Treaty of Amritsar (including the part related to Kashmir valley) after the Standstill Agreement. Hari Singh was indirectly creating a situation in which the Indian Government could legally interfere in case Pakistan attempted to grab his kingdom by force. Instead, Delhi declared that the proposal would be considered only when the Maharaja or his representative came to Delhi to discuss the matter.

On October 22, Pakistan pushed Pashtun and Afridi tribals backed by its Army into the State, having understood that Hari Singh would not accede to Pakistan. The first attack was on Muzaffarabad. On October 23, Maharaja Hari Singh arrived in Srinagar after touring the affected areas in Jammu division; news of the attack on Muzaffarabad had reached the capital by then. The next day was the festival of Dussehra. Hari Singh dispatched his deputy prime minister, Ram Lal Batra, to Delhi with a proposal to accede to India. Besides a letter of accession to India, Batra carried a personal letter to Jawaharlal Nehru and another to Sardar Patel asking for military help in men, arms and ammunition.[10] Ram Lal Batra moved around Delhi with the Letter of Accession, but no one entertained him.

As the valiant soldiers of the State sacrificed their lives to protect its territorial integrity and the lives and dignity of the citizens, Nehru remained obdurate that accession would be accepted only when power was handed over to Sheikh Abdullah. In meetings of the Defence Committee on October 25 and 26, Mountbatten as chairman favoured accession before sending the army. Nehru insisted that power be handed over to Abdullah. On October 26, V.P. Menon, secretary of the States Department, was sent to Srinagar to discuss with the Maharaja, and to bring Mehr Chand Mahajan back with him. Army officer Sam Manekshaw also came to Srinagar along with Menon. Mahajan recalled that Menon came to his residence "and told me that he had come there to take me to New Delhi. Nothing about military aid, he said, could be decided till my arrival there. I told him that we had sent our deputy prime minister to Delhi with a letter of Accession. I reminded him that when I had come to the State to take over as prime minister, I had been assured of military aid whenever I wanted it. He told me, however, that without my going to Delhi, it was difficult to say that military aid will be available in time to save the city of Srinagar".[11]

Nehru wanted Mahajan's assurance that the Maharaja was willing to hand over power to Sheikh Abdullah, for which he wasted vital days from October 22 to 26, during which time the Pakistani army or its tribal vanguard reached Baramulla. The raiders went on an orgy of killing and pillaging. The state army led by Rajendra Singh fought against bitter odds. Hari Singh stood firm in Srinagar, ready to go into the battlefield himself, but Menon feared that the raiders might abduct the Maharaja, in which case it would be difficult to save Jammu and Kashmir from falling into the hands of Pakistan. In such a fraught situation, the Maharaja's safety was of utmost importance, and Menon persuaded Hari Singh to immediately leave for Jammu, a position endorsed by Mehr Chand Mahajan. Moreover, October-November was the time that the State capital normally shifted to Jammu and the "Durbar Move" had already begun, but Hari Singh had remained in Srinagar in view of the crisis. Menon now presented a copy of the Letter of Accession (as drafted by the States Ministry of the Government of India and signed by other rulers who acceded to India), which Hari Singh signed. Menon and Mahajan reached Delhi on October 26 and heeding Menon's advice, Hari Singh and the royal family left for Jammu.

In Delhi, Mahajan found Nehru unwilling to commit military assistance. He said, "Give us the military force we need. Take the accession and give whatever power you desire to the popular party. The army must fly to save Srinagar this evening".[12] As Governor General of the Dominion of India, Louis Mountbatten accepted Hari Singh's accession on October 27, but in the meeting of the Defence Committee, Mountbatten and the chiefs of the three wings of the armed forces opposed sending troops to Kashmir, "but, when Mountbatten saw that the Council of Ministers were adamant about this, he agreed".[13] But now Mountbatten played a trick. He wrote to Hari Singh saying that the accession had been accepted under the condition that when normalcy is restored, the opinion of the people will be sought. This proved to be a turning point in the history of the state. The Indian Independence Act had no provision for attaching conditions after accepting the offer from the ruler of a state. Moreover, this condition was an afterthought; Mountbatten was exceeding his jurisdiction, but Nehru took the bait. This stand by the Governor General revealed a deep-rooted British conspiracy to divide the state and to handover the strategically important Gilgit and Baltistan area to Pakistan, thereby blocking India's land route to Central Asia.

Under pressure of Nehru's obduracy, the Maharaja installed Sheikh Abdullah as the emergency administrator and then as prime minister of the State, though Abdullah was not even a member of the State Legislative Assembly for which elections had been held in January 1947. Nor was he the leader of the Muslims of Jammu as the area was under the influence of the Muslim Conference. Nor was he the leader of the people of Gilgit and Baltistan because Shias were in majority there. Neither did he represent the Hindus and Sikhs of Jammu and Buddhists of Ladakh. His much-vaunted popularity was restricted to the Kashmiri-speaking Sunni Muslims of the Kashmir Valley, excluding Gujjars, Pahadis, Shias and Scheduled Tribes, and Kashmir valley was a very small part of Jammu and Kashmir.

Formation of *Praja Parishad*

As the emergency administrator, Sheikh Abdullah wielded all power and Hari Singh was sidelined in his own state. Soon, slogans such as "*ek Rehnama, Sheikh Mohammad Abdullah, ek Tanzeem National Conference, ek Jhanda, Halwala*" began to reverberate in the State. Jammuites, Ladakhis, Baltis, Dardis, Shias, Gujjars and Pahadis all felt devalued and threatened in the new regime. Under tremendous pressure from Nehru, Hari Singh was forced to appoint Abdullah as his prime minister on March 5, 1948. In these circumstances, Prem Nath Dogra (*Sher-e-Duggar*), Balraj Madhok and others founded the All Jammu and Kashmir Praja Parishad as an alternate political party on November 17, 1947. Hari Wazir was its first president and Hans Raj Pangotra its general secretary.[14]

Meeting of Praja Parishad delegation with Nehru

A large portion of Jammu province (and Ladakh) was still under the occupation of the Pakistani invaders, though they had largely been driven out of Kashmir province. But Mirpur, Kotli, Bhimber, and Poonch were Punjabi-speaking areas where the Muslim League had some influence. Thus, the lives and properties of thousands of Hindus and Sikhs were in grave danger. However, the Army headquarters in Delhi did not allow the officers in the battlefield to go forward as the Indian Army Chief, General Sir Robert McGregor MacDonald Lockhart, was an Englishman. The Army Chief of Pakistan, General Sir Frank Messervy, was also an Englishman. Another Englishman, Sir Douglas David Gracey, succeeded Frank Messervy. It was clearly the strategy of the British government to divide the state strategically in favour of Pakistan.

In these circumstances, a delegation led by Prof. Balraj Madhok and Prem Nath Dogra met Nehru at Jammu airport and apprised him of the situation at Mirpur and requested him to send the Army there; but Nehru asked them to meet Sheikh Abdullah, and ultimately the Army was not sent to Mirpur. Jammu region was abuzz with public discussions that Nehru and Sheikh were taking interest in evacuating the attackers from Kashmir, but not showing much interest in protecting the areas of Jammu from falling under Pakistan's control. On November 2, 1947, a disappointed Mehr Chand Mahajan appealed to Nehru to save the state army garrison in Mirpur, Kotli, Naushera, and Poonch. All these incidents created an impression in the minds of Jammuites and Ladakhis that neither Nehru nor Abdullah was interested in these regions. In fact, Sheikh and Nehru were clearly and doggedly pursuing a separatist line to divide Jammu and Kashmir according to the strategic plans of the British.

India in the Security Council

Nehru took the case of Jammu and Kashmir to the United Nations on the advice and persuasion of Lord Mountbatten on January 1, 1948, and asked it to declare Pakistan as an aggressor; instead, the Security Council began to debate whether the accession of the state to India was valid or not. To make matters worse, India was committing to letting the people of the state decide if they would ultimately go with India or Pakistan. This strategy of Nehru hurt India more than Pakistan, because India was admitting that Pakistan was a stakeholder in Jammu and Kashmir. This flawed approach also put a question mark on the future of the people of Jammu and Ladakh.

As previously mentioned, under pressure from Nehru, Sheikh Mohammad Abdullah was appointed prime minister of the state on March 5, 1948. Thus, Mountbatten completed his agenda in India successfully: failing to secure the accession of Jammu and Kashmir to Pakistan, he divided the state carefully to the strategic advantage of Pakistan (and the West in the context of the looming

Cold War), unleashed the ghost of plebiscite in the valley, and convinced Nehru to put the case of the state as a disputed area in the Security Council. On completing this mission of British imperialism, he departed from India on June 21, 1948. On January 1, 1949, India at UN insistence declared a ceasefire in Jammu and Kashmir and the practical division of the state was complete. Those areas of the state needed to strengthen Pakistan remained with Pakistan. The people of these areas, namely, Gilgit, Baltistan (of Ladakh) and Mirpur, Kotli, etc. (of Jammu) were not pro-Sheikh Abdullah. Keeping these areas out of the State also suited Abdullah.

Article 370

More than 550 Princely States that had acceded to the Indian Union initially acceded only with respect to three subjects, but gradually accepted the federal provisions being drafted for the other states of the erstwhile British India. However, Abdullah did not want all provisions of the Indian constitution to apply to Jammu and Kashmir. His argument was that (1) the accession of the State to the federal constitutional system was conditional and (2) Maharaja Hari Singh had only surrendered three subjects, namely, defence, external affairs, and communications vide the Instrument of Accession to the federal constitutional arrangement. The right to execute an Instrument supplementary to the Instrument of Accession was retained by the Maharaja. It follows that the Government of India should have consulted Hari Singh regarding the signing of a Supplementary Instrument because he was the constitutional head of the State. From a legal standpoint, he alone had the right to take a decision on this matter. There can be no doubt that Hari Singh would have signed such a Supplementary Instrument and this question would have been put to rest for posterity. But Nehru directed Gopalaswami Ayyangar to incorporate the provisions determined by Sheikh Abdullah into the Constitution. There was tremendous opposition from within the Congress, but Nehru insisted, "give Abdullah what he wanted".[15]

Nehru surrendered to all of Sheikh Abdullah's whims, only to have Abdullah turn into an albatross around his neck, but would not deal with Maharaja Hari Singh who could have solved all problems gracefully. Gopalaswami Ayyangar presented Abdullah's stand to the Drafting Committee of the Constituent Assembly on October 17, 1949, in the form of Article 306 (which later became Article 370). Giving a lengthy explanation for Article 370, Ayyangar stated, "This discrimination becomes due to the special conditions of Kashmir. That particular state is not yet ripe for this kind of integration. It is the hope of everybody here that in due course even Jammu and Kashmir will become ripe for the same sort of integration, as has taken place in the case of other states".[16]

However, Sheikh Abdullah's views regarding Article 370 were different from those stated by Gopalaswami Ayyangar before the Constituent Assembly. According to Abdullah,

> In India, new constitution was being drafted for the country. When a lot of work had been done, the Centre thought of co-opting some members from Kashmir. At that time we managed our affairs with the Maharaja's constitution with certain amendments. We needed to determine the status of our state in the Indian constitution after the accession. So talks were held in Delhi on this issue between us and the central leadership. Our side was represented by Bakshi (Ghulam Mohammad), Beg (Mohammad Afzal), Qasim (Mir) and Dhar (D.P. Dhar).
>
> I also attended the talks for a while. We had decided among ourselves that we would not deflect from the provisos envisaged in the Instrument of Accession. But the central leadership desired our complete merger in the Union like the other states. We were not agreeable to this. Our stand was clear. Kashmir with its Muslim majority was the only state to have joined the Indian Union. It shared its borders on three sides with Pakistan, which was another reason why the latter staked its claim to it. Besides, India had agreed to a plebiscite by which Kashmir was to decide its future. The entire issue dominated the United Nations forums where time and again Indian delegates spoke with full throated ease alerting that India did not covet Kashmir but favoured a plebiscite under the United Nations auspices by which the people would choose either Pakistan or India or decide to be independent. Under these conditions, a merger in the Indian Union was out of the question. In view of this, Article 370 was incorporated into the constitution, although we had certain reservations about certain details and terms.
>
> However, when Ayyangar presented it before the Constituent Assembly, the members from the state did not object. It may be borne in mind that the state was represented by myself, Beg, Saeed, and Pandit Moti Ram Begra. When I walked into the Assembly the first time, I was given a warm welcome. Jawaharlal received me personally and made me sit next to him. That very day we were formally sworn in as the members. .
>
> As mentioned earlier, when we were in consultation with the central leaders over the legislation of Article 370, Beg, who with his legal expertise acted as my advisor, and myself, got an impression that our relationship with the

> centre was not going to be a smooth affair. We could see their mental kinks and reservations. They might say anything verbally, but inwardly they intended to treat us the same way as the other states. .
>
> Before independence the rulers of the states of undivided India had struck a deal, after prolonged deliberations, with the leaders of the National Congress and the Muslim League. The deal determined their status in case of their merger into the Indian Federation. Even those conditions were agreed on which the rulers could join either India or Pakistan. It was agreed that such states would transfer to the centre only defence, foreign affairs and communications, and retain their internal autonomy in other matters. Patel had given an assurance that the states would not have to bear defence expenditure. After acquiring power, the Congress leaders failed to keep their promise. They forced the states to merge in the Union. This way the states were asked not to form their own constituent assemblies but to wait for the decision of the Central Constituent Assembly. The intention was that they should adopt the central constitution which would ensure their merger in the Union. To achieve this objective, the states were first divided into various groups. Then each group was placed under the charge of a raj pramukh and upraj pramukh. Thus a great many rajas and maharajas lost their authority.
>
> In the second phase, the raj pramukhs and upraj pramukhs were divested of their administrative authority and made constitutional heads like modern-day governors. In the third phase, the rajas and maharajas were persuaded to completely abdicate their administrative responsibilities. In return, they were offered privy purses and other special privileges enjoyed by them earlier. For this, the central government would have to spend nothing but it kept the rajas' ego inflated. Their privileges included gun salute, separate flags, official security, travel allowances, etc. Already bereft of self-respect and moral rectitude, they fell into the trap and agreed to their self-extinction. It may be that they had sensed the designs of the Indian leaders and so grabbed at whatever came their way. The circumstances in Kashmir were different. Its future was still under discussion before the United Nations Organisation. So it was not possible to make similar changes here.[17]

Thus, according to Sheikh Abdullah, Article 370 restricted the right of Parliament to frame legislation on Jammu and Kashmir beyond the above-mentioned three subjects and this article defined the relationship between the State and the Union. Abdullah's main contention was that in spite of being a Muslim-majority state, Jammu and Kashmir had decided to accede to India and so it should receive special privileges, and hence Article 370. On its part, the Government of India, as enunciated by Ayyangar, held the view that Article

370 was not a privilege but rather a temporary arrangement in view of the special conditions prevailing in the State. New Delhi hoped that Article 370 would cease to exist as soon as these special conditions came to an end. However, Sheikh Abdullah tasted his first success on October 17, 1949, when Article 370 was incorporated into the Constitution of India.

Praja Parishad demands full integration

In early 1949, the Praja Parishad began to protest against the policies of the National Conference government led by Sheikh Abdullah. The Parishad declared its objectives as full integration of Jammu and Kashmir with the rest of India at par with other princely states that had acceded to India; establishment of a political, social and economic order wherein no one suffers discrimination on grounds of caste, colour and faith; and equality of opportunity to all citizens. Its membership was open to all adult residents of the state. Abdullah perceived the Praja Parishad leaders as a threat to his goal of complete autonomy; Prem Nath Dogra and his colleagues were arrested in February 1949. Section 3 of the Ranbir Penal Code (known as "Daffa Tun", i.e., lockup without trial) was slapped on Dogra. Soon, as many as 294 Parishad workers were arrested.[18] Balraj Madhok, a member of the Rashtriya Swayamsevak Sangh (RSS) and one of the founder members of the Praja Parishad, was banned from the state.[19] In May 1949, the Praja Parishad launched a *satyagraha* for the release of Prem Nath Dogra. Abdullah finally yielded to the pressure and released Dogra on October 8, 1949.

Elections to the State Constitution Assembly

Nehru took the issue of Pakistani aggression in Jammu and Kashmir to the Security Council under the Machiavellian advice of Mountbatten; but deliberations in the Council made it clear that the issue was becoming a tool between two blocs in the Cold War, and that Britain was leading the attack on India. But it was too late for India to get out of this mess. Nehru was desperate for a way out of this cul-de-sac while Abdullah was in search of a mechanism to get full control over the state. The Constituent Assembly to draft the constitution of the state was a possible way out. But the Assembly meant different things to the two leaders. Nehru hoped the Constituent Assembly would be a sound and legal substitute for a plebiscite. Sheikh Abdullah saw it as the route to full control over the State, to be in a position to dictate terms to Delhi. Maharaja Hari Singh had been deprived of all power though he was still the titular head of state. A notification for elections to the proposed Constituent Assembly was issued, but Abdullah proved to be far more adroit than Nehru.

The Constituent Assembly (which also served as the state's Legislative Assembly) was to have 100 members, but 25 Assembly constituencies were under Pakistan's occupation and elections could not be held in those areas.[20] The remaining 75 seats were distributed arbitrarily: 43 for Kashmir Valley, 30 for Jammu province and 2 for Ladakh region, even though the population of Kashmir valley was far less than that of Jammu. The elections took place in September-October 1951. Nehru did not allow the Congress party to contest the elections as he considered the National Conference as an ideological branch of the Congress. The Praja Parishad and Akali Dal contested, but withdrew their candidates in protest against the high-handedness of the Abdullah regime. Sheikh Abdullah managed the election to the State Constituent Assembly by getting most nomination papers of opposing candidates rejected on flimsy grounds and driving the opposition parties (Praja Parishad and Akali Dal) to boycott the elections in protest. Not even a single voter entered any polling booth in the state and Abdullah won all 75 seats. This was a feat unparalleled in the annals of parliamentary democracy anywhere in the world. Josef Korbel commented, "No dictator could do better".[21] As a consequence of this so-called election, Nehru lost all power of taking the initiative and Abdullah began wielding total power. Before the elections to the state Constituent Assembly, it used to be said that Sheikh Abdullah was Nehru's man in the valley, but after the elections a new phrase gained currency – that Nehru was Sheikh Abdullah's man in India. Abdullah was not interested in giving democratic rights to the people of Jammu and Kashmir. Sumantra Bose observed that the manner of the elections indicated that the National Conference elites wanted to govern Jammu and Kashmir as a party state. Their slogan was, "One Leader, One Party, One Programme".[22]

Democratic powers have three main sources: the fundamental rights of the citizens, their protection by an independent judiciary, and free and fair elections. Sheikh was not ready to implement these provisions of the Indian constitution in Jammu and Kashmir. Instead, he started taking interest in dismantling the unification process. He demanded a separate flag and constitution for the state. He insisted that the constitutional head should not be nominated by the President, as is done for other states, but elected by the legislative assembly. It seemed evident that Sheikh was following the advice of external forces and burdening the state with autocratic rule. In 1952, Sheikh faced conflict with the people at every turn of the path he was following. The people of the state had to fight for their rights in independent India and also to make sacrifices. The year 1952 became witness to such a struggle and it took a small spark to ignite it.

Speech at Ranbir Singh Pura

Ranbir Singh Pura (RS Pura) is about 35 km from Jammu and only 10 km from the Pakistan border. Before independence, the road and rail link of Jammu to the rest of country passed through RS Pura, but partition put an end to this. The National Conference on April 10, 1952, organised a public gathering here, and Sheikh Abdullah made a long speech. Actually he was addressing both India and Pakistan from the Indo-Pakistan border. He said Kashmir would act as a bridge between India and Pakistan.

> Our merger with the India is of limited nature. Communalism had not stopped in India yet. Kashmir should get a special status. Those who are talking about implementing the full constitution in Kashmir are acting irrationally, petulantly and madly. We can implement the whole of constitution too, if we are convinced that communalism has been eradicated from India. A lot of Kashmiris ask me, if something happened to Jawahar Lal Nehru, what will happen to them. We are practical, so we should be ready for every eventuality. That is why I am saying that those who want to annihilate the separate identity of Kashmir are not aware about the ground situation.[23]

After this, Sheikh Abdullah asked both India and Pakistan to adopt a secular democracy.

He then addressed the media and said, "I am pained that Indian media and some journalists here are wrongly criticizing our desire for special status. If these journalists think that by doing so, they are helping India and Kashmir, then they are in delusion. Instead, they are breaking the chain between India and Kashmir. Even after this, if they do not heed to my warning carefully, they would be breaking the relationship between India and Kashmir". In the end, Sheikh resorted to threats, "National Conference do not want to keep anyone in illusion. I have clearly put forward my view on the political, economic or constitutional autonomy or on the future of dynastic rule. I would like to say something to the Indian media expressively. Sheikh Abdullah is not afraid of anyone. I will not bow my head before India, Pakistan, America or any other nation. It would be good that all these nations understand this well".[24] Sheikh ended his speech thrice chanting, "Jawaharlal Nehru ki jai".

This speech hinted at Abdullah's real intentions and the nationalists in the state grew apprehensive. The Constituent Assembly was busy writing a separate constitution for the state. In the whole scheme of this constitution, Jammu and Ladakh were being marginalised. Seats in the Assembly were allotted disproportionately, with the Kashmir Valley getting 13 seats more than Jammu. Matters came to a head when Abdullah tried to communalise the Jammu and Kashmir issue. The demand for special status was made on the ground that there was a majority of Muslims in the state. The Government of India repeatedly held that it never accepted the two-nation theory. But, in Jammu and Kashmir, it seemed that the National Conference was advocating a three-nation theory, namely, India, Pakistan and an autonomous state of Jammu and Kashmir. For the nationalist forces, this was the last straw.

Satyagraha by Praja Parishad

This movement virtually began with the formation of the Praja Parishad on November 17, 1947, but its intensity was felt only after a prolonged dialogue between Sheikh Abdullah and Jawaharlal Nehru about the future Constitution of Jammu and Kashmir in July 1952. Some newspapers termed these talks as the Delhi Agreement, and it was publicised as a legal document though it was never put to paper or signed. Nehru agreed in these talks that there would be a separate flag for Jammu and Kashmir and the State would have its own *Sadr-e-Riyasat* (Governor) on the pattern of the country's President (Rashtrapati). There was no discussion on autonomy for Jammu and Ladakh, and representatives from Jammu and Ladakh were not even invited for the talks. Rights given by the Constitution of India to all citizens were denied to Indian citizens living in Jammu and Kashmir. Abdullah also decided to discriminate between peoples of different categories in the state, but Nehru was unwavering in his support for Abdullah.

The Praja Parishad declared its opposition to a separate flag and constitution for Jammu and Kashmir as this would encourage fissiparous tendencies by instilling a feeling of separatism. It argued that the safety and security of Jammu and Kashmir lay in accepting the Constitution of India and repealing Article 370 of the Indian constitution.[25] On November 14, 1952, the Praja Parishad launched its struggle with the cry, *Ek desh mein do Vidhan, do Nishan, do Pradhan nahin chelenge, nahin chelenge* ("In one country, two constitutions, two symbols, two heads won't work, won't work"). Rallies and satyagrahas were held in every nook and cranny of the state. The whole of Jammu reverberated with this slogan. The situation deteriorated when Nehru and Abdullah tried to repress the movement by force. Fighting for the unity and integrity of the country, the Praja Parishad opposed the occupation of large parts of the state by Pakistan and demanded complete unification of Jammu and Kashmir State with the Indian Union. Sheikh Abdullah, however, was determined to keep the state outside the jurisdiction of the Indian Constitution, barring the most nominal ties. He moved to crush the movement by banning protests, gatherings, demonstrations and meetings by invoking Article 50 of Jammu and Kashmir Security Act. Instead of listening to the grievances of the people, Nehru took umbrage at the challenge to his dignity. Abdullah had a free hand, and 15 satyagrahis were gunned down by the police.

At this stage, Dr Syama Prasad Mookerji, president of Bharatiya Jan Sangh, entered the arena and took the Praja Parishad agitation to every part of the country, finally entering Jammu and Kashmir State to test the waters. He was arrested on May 11, 1953, and driven to Srinagar, where he was housed in an isolated bungalow. His advocates and even relatives were denied permission to meet him. After 42 days in confinement, Mookerji died a mysterious death in a government hospital on June 23. The State Government kept the death a secret for some time. Even the Sadr-e-Riyasat, Karan Singh, was not informed.

Nehru rejected the demand for an enquiry, but suspicion lingered. The Praja Parishad suspended its agitation after Mookerji's death, and Abdullah triumphed. Sheikh Abdullah "had already given out his idea of valley of Kashmir remaining an independent and neutral state".[26] Nehru invited Abdullah to Delhi, but he refused, Nehru later disclosed.[27] American politician Adlai Stevenson was in Kashmir and Sheikh Abdullah had long talks with him about the future status of the valley, a fact disclosed by Stevenson himself on his return to America. Abdullah was now "suspected of planning a session of the Constituent Assembly, which instead of ratifying the accession of the state of Jammu and Kashmir to India, would declare the vale of Kashmir independent".[23] As Abdullah appeared to be questioning the accession itself, even members of the National Conference became apprehensive. A marathon meeting of the National Conference working committee was held in May 1953 to discuss Sheikh Abdullah's new line regarding Jammu and Kashmir and "a resolution endorsing the accession to India and supporting the Delhi Agreement was passed with a majority of fifteen against four votes".[29] There was an open rift in the cabinet also on these issues. Three out of five cabinet members (Bakshi Ghulam Mohammad, D.P. Dhar and Sham Lal Saraf) submitted a memorandum to the Sadr-e-Riyasat telling him that the cabinet had lost faith in the leadership of Sheikh Abdullah. Karan Singh invited Sheikh Abdullah to discuss the issue and sort out the differences. But a defiant Sheikh refused to attend the meeting and left for Gulmarg with his wife. The Sadr-e-Riyasat dismissed the government and invited Bakshi Ghulam Mohammad to form a new ministry; Abdullah was arrested the same night (August 8, 1953) and placed under house arrest for 11 years. Bakshi Ghulam Mohammad completed the task of framing the independent constitution of the state and was instrumental in getting Jawaharlal Nehru to insinuate Article 35-A into the Constitution of India in 1954. This increased the constitutional distance between Jammu and Kashmir and India, to the detriment of its people.

*

NOTES

1 Bamzai, P.N.K., *Kashmir and Power Politics from Lake Success to Tashkent*, New Delhi: Metropolitan Book Co., 1966, p. 60.
2 Agnihotri, Kuldip Chand, *Jammu Kashmir ke Jan Nayak Maharaja Hari Singh*, New Delhi: Prabhat Prakashan, 2016, p. 277.
3 Johnson, Allen Campbell, *Mission with Mountbatten*, New York: Atheneum Books, 1985, p. 234.
4 Hodson, H.V., *The Great Divide*, London: Hutchinson, 1969, p. 442.
5 Mahajan, Mehr Chand, *Looking Back*, Mumbai: Asia Publishing House, 1963, p. 268.
6 Singh, Karan, *Jammu and Kashmir 1949-1964*, Delhi: Penguin, 2006, p. 312.
7 Christopher Thomas, *Faultline Kashmir*, Middlesex, U.K.: Brunel Academic Publishers, 2000, p. 144. See also, Menon, V.P., *The Story of the Integration of the Indian States*, Mumbai: Orient Longman, 1969, pp. 375-376.
8 Johnson, op. cit., p. 120.
9 Singh, Karan, *Autobiography*, Delhi: Oxford University Press, 2003, pp. 50-51.
10 Mahajan, Mehr Chand, Looking Back, Mumbai:,, op. cit., p. 150.
11 Ibid.
12 Ibid., pp. 151-152.
13 Gopal, S., *Jawaharlal Nehru: A Biography (Hindi edn.)*, New Delhi: Sahitya Academy, 2012, p. 190.
14 Hari Wazir joined the Indian Army as a commissioned officer and died in Kashmir; thereafter, Prem Nath Dogra took charge of the Praja Parishad.
15 Devadas, David, *In Search of a Future: The Story of Kashmir*, New Delhi: Penguin, 2007, p. 79.
16 Constituent Assembly Debates; Volume X, p. 424.
17 Abdullah, Sheikh Mohammad, *The Blazing Chinar*, Srinagar: Gulshan Books, 2013, pp. 357-359.

18 Gupta, Jyoti Bhusan Das, *Jammu and Kashmir*, Springer, 2012, p. 195.

19 Jaffrelot, Christophe, *Hindu Nationalism: A Reader*, Princeton, NJ: Princeton University Press, 2007, pp. 158-159.

20 The 12th Amendment to the J&K Constitution, October 19, 1975, reduced the number of seats assigned to POJK to 24.

21 Korbel, Josef, *Danger in Kashmir*, Princeton, NJ: Princeton University Press, 1966, p. 222.

22 Bose, Sumantra, *Kashmir: Roots of Conflict, Paths to Peace*, Massachusetts: Harvard University Press, 2002, pp. 56-57.

23 *The Tribune*, Ambala, April 12, 1952.

24 Ibid.

25 Bamzai, P.N.K., *A History of Kashmir*, Srinagar: Gulshan Books, 2008, pp. 791-792.

26 Bamzai, *A History of Kashmir*, op. cit., p. 794.

27 Korbel, op. cit., p. 236.

28 Ibid., p. 237.

29 Bamzai, op. cit., p. 794.

ANNEXURES

Annexure I
Post Mortem Report of January 17, 2018

GOVT. DISTRICT HOSPITAL, KATHUA
J&K HEALTH DEPARTMENT
POST-MORTEM EXAMINATION REPORT

No.: 27 Date: 17/1/18 Identified by

Name: Asifa 1. Father ① Mohd Yusuf S/o Shab Din R/o Rasan.

S/o. D/o. W/o.: Mohd Yusuf

Age: 8yrs Sex: F.

Religion: Muslim.

Address: Rasana Teh Hiranagar, Distt Kathua 2. Javed Ahmed S/o Fareed R/o Rasan. Uncle.

Date and Time of Autopsy: 2:30pm on 17/1/18

Alleged cause of death: H/o Kidnapping and dead body received from Jungle after 6 days.

Authority for Autopsy SI P/S Hiranagar

EXTERNAL APPEARANCE

Length of the Body: 110 cm.

Appearance of the body: Average built.

Signs of Decomposition: No signs seen.

Rigor mortis: ++ Partially present in upper and lower limbs resolving

Liver mortis: present over abdomen.

Belongings: Purple coloured frock, purple coloured pajayma, and mustard coloured shoal, Plastic shoes, sand and mud present over frock.

STATE OF NATURAL ORIFICES:

Eyes: Congested

Ears: NAD

Nostrils: Bleeding +

Anus: NAD

Vulva/Vagina: ① Vulval opening wide easily admitting 1 finger.
② Vulval laceration present medially towards posterior fourchette. Blood stained discharge inside vagina

Special Remarks:
③ hymen not intact.
④ Fornices found intact.
⑤ Slides of vaginal smear prepared (4 in no)

[illegible]

Contd. (8) Bluish discolouration over Ear lobule nails.

(2)

II. EXTERNAL AND INTERNAL INJURIES :

(1) Abrasion mark over right side of face.
(2) tongue protruded.
(3) Eyes Congested.
(4) Bluish discolouration over abdomen around umbi
(5) abrasion over thighs.
(6) abrasion over right forearm.
(7) deep lacerated wound behind right Ear.

Attached With Challan

Sr. Supdt. of Police,
Crime Branch, Jammu.

(3)

III. HEAD : No external or internal injury seen.

Scalp

Bones Intact.

Membranes — Intact

Base of Skull NAD.

IV. NECK :

Injuries, Ligaturamarks etc. and No Injury seen.

Dissection finding Nil

V. THORAX :

(i) Wall, ribs and cartilages

Pleura, Larynx, Trachea for

foreign body or disease, etc.

} Small amount of blood stained froth present in trachea. Nil.

(iii) Lungs : — Congested with few petechial haemorrhages.

(iv) Pericardium — NAD

(v) Heart and blood vessels. filled c̄ Blood

VI. ABDOMEN :

(i) Walls, Peritoneum, peritoneal cavity contents — Nil

(ii) Liver, Gall Bladder — Nil

(iii) Pancreas] Nil

(iv) Spleen] Nil

(v) Kidneys] Nil

(vi) Urinary bladder — Empty

(vii) Stomach — filled c̄ digested material.

(viii) Intestines

(4)

VII. ORGANS OF GENERATION : —Nil.

IX. "SPINAL CANAL" Not opened.

Attached With Challan

Sr. Supdt. of Police,
Crime Branch, Jammu.

Date/Hour of death

(as per Hospital record)

Time since death ...... not more than 72 hours

Viscera for :-

Forensic Science Laboratory/Histopathological Department Govt. Medical College, Jammu.

1. Container 'A' (1) Pieces of kidney, Liver, Lung heart spleen (FSL)
2. Container 'B' Stomach with food content (FSL)
3. Container 'C' Uterus in formalin (HPE).

Container D Vaginal smear slide

(1) Dr. Jyoti [signature] 17/01/18
(2) Dr. Madhu [signature] 17/01/18
(3) Dr. Mukul [signature]

OPINION AS TO CAUSE OF DEATH: Opinion kept reserved.

(1) Body and belongings handed with viscera and vaginal smear slides handed over to police.

Annexure II
J&K Forensic Science Laboratory Reports
(letters '219' and '220' written by hand)

J&K FORENSIC SCIENC[illegible]ORATORY

Jammu

[illegible]7502
[illegible]1-2435249

(Admissible as evidence in the court of law)

Report No:- 128/C&T/FSL/2018 Dated:- 17-2-2018

To : **Medical Supdt.,**
Govt Distt. Hospital,
Kathua.

Reported by: **Pawan Kumar Abrol,**
(M.Sc. Chemistry)
Scientific Officer,
FSL Jammu.

Subject: : Viscera of Asifa D/o Mohd Yousuf, age about 08 yrs R/o Rassana Teh Hiranagar, Distt. Kathua.

Reference : Your letter No. MS/DHK/E-IV/3380-90 Dt. 18-01-2018 advancing two sealed Packets which were received in this office on 22-01-2018 through ASI Prabhu Daya No. 825560/EXJ P/S Hiranagar.

The exhibits were found sealed & reached me with 1 seal intact in each respectively.

DESCRIPTION AND LABORTORY MARKINGS:-

Two sealed packets marked as Container A and Container B by you.

Container A : One sealed small plastic container enclosed with adhesive tape bearing 1 seal intact said to contain pieces of Liver, Kidney, Spleen, Lung and Heart which were collectively given the exhibit No. P-187/2018 by me.

Container B : One sealed small plastic container enclosed with adhesive tape bearing 1 seal intact said to contain Stomach and Intestine which were collectively given the exhibit No. P-188/2018 by me.

(The above seals were opened and the contents of the Exhibits were duly examined by me remaining under my immediate custody until the examination was completed.)

RESULT :- The Exhibits were subjected to various Chemical tests and chromatographic examination and the result arrived at is as under :-

1. **Clonazepam** was detected in the Exhibit Nos. P-187/2018 & P-188/2018.
2. **Clonazepam** is a **Anticonvulsant (Drug).**

EXAMINED BY
P Abrol 17/02/2018
(Pawan Kumar Abrol)
(Pawan Kumar Abrol)
Scientific Officer,
HOD(Chemistry & Toxicology)
J&K Forensic Science Laboratory
Jammu

JAMMU UNIVERSITY, NEW CAMPUS ROAD, VIKRAM CHOWK, JAMMU-180004

J & K FORENSIC SCIENCE LABORATORY SRINAGAR

(Admissible as evidence in the Court of Law)

Tel:- 0194-2490528
Fax:- 0194-2490528

Report No :- 41-Bio-Sr. Dated :- 30-1-018

Report By:- Mushtaq Ahmad Bhat,
(M. Sc. Zoology),
Sc. Officer, (Head Bio/ Serology Division),
FSL, Srinagar.

To: - **Medical Superintendent,**
Govt, Distt.Hospital Kathua.

Subject: - **Examination of four slides taken from Vaginal Smear of Asifa D/O Mohd Yousuf Age about 08 yrs R/O RassanaTehsil Hiranagar Distt. Kathua.**

Received on 24-01-2018 one sealed plastic container, enclosed within Adhesive tape bearing **(02)** intact seals , sealed by Gynaecologist Govt. Distt.Hospital Kathua and forwarded for examination by Medical Superintendent, Govt.Distt.Hospital Kathua vide his letter No. MS/DHK/E-IV/3417-19 dated 19-01-2018 sent through SI Krishan Singh EXJ.No.795620.

DESCRIPTION OF THE SEALED PLASTIC CONTAINER:-

1.One Sealed Plastic container :-On opening was found to contain one small packet enclosed within adhesive tape containing four glass slides allegedly Smeared with Vaginal secretion which were collectively marked as Exhibit - No. M-01/2018 in the laboratory.

The above sealed Plastic container was opened in my presence and the contents of the exhibits remained under my immediate custody until the examination was completed.

RESULT:-

"NO SPERMATOZOA WERE DETECTED ON THE EXHIBIT NO,-M-01/2018".

07/2/018

EXAMINED BY,

30/01/18

Mushtaq Ahmad Bhat
Scientific Officer,Head (Bio/ Sero Division),
FSL, J&K, Srinagar.

Annexure III

Second Post Mortem Report also dated January 17, 2018 (letters '221' written by

GOVT. DISTRICT HOSPITAL, KATHUA

J&K HEALTH DEPARTMENT

POST-MORTEM EXAMINATION REPORT

No.: 27 Date 17/1/18 Identified by

Father

Name: Asifa 1. Mohd Yusuf

S/o D/o W/o: Mohd Yusuf S/o ShabDin

Age: 8 yrs Sex: F R/o Rasan.

Religion: Muslim

Address: Rassana Teh- Hiranagar, Distt Kathua 2. Javed Ahmed

S/o Fareed.

R/o Rasan.

Uncle.

Date and Time of Autopsy: 2:30 pm. on 17/1/18

Alleged cause of death: H/O Kidnapping and dead body received from jungle after 6 days.

Authority for Autopsy: SI P/S Hiranagar.

EXTERNAL APPEARANCE

Length of the Body: 110cm

Appearance of the body: average built.

Signs of Decomposition: No Sign Seen.

Rigor mortis: ++ Partially present in upper and lower limbs resolving

Livor mortis: on abdomen.

Belongings: Purple Coloured frock, Purple coloured pajayma and mustard coloured wrap, plastic shoes, Sand and mud present over frock.

STATE OF NATURAL ORIFICES:

Eyes: Congested

Ears: NAD

Nostrils: Bleeding +

Anus: NAD.

Vulva/Vagina: (1) Vulval opening wide, easily admitting 1 finger. Vulval laceration present medially (towards posterior fourchette). Blood stained discharge inside vagina.

Special Remarks:

(2) Hymen not intact

(3) Fourchette found intact.

(4) Slides of vaginal smear prepared (4 in No) sent for HPE.

(5) [illegible] sample also sent.

(6) [illegible] abrasions, Blood stained present on the labia and vulva.

[illegible] discolouration over face [illegible] ~~and bed of nails seen~~

(2)

II. EXTERNAL AND INTERNAL INJURIES :

(1) abrasion mark over right side of face seen.

(2) tongue protruded

(3) Eyes Congested

(4) Bluish discolouration over abdomen around umbilicus

(5) Bluish red abrasions over thigh seen.

(6) Bluish red abrasions over right forearm seen.

(7). deep lacerated wound appox 2cm x 0.5cm behind rig Ear seen. (Reddish Brown in Colour).

(8) Bluish discolouration over Ear lobules and nails.

Attached With Challan

Sr. Supdt. of Police,
Crime Branch, Jammu.

(3)

III. HEAD :

Scalp — No External or Internal Injury Seen.

Bones — Intact

Membranes — Intact

Base of Skull N.A.D.

IV. NECK :

Injuries, Ligaturamarks etc. and — No Injury Seen.

Dissection finding Nil

V. THORAX :

(i) Wall, ribs and cartilages NAD.

(ii) Pleura, Larynx, Trachea for — Small amount of blood stained froth present in trachea.

foreign body or disease, etc.

(iii) Lungs : — Congested with few petechial haemorrhages.

(iv) Pericardium Nil

(v) Heart and blood vessels. filled c̄ Blood.

VI. ABDOMEN :

(i) Walls, Peritoneum, peritoneal cavity contents

(ii) Liver, Gall Bladder NAD

(iii) Pancreas NAD

(iv) Spleen NAD

(v) Kidneys NAD.

(i)–(v): NAD.

(vi) Urinary bladder NAD.

(vii) Stomach — Empty

(viii) Intestines — NAD.

(4)

VII. ORGANS OF GENERATION : Nil. Original report of postgraduate department of pathology GMC Jammu, Patho No/18/1471 dated 14/3/18 bearing Signature of Consultant Pathology (Dr. Navneet Naz, Lecturer, Deptt of Pathology) is enclosed.

IX. "SPINAL CANAL" not opened.

Attached With Challan

[signature]

Sr. Supdt. of Police,
Crime Branch, Jammu.

Date/Hour of death

(as per Hospital record)

Time since death not more than 72 hours.

Viscera for :-

Forensic Science Laboratory/Histopathological Department Govt. Medical College, Jammu.

1. Container 'A' ① Pieces of kidney, liver, lung and heart spleen (Sent for chemical analysis to FSL Jammu.
2. Container 'B' ② Stomach with food contents.
3. Container 'C' ③. Uterus in formalin 10%, sent for HPE to GMC Jammu.

① Original report of J&K Forensic Science laboratory Jammu Report No 128/CST/FSL/2018 dated 17/2/2018 bearing Signature of HOD (Chemistry and Toxicology) J&K Forensic Science Laboratory Jammu is enclosed.

OPINION AS TO CAUSE OF DEATH :

② Original report of J&K Forensic Science Laboratory Srinagar Report No-41-BioSer dated 30-1-2018 bearing signature of Head Bio/Sero Division FSL J&K Srinagar enclosed.

① Body and belongings with viscera and vaginal smear slides handed over to police.

After conducting the Autopsy we are of the opinion that the deceased died because of Asphyxia leading to cardiopulmonary arrest. Board of Doctor ① Dr Jyoti [signature] 19/3/18.
② Dr. Madhu [signature] 19/3/18
③ Dr. Mukul [signature] 15-3-18

Annexure IV
Vishal Jangotra Handwriting Forensic Report, dated July 26, 2018

J&K FORENSIC SCIENCE LABORATORY SRINAGAR, KASHMIR

(Admissible as Evidence in the Court of Law)

Tel: 0194-2490528
Fax: 0194-2490528

Report No. 121-Doc **Dated:** 26-7-18

Report by: **Farhat Aman Kar**
Document Expert,
Documents Division J&K FSL Srinagar.

Material submitted for Examination by: Superintendent of Police, Incharge SIT, Crime Branch Jammu in case FIR No. 10/2018 U/S 363, 343, 376-D, 302, 120-B, 201/RPC of P/S Hiranagar referred vide letter No. CBJ/FIR-10/2018/Hiranagar/513, Dated:-17-07-2018 to Director J&K Forensic Science Laboratory Srinagar Kashmir through ASI Madan Lal No. EXK-826384 of Incharge SIT Crime Branch Jammu. The case was received at FSL Srinagar on 19-07-2018 vide FSL Sgr. case receipt No. FSL/Legal/Sgr-1100-Doc.

The original documents in the form of three (03) volumes of Answer Scripts of this case have been examined carefully and thoroughly with the help of available Scientific Aids like Illuminated Magnifiers; Stereozoom Microscope and Ultra Violet Light arrangements and the following opinion has been arrived at:

Results of the Examination:

On comparison of blue enclosed Admitted writings stamped and marked as A1A to A7A and red enclosed Questioned writings similarly stamped and marked as Q1A to Q20A have been found that the Admitted writings and Questioned writings have been written by one and the same person due to the reason that the similarities are observed between the Questioned and Admitted writings in the individual writing habits and some of the general writing habits of movement, skill and alignment.

Inter-spacing between the letters and words in the Questioned writings marked as Q1A to Q20A have been written with wide hiatus between letters and words as compared to Admitted writings. This aspect reveals that extent of natural variation in the Questioned writings is more personified and profound. Such personified and profound natural variation can occur in the writings of a person when there is lack of neuro-muscular coordination of the writer and such lack of neuro-muscular coordination is found due to various psychological and physical conditions.

EXAMINED BY

FARHAT AMAN KAR
Assistant Scientific Officer
Documents Division
J&K Forensic Science Laboratory
Srinagar, Kashmir

Index